FAITHS IN CONFLICT?

VINOTH RAMACHANDRA

FAITHS IN CONFLICT?

CHRISTIAN INTEGRITY IN A MULTICULTURAL WORLD

LONDON LECTURES IN CONTEMPORARY CHRISTIANITY

Inter-Varsity Press

INTER-VARSITY PRESS
38 De Montfort Street, Leicester LE1 7GP, England

© Vinoth Ramachandra 1999

First published 1999
Reprinted 2000

British Library Cataloguing in Publication Data
A catalogue record is available from the British Library.

ISBN 0-85111-650-7

Set in Minion Condensed
Typeset in Great Britain
Printed and bound in Great Britain by Creative Print and Design (Wales),
Ebbw Vale

*Inter-Varsity Press, is the book-publishing division of the Universities and
Colleges Christian Fellowship (formerly the Inter-Varsity Fellowship), a student
movement linking Christian Unions in universities and colleges throughout Great
Britain, and a member movement of the International Fellowship of Evangelical
Students. For information about local and national activities write to UCCF,
38 De Montfort Street, Leicester LE1 7GP.*

FOR KARIN

CONTENTS

Preface

Our planet is fast becoming a web of criss-crossing influences. Travel and technology have brought about a mingling of peoples and cultures on a scale that our parents, let alone our forebears, never imagined. Far from the East being East and the West remaining West, the two have borrowed from, and interacted with, each other for centuries. But the pace of interaction has accelerated enormously. New, sometimes bewildering, hybrid cultures seem to be emerging – a world of tandoori pizzas and *ninja* ballets, of Silicon Valleys in Bangalore and Zen monasteries in California. Lovers of music in America are more than likely to be listening to their favourite works of Mahler and Mendelssohn performed by a Mehta, a Midori or a Ma. The best writers of English literature these days all seem to be of Asian origin – Salman Rushdie, V. S. Naipaul, Amy Tan, Kazuo Ishiguro, Vikram Seth, to list but the more famous names – and a new talent from the Indian subcontinent emerges, with increasing regularity, to claim a major literary prize in the West.

The encounter between cultures can be exhilarating, but it can also be fraught with tension. At times it erupts in violence. This is especially the case where economic disparities between cultures shape the direction in which cultural influence takes place. Travel is still limited to a relatively affluent minority of the world's population, and, sadly, mass tourism from the West has rarely led to a deeper appreciation of non-Western peoples. Tourism has, more often than not, come to mean luxury hotels and holiday homes, drugs and prostitutes, and polluted beaches. Communications technologies, like other economic resources, are unevenly distributed. It is a sobering fact that nine out of ten people in the world have never made a telephone call in their lives; that, despite the propaganda of Bill Gates and other computer salesmen, ninety-nine out of every hundred do not have access to the Internet; that Tokyo, with a population of 23 million, has three times as many telephone lines as the whole continent of Africa with 580 million people.

Moreover, the explosion of information technology has not necessarily been accompanied by greater awareness of the economic plight of nations outside Europe and America. The histories of those nations still tends to be taught in an ethnocentric manner. As computers, TV and other mass media come to be controlled by a few giant financial empires, serious journalism withers and the banal, the trivial and the salacious become transformed into 'global news'. Monica Lewinsky, Louise Woodward and Princess Diana have burst into every living-room and rural village touched by TV, while the vast majority of Europeans and Americans are blissfully ignorant of how their histories, policies and lifestyles have led to wars, coups and economic meltdowns in other parts of the world. As Noam Chomsky and others have demonstrated, the media in democratic countries are often agents of thought-control on behalf of the ruling élites and big business. Xenophobia, deep-seated prejudices fuelled by economic anxieties, and archaic stereotypes of other nations and cultures persist in societies that claim high levels of education and mobility. We tend to be exposed to the *worst* in each other's cultures. Those who seek to build bridges of mutual learning and understanding are in short supply.

Many cultures are remarkably resilient, and many observers would regard the examples given at the beginning of this preface as rather superficial and exceptional instances of cultural blending. Conflict, rather than blending, seems the norm of the day. At the same time as we become aware of our global inter-dependence, we also experience the erection of new barriers between peoples. Ethnic nationalisms are on the rise, from Quebec to Fiji. From a global perspective, both 'Little England' and 'Fortress Europe' are birds of the same feather.

Religion, which lies at the heart of most cultures, seems to be the most powerful source of such conflict. Many voices, secular and Christian, have warned of the imminent threat to Western civilization and 'Western values' posed by the 'resurgence of Islam' around the world. Rapid church growth in countries like Indonesia has led to waves of anti-Christian rioting in recent years. Muslims in Bosnia and Kosovo have suffered unspeakable atrocities at the hands of Orthodox Serbs. Christians and other religious minorities in India have experienced violence and discrimination at the hands of Hindu nationalists. In the aftermath of the controversial Indian and Pakistani nuclear explosions in May 1998, an article in Britain's *The Independent* newspaper declared, with splendid self-assurance, that 'India's bomb was a *Hindu bomb*. Pakistan's bomb was a *Muslim bomb*'. Religion, long banished to the margins of political discussion, has now seized the centre stage.

Religion is also a source of moral order. Many politicians in the West have recently been calling for the reinforcement of religious education in schools in an attempt to inject a moral sensibility into what is increasingly perceived as an anomic society. Most members of faith-communities would reject this functionalist approach to their traditions and question the separation of moral values from fundamental religious convictions about the world. However, what is of significance is that 'religion' and particular religious discourses are now deemed to be politically important even in so-called 'secularized' societies. That, surely, is a development the architects of the French Enlightenment could never have forseen, let alone desired.

Suspicion, fear and hostility between faith-communities (whether 'religious' or 'secular') are not confined to the Indian subcontinent or the Middle East. Muslims living in Europe have often complained that European peoples are not only racist but 'Islamophobic'. European and American media frequently run scare-stories highlighting the presence of 'Islamic terrorists' or 'Muslim fanatics' on the West's doorstep. New Age gurus offer ecologically-sensitive new religions as antidotes to the seemingly inevitable violence engendered by the Semitic faiths.

What are the sources of such fears and hostility? And how can the risks of violent confrontation be reduced, as diverse religious traditions and communities seek to orient themselves in a fast-changing, pluralist world? The issues raised for Christians in the West are particularly acute. Does tolerance require the abandonment of belief in universal truths? What is the distinctiveness of the Christian message in a world of many faiths? And what can Christians in the West learn from non-Western Christians and their struggle to live with integrity and faithfulness as minority communities?

This book is an attempt to respond to such challenging issues. It comes out of four lectures delivered in November 1998 at the School of Oriental and African Studies, London, under the auspices of the Institute of Contemporary Christianity. The London Lectures in Contemporary Christianity are an annual series founded in 1974 to promote Christian thought on contemporary issues.

In chapter 1, I discuss the global 'Islamic resurgence' of recent decades and the alleged threat it poses to the West. One of the most competent exponents of the view that 'Islam' and the 'West' are mutually hostile and irreconcilable is Samuel Huntington, a politics professor at Harvard University and adviser on international relations to US governments. In the post-Cold War world,

Huntington argues, religious or civilizational clashes have replaced wars fought for economic or strategic reasons. This chapter combines a critique of Huntington with an examination of the West's perception of Islam and the misleading rhetoric of Islamist movements. It also explores how dangerous stereotypes are generated in both Western and Islamic societies. It concludes with some challenging questions for Muslims and Christians alike.

Over the past fifty years India has wrestled with a host of issues which are only now surfacing in North America and Europe – multiculturalism, affirmative action, group rights, and so on. Is India's recent history a window into the West's own future? Chapter 2 examines the interaction between the secular and religious visions of nationalism within the Indian context. What is 'Hinduism', and how is the Hindu identity being shaped today? And, is it true, as many Hindu and liberal intellectuals allege, that the Christian mission has failed in Indian society?

A fascination with Jesus Christ and inspiration from the Gospels has marked many Hindu reformers in India. Jesus continues to attract and scandalize people of all cultures today. What are the reasons for such attraction? Chapter 3 begins by looking at the 'foolishness' of early Christian preaching. It goes on to consider the story of Israel's election in the Hebrew Bible: is this an unnecessary obstacle to healthy inter-faith relations, or is it indispensable to our understanding of who Jesus was and his significance today? The chapter explores the unique combination that we find in Jesus of an other-centred lifestyle with self-directed claims, and draws out the implications of this for the world of religions. (Much of the material in this chapter has been adapted from my earlier book *The Recovery of Mission*, Carlisle: Paternoster; Grand Rapids: Eerdmans, 1996, ch. 6.)

How do the major world faiths handle the facts of diversity and conflicting truth-claims? Chapter 4 responds to various accusations levelled at Christians who assert that what God did in Jesus of Nazareth was normative and decisive for all peoples. I try to sort out some of the conceptual fuzziness involved in such accusations, and then go on to rebut another common charge: namely, that traditional Christian emphasis on mission and conversion is a threat to cultural pluralism.

No discussion of religious conflict can avoid the argument of whether a secular society is necessary for genuine dialogue and harmony between peoples. In Chapter 5 I untangle some of the threads that have become interwoven in discussions of 'secularism', and argue for a contextual approach to issues of civility and the common good. Finally, a brief epilogue draws together the implications of some of the foregoing for an authentically Christian discipleship in the late modern world.

1
Islam and new religious wars?

The 'Clash of Civilizations' argument

Samuel Huntington's book *The Clash of Civilizations and the Remaking of World Order* is an ambitious, influential and highly acclaimed attempt to articulate a framework that would make sense of our post-Cold War world.[1] Huntington is a professor at Harvard University and has served as adviser on international relations to US governments. So his work is, at one and the same time, a political narrative and a blueprint for American foreign policy in the new millennium.

Huntington's main thesis is straightforward. 'In the post-Cold War world,' he writes, 'the most important distinctions among peoples are not ideological, political, or economic. They are cultural.'[2] In this new world order, 'the most pervasive, important and dangerous conflicts will not be between social classes, rich and poor, or other economically defined groups, but between peoples belonging to different cultural entities.'[3]

As the dominance of the West declines, other ancient civilizations assert their global influence. A civilization is the broadest level of cultural identity people have, and religion is a central characteristic of all civilizations. 'Civilizations are the biggest "we" within which we feel culturally at home as distinguished from all the other "them" out there.'[4] Huntington identifies six major contemporary civilizations that have increasing political influence in this new 'multipolar' world order: Western (Europe and North America), Sinic,

13

Japanese, Hindu, Islamic and Orthodox. Five of these civilizations have dominant 'core states' (USA, China, Japan, India and Russia) but Islam does not. While states remain the key actors in global politics, they increasingly define their interests in civilizational terms. Non-Western civilizations reject Western values in favour of their own cultural norms, and as the material superiority of the West diminishes its cultural appeal for non-Western peoples also fades. He writes:

> Spurred by modernization, global politics is being reconfigured along cultural lines. Peoples and countries with similar cultures are coming together. Peoples and countries with different cultures are coming apart. Alignments defined by ideology and superpower relations are giving way to alignments defined by culture and civilization. Political boundaries increasingly are redrawn to coincide with cultural ones: ethnic, religious, and civilizational. Cultural communities are replacing Cold War blocs, and the fault lines between civilizations are becoming central lines of conflict in global politics.[5]

The political scenario that emerges from this is clear. Conflicts are likely to occur in what Huntington calls 'cleft countries' – states which contain people from two or more different civilizations, as in the Ukraine – and along 'fault lines' which divide one civilization from another. Conflicts that take place across lines dividing different civilizations are likely to be complex and interminable as local antagonists rally support from their brethren belonging to the same civilization. The chief danger lies in the possibility of a 'fault-line' conflict within a core state escalating into an inter-civilizational war involving several countries.

Huntington is as concerned about the 'Islamic resurgence' and the 'Asian Affirmation', as much as he is about the Western belief in the universality of Western culture. While the rise of East Asia has been fuelled (until recently) by spectacular rates of economic growth, the resurgence of Islam has been fuelled by equally spectacular rates of population growth. Both China and Islam represent what he calls 'challenger civilizations' to the West. In the case of Islam, the demographic explosion, historic and ingrained animosity towards the West, and the absence of a strong core-state combine to create a high potential for violent conflict. 'The dangerous clashes of the future', he maintains, 'are likely to arise from the interaction of Western arrogance, Islamic intolerance, and Sinic assertiveness.'[6]

What is required, then, is a mutual accommodation between diverse civilizations and the refusal on the part of Huntington's 'core states' to interfere in conflicts based in other civilizations. 'In the emerging era,' he maintains, 'the clashes between civilizations are the greatest threat to world peace, and an international order based on civilizations is the surest safeguard against world war.'[7] Huntington's civilizational paradigm has the merit of simplicity. There is also much in his book that is insightful, and his arguments are presented with great anecdotal skill and memorable sound-bites (as, for instance, his observation that 'in Islam, God is Caesar; in China and Japan, Caesar is God; in Orthodoxy, God is Caesar's junior partner'). His analyses of 'fault-line' conflicts and 'cleft societies' are often intriguing. And I agree with his rebuttal of the common belief that modernization is tantamount to Westernization and leads to a convergence of all cultures.

Why does his thesis carry a prima facie plausibility? We all know from personal experience that cultural differences can breed mutual suspicions and misunderstandings. Moreover, almost all the major events we read about in our newspapers seem to involve different cultural identities: the US and Muslim Iraqis; Hindus and Muslims in India; 'Western' Croats, 'Orthodox' Serbs and Muslim Albanians in the Balkans; 'Orthodox' Russians and Armenians fighting Muslim Chechens and Azerbaijanis; Arabs and Jews on the West Bank; China and the West over human rights, and so on.

However, despite its insights and initial plausibility, Huntington's thesis is, I believe, seriously flawed. The 'clash of civilizations' is an unreliable guide for understanding the world in which we live. It is also a dangerous blueprint for Western foreign policy. Rather than attempting a detailed refutation, I shall illustrate my dissatisfaction with the whole approach typified by Huntington by focusing on the treatment of 'Islam' as a civilizational category – and situating the discussion around a wider perception, increasingly common in Western and Islamic circles alike, of mutual confrontation. I shall then go on to raise some specifically Christian concerns about Muslims and Islam, arising from both Western and non-Western societies.

The Islamic threat?

For those in the West who seek new demons, the communist threat has been replaced by the ideological, political and demographic threat of Islam.

When the Oklahoma City bomb exploded in April 1995, the immediate response of both the police and the media was that the blast was the work of Islamic terrorists. Men of 'Middle Eastern complexion' were summarily arrested; there were calls for pre-emptive strikes on Middle Eastern countries, and a wave of attacks took place on both mosques and Muslims across the United States. The British papers quickly followed the American lead. The tabloid *Today* ran the banner headline 'IN THE NAME OF ISLAM', while the *Daily Mail* said that the carnage bore 'all the hallmarks of the work of Islamic fundamentalists with a fanatical hatred of America'. (On 24 August 1998, the same popular newspaper carried a front-page headline 'MOSLEM FANATICS IN GERM ATTACK THREAT', warning of an imminent plot to strike Western cities with biological and chemical weapons. This was, presumably, to justify the US missile attacks, four days earlier, on the elusive Saudi-born Osama bin Laden's alleged training bases in Afghanistan and Sudan.)

Identical prejudices, conspiracy theories and ludicrous stereotypes of the 'West' are found in the media of Middle Eastern countries. Both popular and intellectually serious Islamic publications repeatedly describe what are alleged to be Western plots to humiliate Muslims and undermine Islamic traditions and culture.[8] When the Americans sent troops to the Saudi Arabian desert following Saddam Hussein's invasion of Kuwait in 1990, a communiqué issued by the Palestinian Islamic movement, Hamas, declared it to be 'another episode in the fight between good and evil' and 'a hateful Christian plot against our religion, our civilization and our land'.[9] Following the death of Princess Diana, the Libyan leader Colonel Qaddafi openly accused the British secret service of having engineered the car crash in order to prevent the marriage of British royalty to a Muslim. Other demagogues in the Middle East took up the charge: this was yet a further example of Western hostility towards Islam and part of a conspiracy to silence the voice of Muslims.

At first glance, all this may lend credence to Huntington's thesis. Are we not witnessing the latest manifestation of atavistic and irreversible animosities between the civilization of the 'West' and what is commonly called 'the world of Islam'? But none of the examples quoted above is exactly representative of any civilization, ancient or modern. Terrorism, jingoism and racial stereotyping are neither uniquely 'Islamic' nor uniquely 'Western'. Moreover, what is often presented in the language of 'ancient and fundamental differences' are, in fact, concoctions of recent political and social origin. 'Civilizations', 'nations', 'traditions', 'communities' – terms that claim a timeless reality and authority often turn out, on closer inspection, to be both less rigid and more modern than we thought.

Much confusion surrounds the rhetoric of both Islamists (or 'Islamic fundamentalists', as they are popularly, but misleadingly, called) and their critics in the non-Muslim world. Much of this confusion has to do with the way 'Islam' as a way of life, a system of beliefs and practices, is conflated with 'Islam' as a specific, timeless, social and political programme. The claim of Islamist movements and Islamically oriented governments is that the latter is derived from the former in a way that is logically necessary and historically universal. 'Islam' is then presented as a monolithic, unchanging reality; and all programmes for social and political change are justified in terms of this 'Islam' (Islamic economics, Islamic computing, Islamic dress codes, and so on). This is what distinguishes Islamists from other Muslims.

Huntington plays into the Islamists' hands by basically accepting their redefinition of Islam. The threat to the West does not come from a small group of extremists on the lunatic fringe, but from 'Islam' itself. He writes: 'The underlying problem for the West is not Islamic fundamentalism. It is Islam, a different civilization whose people are convinced of the superiority of their culture and are obsessed with the inferiority of their power.'[10] On this assumption, he tries to explain the dealings of contemporary Islamic societies with the West in terms of the enduring civilization of 'Islam'.

However, whenever groups of people invoke religious texts to justify specific political action, they are reflecting particular forces within their societies. These groups are responding to specific, historical problems, often of a social and political nature, *not* engaging in some universal crusade against other peoples. Whether in Iran or Algeria, Pakistan or Sri Lanka, the rise of religious nationalisms has been directed less against direct foreign domination than against the post-colonial state that has failed to resolve the problems of the society it rules. The inability of these states to meet either the economic expectations or the cultural aspirations of their people has been the context in which Islamist movements have emerged.

The Islamic resurgence

The term 'the Islamic resurgence' or 'the Islamic revival' has come to be applied to the re-emergence of Islam as an ideological force in Muslim politics since the late 1960s. From Morocco to Indonesia, governments in Muslim-majority countries and opposition movements have increasingly sought to legitimate their policies and muster popular support by appealing to Islam. Islam has been invoked in nationalist struggles and resistance movements in Afghanistan, in the Muslim republics of the former Soviet Central Asia, in Kashmir, and in the communal politics of Lebanon, India, Thailand and the Philippines. Islamist organizations have become the major opposition groups in Egypt, Tunisia, Algeria, Turkey, Morocco, the West Bank and Indonesia. The Iranian Revolution of 1979, the Iran–Iraq War, the Gulf War, and the Rushdie affair have not only sent shock waves throughout the Muslim world but brought Islam and Islamist movements to the centre stage of the world's media.

In any appraisal of Islamist movements, the local context is of primary importance. The many studies of the social origins of the activists in these movements reveal a profile that is fairly typical: they come from the lower middle class; they have a university education, usually in the natural sciences, engineering or medicine; and although they are city-dwellers when they join the organization, their origins are usually rural.

This is how Azmy Bishara, a philosophy professor at the Bir Zeit University in the Occupied Territories of the West Bank, explains this profile:

> Young adults who have left the villages usually live in slums on the outskirts of the metropolis. There, in the mosques of the suburban slums whose very architecture proclaims a terrible loss of identity, the migrants find a welcome and begin organizing themselves. Structural barriers keep these embittered students from integrating into the affluent classes that are reaping the fruits of modernization. But modernity itself, higher education, the demand for political organization – these are what provide them with the means to do battle against the status quo. They take up an offensive posture, looking back to a past utopia. This escape is not conducted as a retreat but as an attack. Those who espouse it are not conservatives but rather a unique product of modernity: modern individuals with a split and alienated consciousness, enlightened persons alienated from 'enlightenment'.[11]

None of these problems – whether they have to do with rapid urbanization, competition for educational and employment positions, the growing authoritarianism and corruption of the state, or the changing status of women – is specific to the Islamic world. If one wishes to understand the rise of Islamist movements in Algeria, Afghanistan, Egypt, Indonesia or elsewhere, it would be more fruitful to begin by examining the problems facing the populations of these countries, rather than by studying Qu'ranic texts or invoking the general influence of Islam. For that would be to play the same game as the Islamists. If, in Western Europe, immigrants from various Islamic countries have come to define themselves increasingly in Islamic terms, this may be not so much a reassertion of some global Muslim identity as a response of fear engendered by growing racist attacks, employment discrimination and social alienation that they experience in their adopted countries.

Islam in danger?

Some of the most incisive and balanced observations on these themes come from the pen of Professor Fred Halliday of the London School of Economics.

Halliday is the author of a number of outstanding analyses of Middle Eastern societies as well as of immigrant communities in Britain. In his book *Islam and the Myth of Confrontation*, he points out that 'Myths of "Islamic threat", like myths of legitimacy or nationalism, are part of the rhetorical baggage of political struggle, employed by both those who wish to remain in power and those who aspire to attain power.'[12]

The fact that most Muslims are not supporters of Islamist movements is obscured, as are the conditions under which people who are Muslims do turn to this particular option. The myth of the 'Islamic threat' fails to distinguish between the militant stridency of the few and the legitimate aspirations of the many. As with other political myths, however, once these ideas are propagated they gain a certain reality – for those whom they are designed to mobilize, and also for those against whom they are directed. The myth of confrontation pertaining to Muslims is taken up by Islamist movements to justify their own causes.

The opponents and proponents of the Islamic movement were in agreement that 'Islam' itself was a total, unchanging system, that its precepts operated over centuries, in all kinds of societies, and determined the attitudes of diverse peoples towards politics, sexuality and society. Both sides shared the view of a historically determined, essential 'Islam', which is supposedly able to account for all that Muslims say, do, and should say and should do. Khomeini, Turabi, the Muslim Brothers and the rest are as insistent on this score as any anti-Islamic bigot in the West. Whatever else, the image of a timeless 'Islam' is not just the fabrication of fevered Western minds.[13]

Memories of Western imperialism and exploitation, followed by continued support from the West for autocratic and oppressive regimes, have left deep scars and resentments in the psyche of many Arabs and Iranians. These 'became both easy excuses for societal failures and combustible materials in Muslim politics. If there is an Islamic threat, many Arabs and Muslims believe there has also been a Western threat – of political, economic, and religio-cultural imperialism, a political occupation accompanied by cultural invasion. As a result many in the Muslim world, like their counterparts in the West, opt for easy anti-imperialist slogans and demonization. At its worst, both sides have engaged in a process of "mutual satanization".'[14]

Many of the phenomena identified as specifically Islamic are not unique to the Islamic world, whether they be tribal regimes, fragile democracies, religious bigotry, oppression of women, or intolerance of minorities or of political dissent. The particular form which the Islamist movement in a particular society takes is determined by the problems that society confronts. For example, although neighbours, Iran and Afghanistan produced very different Islamist movements. Iran's Islamism was urban-based and led by traditionalist clergy, acting through mass political mobilizations; Afghanistan's was rural-based, but led by modernized intellectuals acting through guerrilla war.

Halliday also reminds us that most Islamist movements are concerned with what is going on within the Islamic world and with competition between Islamic states and parties, rather than with the outside world. 'It is worth recalling that Ayatollah Khomeini's rhetoric was not one calling for a *jihad* to conquer or convert the non-Muslim world, but was a cry of concern: "Islam is in danger." If there is any common thread running through these movements, it lies here.'[15]

This sense of Islam being in danger and at risk of corruption is felt among many of the older immigrants from Islamic countries to Western Europe. The tightening of immigration controls has made it evident to those now resident in Europe that they are there to stay. The rise of racist attacks in Britain, France and Germany have led many, especially second-generation immigrants, to give up all hope of full integration in their countries of reception. International events such as the Iranian revolution, the US attacks on Libya and alleged terrorist targets in other Islamic states, Indian army atrocities in Kashmir, and the genocide in Bosnia, have also served to encourage increasing religious identifications among such immigrants. This greater religious visibility has led to campaigns on issues such as special Islamic schools for Muslim children, the veiling of women and girls, the provision of places of worship and the availability of halal meat. In France, Islamic organizations are already a political force, and that may be the way of Britain in the not-too-distant future.

Many of these campaigns, however, reflect concern over how to maintain control within the community, rather than over an external threat to the survival of Islam. Many of the self-appointed leaders of Muslim immigrant communities express anxiety over the extent to which the younger generation will continue to respect the faith. Salman Rushdie's controversial novel *The Satanic Verses* gave expression to the migrant's experience of alienation both from his country of reception (e.g. his reflections on the racism of the British police) and from the customs and traditions of the country he has left permanently. As Fred Halliday notes, the reaction of outrage to the novel itself gave expression to a sense of 'erosion, real or imagined', for 'Rushdie's main challenge to the Islamic world, beyond his Rabelaisian account of early Islam, is to have broken away from it'. Khomeini accused him of *kufr*, which can mean not only atheism or blasphemy but also apostasy. 'It is this latter charge that is the most serious since, in writing as he did of Mohammed, of doubt, of the profane masquerading as the religious, Rushdie represented a challenge from within that embattled religious leaders, in Bradford as in Tehran, could not accept.'[16]

> What this suggests above all is that for all their assertiveness the Muslim communities in Western Europe feel themselves to be under threat: it is the fear of loss of social control that animates the activities of their leaders, traditional and new. Here, of course, their concern has been shared by many of the most vocal leaders of the Islamic world, including Khomeini. Aggressive and aggrieved as they may sound, theirs is a defensive cry ... Islam is 'in danger', and it is seen to be under threat not so much from without, something that has always been the case, as from the loss of belief and of submission emerging from within.[17]

The myth of unity

Another myth propagated by Muslims and non-Muslims alike is the supposed unity and equality of the 'community of believers' (*ummah*) or the 'household of Islam' (*dar-ul Islam*). This has never been true of the Muslim world since the time of the first caliph, Abu Bakr. Within twenty-five years of the death of Muhammad, Muslim believers were killing each other on the field of battle. From the beginnings of the Muslim conquests, discrimination on the grounds of ethnicity and colour was routinely practised in the community. The superiority of Arab Muslims over non-Arab Muslims (converts from the local populace) was taken for granted in rules pertaining to marriage and military leadership. The reign of the first four 'rightly-guided caliphs',[18] often referred to by Sunni Muslims as the Golden Age of Islam, was marked by intrigue, treachery, assassinations and family rivalry.

Even during the medieval period in Europe, when Islamic civilization was at its zenith, the 'Abbasid caliphate' in Baghdad was contested by caliphates in Spain and Egypt. The Ottoman Turks claimed the caliphate for their sultans in the fifteenth century and ruled most of the Middle East and the Balkans until the First World War. After Kemal Ataturk, the Turkish nationalist leader, abolished the caliphate in 1923, the *dar-ul Islam* has been the arena for some of the bloodiest struggles for supremacy in the Middle East (for instance, the war between Iran and Iraq).

Some of the most terrible acts of repression and genocide have been perpetrated within Islamic states against Muslim religious minorities seen as deviations from the true faith. Despite its rhetoric, the Organization of the Islamic Conference has been unable to mobilize a united and effective Muslim response on issues from Palestine and Afghanistan to the Gulf War and Bosnia. Libya's Muammar Qaddafi, Egypt's Anwar Sadat and Sudan's Muhammad Nimeiri were all bitter enemies of each other while vociferously projecting an 'Islamic' image. National interest and regional politics, rather than religion, remain the primary consideration in the formulation of foreign policy. Thus, to talk of some enduring, transhistorical conflict between a monolithic Islam and a monolithic West is to inhabit a world of fantasy.

The Muslims of Western Europe, who appear a homogeneous culture to the outside world, are also fragmented into various religious sects in addition to ethnic, linguistic and political groupings that reflect the wider 'world of Islam'. In Britain there are Pakistanis, Bengalis and Indians, as well as Turkish Cypriots and a variety of Arabs. Each national category conceals local and linguistic differences – Punjabis, Sindhis, Pathans, Gujeratis and Baluchis among Pakistanis, for example. Attendance at mosques breaks down almost entirely into such ethnic or regional lines. Islamic states such as Iran, Libya and Saudi Arabia vie with each other for leadership of the world's Muslims, and have sought to influence migrant communities in the West with financial inducements. Massive donations towards the building of mosques and the publication of Islamic literature is one way of seeking to exercise control over those from other communities as well as one's own country. Ayatollah Khomeini's campaign against Rushdie was, in part, aimed at strengthening his claim to be the spiritual leader of all Muslims, Sunni as well as Shi'a. Kalim Siddiqi's misnamed 'Muslim Parliament' in Britain spoke for no-one but its own members, and its support for Iran in the Iran–Iraq War was intended to hit back at the Saudi regime.

The myth of separation

A further weakness in the views represented by writers such as Huntington is the lack of appreciation for the way cultures and civilizations, far from being sealed into watertight compartments, have always interpenetrated and borrowed from each other. In the case of Islamic civilization, for instance, such interdependence has existed from the earliest times. Some familiarity with Jewish and Christian traditions is evident in the Qur'an. The mystical tradition within Islam, known as Sufism, was strongly influenced in its organization and disciplines by the Christian monastic orders. (Indeed, the word *sufi*, meaning 'wool', is very likely derived from the long woollen robes worn by Christian hermits in the Syrian desert.) Christian Neo-platonism found its way into

Muslim theological writings and even influenced the way some thought of Muhammad in terms of a created *Logos* of God. The Arabs were impressed by Persian and Byzantine architectural styles in the lands of their conquest and readily incorporated them into the design of their mosques, especially the domes and arches.

Christians, Jews and Zoroastrians lived in the new Arab empire as tax-paying religious ghettos (*dhimmis*). They provided the administrators, secretaries, scholars, craftsmen and peasants, teaching their nomadic conquerors the skills of governance and urban planning. The best-known and most far-reaching influences came through the translation of Greek works of philosophy, science and medicine into Arabic. These translations were, at the beginning, almost exclusively the work of Christian priests and physicians employed in the courts of Muslim rulers. The first translations from Greek to Arabic were via Syriac, the language of the Persian Christian churches.

Muslim scholars were quick to exploit the value of these writings and they, in turn, paved the way for the scientific revival in Europe by pioneering modern mathematical techniques such as algebra and scientific instruments, e.g. the astrolabe, and by making outstanding astronomical observations. Europe received the fruits of Islamic learning mainly from Muslim Spain. The first Latin translations of Aristotle were made from the Arabic, and for more than three hundred years European scholars read Aristotle with the help of the commentaries of Islamic philosophers, most notably that of the Spaniard, Ibn Rushd (better known in Western philosophy textbooks as Averroës, who died in 1198).[19]

Much of this is acknowledged in secular history books. What is rarely acknowledged, however, is the influence of non-Western Christians and Jews on the development of both Islamic and European civilization via the Arabs. The Egyptian-born Jewish scholar Bat Ye'or has provided a fresh perspective on this process. She points out that Islamic civilization 'glowed in the full blaze of its glory', not in Mecca or Medina but 'in the lands of dhimmitude, in periods when the dhimmis still formed majorities subject to the conquering Muslim minorities. Under the Arabs, it reached its apogee in the Christian East and in Spain. Similarly, it was not in their Central Asian homeland that the Seljuks and Ottomans founded a prestigious empire, but in Anatolia and the Balkans, through the subjection of its Christian Orthodox populations'.[20]

Zoroastrians, Jacobites (Copts and Syrians), Nestorians, Melchites, and Jews translated into Arabic treatises on astronomy, medicine, alchemy, and philosophy, as well as literary narratives and stories. This work necessitated the invention of new words and the forging of the Arabic language and grammar into new conceptual moulds, not only philosophic, scientific, and literary, but also administrative, economic, political, and diplomatic.[21]

The first known scientific work in Arabic was a treatise on medicine, written in Greek by Ahrun, a Christian priest from Alexandria, and translated from Syriac into Arabic in 683 by a Jewish doctor from Basrah (Iraq).[22]

Later, some of those whose cultures and communities had been ravaged by the Arab armies went into exile:

> The elites who fled to Europe took their cultural baggage with them, their scholarship and their knowledge of the classics of antiquity. Thenceforth, in the Christian lands of refuge – Spain, Provence, Sicily, Italy – cultural centres developed where Christians and Jews from Islamized lands taught to the young Europe the knowledge of the old pre-Islamic Orient, formerly translated into Arabic by their ancestors.[23]

By this account, then, the classical heritage was preserved by Christians and Jews who had integrated the Hellenistic culture with biblical spirituality and then fled to Europe as refugees from Muslim lands. One does not have to accept every aspect of Bat Ye'or's work to recognize that the contribution of Christians to the creation of Islamic civilization has been largely ignored by Muslims, Western Christians and secular writers alike.

'Islam' revisited

In the light of these historical realities, let us consider the following statements:

> (a) 'Islamic culture explains in large part the failure of democracy to emerge in much of the Muslim world.'

> (b) 'The idea of sovereign nation states is incompatible with belief in the sovereignty of Allah and the primacy of the *ummah*.'

These statements are typical examples of what over the past thirty years has come to be criticized as 'orientalism' – the creation (or exaggeration) by some Western scholars of 'the difference between the familiar (Europe, the West, "us") and the strange (the Orient, the East, "them")'[24] and justifying the denigration or suppression of the latter by the former.

Thus, consider this modern example: In his book *De l' Islam en general et du monde moderne en particulier,* the French author Jean-Claude Barreau writes: 'What could be described as the "great humiliation", and what is indeed present in *the basic disposition of the Muslims* can be explained by the origins of their religion: it is warlike, conquest-hungry and full of contempt for the unbeliever.'[25]

Such 'orientalist' assumptions are liberally sprinkled throughout Huntington's treatment of Islam; in fact, both statements are direct quotations from Huntington's text (pp. 29 and 175 respectively). The irony here is that Huntington, as has been pointed out earlier, has uncritically swallowed whole the image of 'Islam' that is sold by Islamist thinkers and organizations.

Much of what passes for Islamic legal codes and traditions is a modern and arbitrarily formulated set of views projected back on to a mythical past; or it is local tradition dressed up as authoritatively 'Islamic'. Examples of the latter are the practice of clitoridectomy or female circumcision, found in parts of Africa and Arabia, and the complete veiling of women. Neither has anything to do with Islamic doctrine. Equally without Quranic basis is the policy implemented in a number of Muslim countries that bans women from being judges. These reflect male-dominated local cultural prejudice, not the eternal teaching of Islam. The Palestinian writer, Azmy Bishara, argues that the word used in modern Arabic to refer to government or regime, *nizam* ('order', 'system'), does not appear anywhere in the Qur'an. 'When Islamic political movements speak today of *nizam hukm islami* (an Islamic system of government) they are expressing a formulation that never existed in the Koran or in the Sunna. The modern demand for social and political life to be governed according to *nizam islami* reflects an approach totally foreign to early Muslims.'[26] Similarly, Khomeini's notion of direct political rule by the religious scholars, far from carrying scriptural or traditional authority, was a radical innovation within Shi'ite Islam.[27]

What we are dealing with, then, is not an established, unchanging tradition, legal or otherwise, but a set of discourses and interpretations that are created by contemporary, secular forces. If we want to know why most Muslims hold the views they do about sexuality, economics, democracy and the like, it is not 'Islam' alone that can explain it. 'Islam' lends itself to multiple interpretations; in the twentieth century it has been used to support democracy and dictatorship, republicanism and monarchy. Moreover, the political realities of the Muslim world have not been conducive to the development of healthy, democratic institutions. The national boundaries of most modern Arab states were drawn up by colonial powers, and the first post-colonial rulers either were appointed by those European powers or seized power for themselves in military coups. 'If there are in a range of Islamic countries evident barriers to democracy,' Fred Halliday observes, 'this has to do with certain other features that their societies share. These would include low levels of development, entrenched traditions of state control, political cultures that inhibit diversity and tolerance, the absence of a tradition of private property, and the lack of separation of state and law.'[28]

The nature and scope of democracy have been vigorously debated in many Muslim communities in the modern era. While the more radical Islamist groups reject any form of democracy as 'Western' and 'un-Islamic', many Islamic activists have given an Islamic rationale for parliamentary democracy and clamoured for it in their opposition to incumbent regimes. Islamic organizations such as the Muslim brotherhoods in Egypt and Jordan, the Jamaat-I-Islami in Pakistan, Kashmir and Bangladesh, Turkey's Welfare Party, as well as Algeria's Islamic Salvation Front, Tunisia's Renaissance party, Kuwait's Jamiyyat al-Islam (Reform Society), among others, have, where permitted, participated in parliamentary elections. In contrast, secular regimes in Egypt and Algeria have brutally repressed Islamist organizations that have massive popular support. Attaturk's reforms in Turkey were imposed harshly, with the solid approval of Western powers, even to the extent of banning the use of traditional dress. The present secular government in Turkey seeks to exclude the popular Islamist movement from the electoral process. It is ironic that religious fanaticism is vilified in the Western media while secular fanaticism is either ignored or commended in the name of democracy!

Moreover, political cultures and institutions are not transformed overnight. Europe moved from being an aggregation of feudal monarchies to representative democracies over several centuries, and the process was often violent and fragmentary. Democracy has also meant different things at different periods and to different groups in Western history. Despite having a constitution that enshrined democratic values, American blacks, natives and women began to enjoy equal rights only in the second half of the twentieth century. Only time will tell whether the experiment in parliamentary democracy in Iran will lead to a genuine respect for minority rights; or whether participation in the electoral process by Islamist movements is purely a means to seizing power or represents a serious reinterpretation of religious tradition arising from recent experience.

Halliday also notes that:

> As on many other issues, the main texts of Islam are silent on whether it is desirable for societies to be organized around nationalism or pan-Islamism; capitalism or socialism or, for that matter, slavery; state

control of the economy or private ownership. Nor does Islam tell us about the circumstances in which the state should be opposed or supported; whether there should be one state or many; whether believers should embrace modernity or tradition.[29]

The only parts of the Islamic traditional texts that are sacred are the Qur'an itself, which is said to be the word of God, and the *Sunna*, or the record of the sayings and actions of the prophet Muhammad which were first collected and codified a couple of centuries after his death. Azmy Bishara reminds us that the Muslim religion is primarily not one of legislation and law – unlike Judaism, in which *halakah* orders cultural relations down to the minutest detail. He writes:

> The Koran has 6,000 verses, of which 700 deal with religious laws governing *ubadah* and *mu'amalat* (i.e. matters between persons and God and matters between persons and their neighbours). Only 200 of these actually prescribe 'laws' dealing with matters of conjugal life, inheritance and criminal law. In addition, the validity of some verses is cancelled out by others, so that, all in all, there are no more than 80 verses that actually can be said to 'lay down the law' in any unequivocal sense. From these 80 verses Islamic law must derive the inspiration for its endeavour to order modern society and its problems.[30]

Other sources of Muslim law are the *ijma*, or consensus (lit. 'convergence') of the community, and *qiyas*, a process of analogical reasoning whereby – in the case of no clear ruling in either the Qur'an or the *Sunna* – scholars (the *ulema*) try to find some comparable ruling that suggests an appropriate parallel in the contemporary situation. Four major schools of law developed between AD 800 and 950, giving different weight to each of these sources.[31] All accepted the primacy of the Qur'an and the *Sunna*, while the most conservative reject the authority of both *ijma* and *qiyas*. The finality of these four schools of Islamic jurisprudence have been challenged since the nineteenth century by Muslim scholars responding to modern conditions and other systems of law.

It is this humanly evolved and variously codified body of legal material that has come to be referred to by the misleading term *shari'a*. Islamist movements claim that *shari'a* law is a divinely given code which is quite sufficient for Muslim society and which requires no revision by subsequent cultural, legal, or ethical considerations. The term *shari'a*, literally 'path' or 'way', did not initially denote a legal code at all, but was used in a more general way to speak of good order, perhaps like the Hindu concept of *dharma*. What is today invoked as an unchangeable and sacred body of law is, even in Islamic terms, nothing of the sort. The late Sir Norman Anderson, a universally recognized authority on Islamic jurisprudence, has described *shari'a* as 'an amorphous volume of partly contradictory doctrine, to which lip service, at least, was invariably given and which came to stand, like a sentinel, to bar the path of progress'.[32]

What about the so-called *hudud* punishments (the word means 'limits'), punishments that are considered 'fixed' and therefore binding on all Islamic courts for ever? These are not in fact prescribed in the Qur'an, and have been introduced on the basis that they are found in the *Sunna*. For instance, neither the penalty of eighty lashes for consuming alcoholic liquor nor the stoning to death of adulterers is prescribed in the Qur'an. Both these so-called *hudud* punishments are taken from the *Sunna*. Michael Nazir-Ali, the Pakistani-born Bishop of Rochester in England, observes that the other three *hudud* punishments, namely, the cutting off of the hand for theft of goods worth over a certain value, the lashing of those who accuse a woman falsely of adultery, and the cutting off of the hand and the foot of the opposite side for robbers 'are mentioned in the Qur'an (5.41, 24.4 and 5.36), but immediately following in each case is an injunction to forgive such criminals if they repent of their misdeeds'.[33]

Nazir-Ali also comments:

> It is only fair to point out that even when *hudud* punishments *are* enforced, the law of evidence is so strict that it is extremely difficult to obtain a conviction. For example, in the case of adultery four eyewitnesses to whom *no* major sin can be imputed must testify that penetration has taken place. A husband's testimony may be received on its own but the wife is to be acquitted if she denies the charge under oath.[34]

It seems that any application of the *shari'a* can only be selective, even in the most rigid of Islamic states. In Saudi Arabia, for all its vaunted adherence to tradition, slavery was abolished in 1962, and the rules of the *shari'a* which applied to insurance and certain other commercial contracts have been relaxed. As Anderson notes: 'It must, after all, be realized that to go right "back to the Shari'a" would be, *inter alia*, to go back to a very detailed law of slavery, polygamy, arbitrary divorce, male chauvinism and cruel physical punishments – together with the death penalty for those Muslims who renounce Islam or embrace any other religion.'[35] (Ironically, the Kuwaiti government discarded the *shari'a* rule stating that a Muslim woman loses her civic status [including the dissolution of her marriage] on abandoning Islam, in order to prevent women converting to other faiths as a way of escaping oppressive marriages. Thus the *shari'a* is conveniently ignored whenever male interests are threatened!)

Similarly, the blasphemy law of section 295-C of the Pakistan Penal Code is a relatively recent invention ushered in by the late President Zia ul-Haq. The original law, enacted in 1986, stipulated 'death, or imprisonment for life and fine' for 'derogatory remarks … by words, either spoken or written, or by visible representations' intended to 'defile the sacred name of the Holy Prophet'. In October 1990, the Federal *shari'a* Court declared that the 'penalty for contempt of the Holy Prophet … is death and nothing else'. The legitimacy for such a law of blasphemy, that demands a mandatory death sentence, can come only from two sources: the Qur'an and the directive of the Prophet himself. There is nothing in either that gives support for such laws. Where the Qur'an does mention blasphemy, it is never associated with speaking ill of Muhammad. In the case of wrong teachings about God, it prescribes no earthly punishment but points instead to the day of final judgment (e.g. Qur'an 5.76).

This is why the description of Islamic militancy as 'fundamentalist' can be so misleading. If 'fundamentalism' is taken to mean a *sola Scriptura* position when it comes to political and legal arrangements, Islamists and regimes committed to programmes of 'Islamization' are far from fundamentalist. The poet-philosopher Muhammad Iqbal (1873–1938), revered as the spiritual father of Pakistan for his eloquent advocacy of a separate state for Indian Muslims, was one Muslim reformer who, arguing from a strict position of *sola Scriptura*, opposed the reintroduction of the *shari'a* penal code. As for *ijma*, the 'convergence' of the community which had first been applied to all the inhabitants of Mecca and Medina and was later applied to the consensus of the doctors of law (*ulema*) in a particular period, Iqbal believed that in a modern Islamic state it should be vested in an elected legislature which would be 'guided' by some members of the *ulema* who would also belong to the legislature. Thus, ironically, it seems that those most open to the acceptance of democratic political principles have been those who have stood closest to the primacy of the Qur'an.

The strongly Islamist Saudi regime, for instance, is influenced more by the eighteenth-century Wahahbi movement in Arabia than by any 'pure' Quranic teaching. Some of its harsh punitive practices which attract the attention of the world media, such as beheading for adultery, are prescribed neither in the

Qur'an nor in any tradition. 'Abd al-Wahhab (1703–92) and his followers rejected not only 'superstitious' practices of what is commonly called 'folk Islam' – such as the veneration of saints and visits to the tombs and relics of saints – but also the devotional works of Sufi poets.

Consequently, we should not identify Islamism with either the conservatism of the established *ulema* or the popular Islam of the masses. Azmy Bishara points out that the Egyptian *ulema* establishment, for instance, 'does not accept change; nor are they capable of introducing or promoting changes which have not already permeated the ruling elites. When they do issue rulings in favour of change, they do so unwillingly.'[36] Antagonism between elitist religious-political movements and the community of ordinary believers is also much more common than is depicted in the Western media and by Islamist propagandists alike. The declaration by the founder of the Muslim Brotherhood in Egypt, Hassan al-Banna, is relevant here: 'Our task is in fact nothing more than an offensive against widespread customs and a transformation of traditional practices.'[37]

Traditionally, it is *ijma* (consensus) that determines what the *Sunna* is, and how it is to be interpreted and applied. In regard to the Qur'an itself, there has been a long debate about whether some verses have been abrogated by others, as most Muslims believe, and, if so, which verses were abrogated by which. The greater part of the *shari'a* was developed by jurists from *ijma* and *qiyas* (analogy) – hence the deep ambiguity in statements enshrined in several Islamic constitutions, such as in Pakistan, demanding that all laws be 'in conformity with the Holy Qur'an and *Sunna*'.

Islam and human rights

One area in which Western critique of the dominant Islamic tradition *does* seem to be valid concerns the adaptability of Islamic doctrine and practice to modern ideas of human rights. Seventy per cent of the world's Muslims live in about fifty countries, where Muslims are the majority and the law of the state is based either on *shari'a* alone, or on a combination of *shari'a* and Western law of some kind. Almost all these states have been systematic violators of human rights, even by their own limited definitions. Projects to 'Islamize' law, as in Pakistan and Sudan, are calculated attempts by regimes to consolidate their own power by silencing critics and social groups targeted by these laws.

There have, of course, been those within Muslim-majority states who have campaigned courageously for human rights, but many of them are either in exile or imprisoned. The concept of human rights and the question of how the safeguarding of such rights relates to the Islamic tradition remain contested issues in the Muslim world. At one extreme are those Muslims, usually resident in the West, who maintain that Islam easily accommodates international human-rights norms.[38] At the other extreme are Muslims, perhaps the majority, who claim that these norms are completely alien to and incompatible with Islam and Islamic law.

Recent years have witnessed the rise of Muslim groups who assert that Islam is the only proper ground for a doctrine of universal human rights – rights which, it is either alleged or implied, do not conflict with the premodern *shari'a* rules. They have formulated various schemes of 'Islamic human rights' as alternatives to the internationally recognized human-rights charters. However, in a careful study of these Islamic human-rights schemes, the legal scholar Ann Mayer observes that they are an awkward *mélange* of selective borrowings from both the Islamic heritage and international norms:

> The authors lack any clear theory of what rights should mean in an Islamic context or how to derive their content from the Islamic sources in a principled and consistent fashion. Instead, they merely assemble pastiches of ideas and terminology drawn from two very different cultures without determining a rationale for these combinations or a way to reconcile the conflicting premises underlying them.[39]

A major issue facing Islamic movements is their ability, if in power, to tolerate religious diversity and political dissent. Recent experiments in Pakistan, Iran, the Sudan and Afghanistan raise serious questions about the rights of women, Muslim dissidents and non-Muslim minorities under Islamically oriented governments. The growth of Islamic revivalism has often gone hand-in-hand with attempts to restrict the roles of women in society, to separate women and men in public, and to impose and enforce veiling. This raises legitimate fears among many Muslims and non-Muslims alike and challenges the credibility of those who call for the Islamization of state and society.

Surely one of the most significant tests of human rights is the freedom of religious conversion. Islam, both in practice and in theology, does not find it easy to accept the idea of Muslims becoming Christians. 'Conversion to Christianity (or to any other religion) is generally regarded as a betrayal of family and community, and as apostasy which deserves the severest punishment.'[40]

This is how Colin Chapman humbly but clearly expresses the challenge to Islamic societies:

> It is hard to draw a clear dividing line between what happens in a local

community and what is done by the group in the name of Islam. However charitable we want to be, we have to reckon with the fact that in the majority of cases Muslims who want to become disciples of Christ are thought of and treated as apostates and outcasts from their family and community.[41]

Once again it is dependence on the *Sunna* literature that seems to be the overriding obstacle. The Qur'an does speak of punishment for apostasy, but it is an eschatological punishment (Qur'an 3.85f.; 16.106ff.). However, several traditions ascribe to the Prophet sayings about apostasy deserving the death penalty, and it is these that were taken up by all the four Islamic schools of jurisprudence. All are agreed that an adult male Muslim who changes his religion must be put to death, provided he is in full possession of his faculties and has not acted under coercion. In the period of the so-called 'righteous caliphs', the neighbouring political empires of Persia and Byzantium were defined by a single religion (Zoroastrianism in the case of the former, Christianity in the latter); and so it is understandable why conversion to another faith was considered an act of treason, punishable by death.

Moreover, demands by Western powers that non-Muslim minorities be exempt from *shari'a* regulations are still associated in most Muslims' minds with the ugly story of European imperialism in the Middle East. In the nineteenth century, European powers appointed themselves the protectors of the various local Christian minorities, using allegations of mistreatment of non-Muslims as pretexts for interfering in Middle Eastern politics.[42] The treatment of non-Muslims thus became the focus for contentions about legitimacy between Middle Eastern rulers and European countries with imperialist ambitions. European dominance in Middle Eastern societies favoured non-Muslim minorities, as in Britain's use of its mandate over Palestine to foster the development of a Jewish homeland, and such rule was usually justified as necessary for the protection of non-Muslims from Muslim oppression.

> Since European powers were notably lacking in sympathy for the aspirations of freedom on the part of the Muslim population of the Middle East and concern for Muslim rights and well-being ... Muslims, when reviewing past Western disregard for the rights of Muslims, may respond with anger to contemporary Western criticisms that judge the human rights policies of independent Muslim countries in a hypocritical and self-righteous manner.[43]

The context of today's debate has significantly changed, however. Most Islamic states are signatories to the UN Declaration on Human Rights, and Article 18 of the UN Declaration on Human Rights states: 'Everyone has the right to freedom of thought, conscience and religion; this right includes freedom to change his religion or belief, and freedom, either alone or in community with others and in public or private, to manifest his religion or belief in teaching, practice, worship, and observance.'

Consequently, those Muslims who demand the adoption of Islamic forms of government and the imposition of laws discriminating against non-Muslims, are not fighting alien forces bent on colonial domination but fellow Muslims in their own societies who believe that being a Muslim is compatible with support for constitutional government and equality of citizens. The Republican Brotherhood in Sudan, for instance, argued that Islam established an egalitarian order in which men and women, Muslim and non-Muslim, would enjoy equality before the law. The leader of the Republican Brothers, Mahmoud Muhammad Taha, taught that *shari'a* rules were not timeless but contextual, intended to deal with problems in the early Muslim community. Thus, he discarded those rules that conflicted with modern human-rights norms, arguing that they were not permanently binding on Muslims everywhere.[44] Inevitably, this led to conflict with the Nimeiri regime, notorious for its brutal record on human rights, and Taha himself was executed in 1985.

Thus, the question of the rights and treatment of non-Muslim minorities is also highly relevant for the scope of religious freedom accorded to Muslim dissenters and sects within Islam which are opposed to the version of Islam endorsed by an Islamic government. The Baha'is in Iran, the Ahmadis in Pakistan, and the Republican Brothers in Sudan have all been victims of gross violence in the name of Islam. As Ann Mayer notes, all the Islamic human-rights schemes are evasive on the issue of religious freedom and do not offer any protection for religious minorities comparable with those in international human-rights law:

> The failure of a single one of these Islamic human rights schemes to take a position against the application of the *shari'a* death penalty for apostasy means that the authors of these schemes have neglected to confront and resolve the main issues involved in harmonizing international human rights and *shari'a* standards.[45]

The chilling words of Mawlana Mawdudi (1903–79), founder of the influential Islamist organization *Jama'at-I-Islami* (Community of Islam), thus seem to be representative of Islamic history and tradition: 'Islam is a one-way door; you can enter through it but you cannot leave.' Kenneth Cragg sharply sums up a Christian response to Mawdudi: 'A faith which you are not free to leave becomes a prison, and no self-respecting faith should be a prison for those within it.'[46]

Occidentalism?

Now, let us consider the following statements:

(a) 'Hatred of Islam and of Muslims is *endemic* to the European psyche.'[47]

(b) 'There is an *inherent* tendency in Western society to view women as hate objects.'[48]

These quotations represent the mirror-image of 'orientalism' and perhaps should be labelled as examples of 'occidentalism'. It is a prominent feature of Muslim writings, both serious and popular: the West is depicted as a monolithic entity, irredeemably materialist, immoral and decadent, and characterized by aggressiveness, expansionism and intolerance towards Islam and Muslims.

These clichéd images of the West show remarkable similarities to the clichéd images of Islam that appear in some Western writings and which Muslims correctly denounce. There is little sense of the complex history of the West and the rich interaction of movements, forces and ideologies that have shaped the present European and American peoples. 'Divinely guided society' is society organized along divinely sanctioned *shari'a* law; anything contrary is demonized. In the 'West' spiritual barrenness and moral corruption prevail, and women are degraded as sex objects. The repugnant materialism of wealthy Arabs, Pakistanis, Malays and Indonesians is either ignored altogether or blamed on ubiquitous 'Western values'. So is the fact that many Western women suffer sexual harassment in states that call themselves Islamic, and many high-class prostitutes in London and other European capitals are kept in business by Arab playboys who, at the same time, run their private serfdoms in the Gulf. In any case, both orientalism and occidentalism reduce complex cultures and peoples, and the historically contingent relations among them, to monochrome stories of unchanging 'essences' and 'psyches'.

It is ironic that statement (b) above stems from one of the more irenic, liberal Muslims resident in Britain, the Pakistani-born social anthropologist Dr Akbar Ahmed. Professor Ahmed is also one of the authors of a report on

Islamophobia issued by the Runnymede Trust in October 1997.[49] The report extensively documents cases of anti-Muslim prejudices in the British media, educational institutions and employment. The term 'Islamophobia' is now commonplace among Muslims in the West as a description of all such anti-Muslim attitudes and behaviour. But such Islamophobia cannot be discussed in isolation from the numerous instances of 'Westophobia' that occur in Muslim countries and among Muslim groups in Britain and other Western nations. And, if Muslims rightly resent the negative stereotyping of a monolithic Islam by Western writers, then they need to look with equal dismay at the identical stereotyping that is widespread in the Muslim world, and no less among the authors of the Runnymede Report.[50]

Anti-Western polemic often blends with anti-Christian sentiments, even in the more serious Muslim literature. Moreover, Kate Zebiri, a lecturer in Arabic and Islamic Studies at the University of London, has noted that 'the study of Christianity by modern Muslims does not, on the whole, compare favourably with that of the medieval scholars', many of whom considered it important to understand the arguments and doctrines of Christianity on their own terms before seeking to refute them.[51] Ironically, 'Christianity is sometimes portrayed in the very same terms that have been used of Islam in both earlier orientalist scholarship and the contemporary media: as power-seeking and war-mongering on the one hand, and irrational, obscurantist, backward-looking, and in need of reformation on the other.'[52]

Zebiri's observations on Muslim bookshops in Britain also apply to many other parts of the world:

> Muslim anti-Christian polemic goes relatively unnoticed, even in the age of the mass media, because it occurs within an almost exclusively Muslim market, and is rarely subject to critical scrutiny. Where Muslim bookshops stock books on Christianity authored by non-Muslims, they tend to be selected titles, often bestsellers, which are deemed either to cast aspersions on the origins of Christianity or to reflect badly on Christians by exposing some scandal ... So long as such outlets continue to be selective in this way, and to stock the works of Ahmed Deedat to the exclusion of books which provide accurate objective information on Christianity, and so long as Muslims do not in any significant numbers acquire such information by other means, the process of disinformation will continue.[53]

Occidentalism, moreover, is not confined to some Muslim scholars or the propaganda of Islamist organizations. It was rampant in the speeches of men like Lee Kuan Yew of Singapore, Mahathir Mohamad, Prime Minister of Malaysia, and the late Deng Xiao Ping in China, in the late 1980s and early 1990s. Until the East Asian economic 'bubble' burst in late 1997, it was common to hear these men expounding the superiority of 'Asian values' (and in the case of Lee, specifically 'Confucian values') in defence of their highly authoritarian or patronizing styles of leadership. It was a discourse of resistance to sharp criticisms from the USA and Europe of the terrible human-rights records of countries such as China, Myanmar and Indonesia. By 'Asian values', they meant not only the virtues of family loyalty and hard work (which presumably are not confined to Asia), but, much more dubiously, the rejection of participatory democracy and all political dissent. Here, writ large, is the classic orientalist image of the 'Asian despot', propagated not by Western colonialists but by self-appointed spokesmen for the peoples of Asia. Mahathir took the rhetoric even further: 'Asian values are universal values. European values are European values,' he asserted at a summit of European and Asian governmental heads in 1996.[54]

Huntington, of course, tends to perpetuate the myth. 'East Asian economic success has its source in East Asian culture,' he declares with incredible self-assurance. He continues, '… as do the difficulties East Asian societies have had in achieving stable democratic political systems.'[55] For Huntington, peoples as disparate in historical background and general outlook as the Thais and Singaporeans all come under an all-embracing 'East Asian culture'. What constitutes this 'East Asian culture', and how it is unique, let alone how it serves as an explanatory factor for economic and political developments, are never clarified. More damagingly, there is hardly any recognition that the economic success may have been due to factors other than indigenous culture – e.g. the character of immigrant societies (typically self-reliant and hard-working), the massive investment (military and economic) in the region by the US to counter the threat of communist aggression – or that the failure of democracy owes as much to persistent US intervention in internal politics and the backing of brutal dictatorships almost until the end of the Cold War as it owes to the nature of East Asian culture.

Huntington identifies the economic prosperity of Asian economies as the source of the rhetoric of moral and cultural superiority. But this is a partial truth. The 'assertiveness' of East Asian cultures really boils down to the hubris of a few power-hungry politicians and army generals, all of them male and all of them old. The economic prosperity of Chinese peoples in Hong Kong or Singapore had little to do with the teachings of Confucius. Nineteenth-century intellectuals in China, as well as twentieth-century communists, denounced Confucianism as the biggest stumbling-block to economic advancement. If

Confucianism is now being rehabilitated in these countries, it is more a strategy of resistance both to the attractiveness of Christian teachings among Chinese intellectuals and the pressure (emanating from both Christian and secular sources) for greater freedoms of political expression.

Unbridgeable differences?

Perhaps we can now delineate the flaw in Huntington's overall argument. There are two separate issues which need to be clearly distinguished. The first has to do with the observation that justifications for political actions which appeal to culture or religion are more common now than they were in international politics a decade or so ago. The second issue is whether, in fact, differences of culture or religion *are* what precipitate international conflicts and determine the forms of international co-operation. Huntington fails, for the most part, to recognize this crucial difference.

On Huntington's policy recommendations, the United States must not try to impose a Western language of 'human rights' on the rest of the world. The US must aim to consolidate its affinities with Europe, and not with Asia or the Middle East as these belong to incompatible civilizations. By portraying the contemporary world as one of mutually contradictory and intrinsically hostile cultural communities vying with each other for global power, Huntington runs the risk of making the 'clash of civilizations' a self-fulfilling prophecy. The more we believe it, the more likely it is to come true. States such as Turkey and Egypt which are friendly towards the West will be pushed more and more towards the camp of the Islamists. Also, since Islamist movements thrive on local economic inequalities and deepening social misery, discriminatory practices against Muslims in Europe and the US, and the unwillingness to confront military aggression and the killing or imprisonment of Muslims abroad will only fuel the growing appeal of militant Islamism worldwide.

Huntington is, of course, quite right that despite all claims to the contrary – be they Islamic, Confucian, Gandhian, or other – the international codes on human rights arose in Western societies and were codified and promoted largely by Western states and non-governmental organizations. However, the fact that concepts such as human rights and democracy may have originated in European societies does not deny their universal validity, any more than in the case of natural science. This is a fallacious argument. Since 1948 many non-Western governments have come to embrace universal declarations on civic and political rights.

The fact that those states and societies which proclaimed human rights most loudly were also dominating and exploiting the rest of the world for centuries – and still seek to mantain a hegemony over the international economic system – does not mean that the West must now deny the validity of these ideas out of guilt over its hypocrisy and a new commitment to 'multiculturalism'. What it requires, instead, is that Western states and societies learn to practise them more consistently within their own borders and in their relations with others.

Moreover, talk of incompatibility between Western civilization and Islamist militancy is contradicted by recent history, which affords countless examples of American complicity with brutal Islamist regimes and movements. Consider Western policy towards Pakistan. In the 1980s the USA gave massive support and arms to Zia ul-Haq, a general who came to power in a military coup. Zia was responsible for a repressive programme of Islamization under which many Muslims as well as non-Muslims suffered the loss of civic rights. His dictatorship was involved in heroin smuggling and the building of nuclear missiles. But, because they needed his territory as a base from which to support the *Mujahidin* in Afghanistan, the American government turned a blind eye to these peccadilloes.

Support of the Afghan *Mujahidin* with goods and arms against the Soviet Union, and, following the Soviet withdrawal, against the secular government of President Najibullah, was the largest and most successful operation ever undertaken by the CIA. The *Mujahidin* received massive amounts of arms and financial aid from the CIA, regardless of their political orientation or Islamist zeal. It did not seem to worry the CIA that the arch-fundamentalist Gulbuddin Hekmatyar's party was openly not only anti-Soviet but also anti-American, and that it was responsible for massacres, torture, heroin trafficking, and just about every conceivable human-rights abuse. It was only when he openly took Saddam Hussein's side in the Gulf War that the Americans distanced themselves from him. Similarly, in the case of the Sudan, Ja'far Nimeiri's unpopular regime enjoyed strong support from the US, even during its harsh programme of Islamization in 1983–85.

The Gulf War itself contradicts Huntington's prediction that conflicts between civilizations will be more likely than conflicts within the same civilization. In the Gulf War, civilizational identities were irrelevant. One Islamic state attacked a fellow Islamic state. Some misguided Islamic intellectuals in the West and in other Islamic countries may have rallied around Saddam Hussein, but the fact remains that a coalition of Western states defended feudal and repressive Islamic regimes in Kuwait and Saudi Arabia against a secular Iraq. Saudi Arabia, which is the strongest ally of the US and Britain in the Middle East, next to Israel, is the most intolerant state one could imagine. No Christian, even though he be a foreigner, can carry a Bible in the country. No Christian churches can be built, and even prayer meetings in private homes are likely to be broken up by the religious police. The Saudi leadership has also traditionally been committed to exporting its own brand of Islam. The Islamists in Sudan and other countries have been nurtured with Saudi money. As far as the Gulf is concerned, it is not religion that matters as much as power and strategic interests.

These examples undermine any notions of intrinsic incompatibility between 'American interests' and 'Islamist values'. In fact where foreign policy is concerned, both American and Middle Eastern heads of state disguise their pragmatic actions in religious rhetoric. American presidents like Reagan, Bush and Clinton have liberally sprinkled their foreign-policy speeches with references to 'God' and biblical allusions. Moreover, the Middle East is a region where political statements are couched in religious or quasi-religious language, much stronger than that used by Washington. Baghdad and Tehran both want to control the Gulf region and so does the USA. All three have enough economic, political and strategic reasons without needing a religious one. Nevertheless, none of these states would openly admit to this. Significantly, both Saddam Hussein and George Bush formulated their battle for supremacy in the Gulf in religious terms: *jihad* versus moral crusade.

Religious rhetoric

In their well-known study of American 'civil religion', *Habits of the Heart,*[56] Robert Bellah and his colleagues drew attention to the way the inaugural addresses of most American presidents are peppered with references to God and with biblical allusions. President Carter was one president whose faith went beyond a vague civil religion to embrace a more biblical Christianity. In his efforts to reach an agreement between Israel and Egypt at Camp David, Carter seemed motivated by religious considerations: 'I think the fact that we worship the same God and are bound by basically the same moral principles is a possible source for resolution of differences. I was always convinced that if Sadat and Begin could get together, they would be bound by that common belief.'[57] Here Islam does not appear to be a threat; the common ground between Islam, Judaism and Christianity is seen as a precondition of the Camp David Agreement.

In 1898, President McKinley recounted to a group of visiting clergymen how he had come to the decision to annex the Philippines: 'I walked the floor of the White House night after night until midnight', and more than once 'went down on my knees and prayed Almighty God for light and guidance'. One night he received God's answer: there was no question of turning the

Philippines over to America's commercial rivals, France or Germany, for 'that would be bad business', nor of leaving them to themselves. McKinley concluded: 'There was nothing left for us to do but to take them all, and to educate the Filipinos, and uplift and civilize and Christianize them and by God's grace do the very best we could by them, as our fellow men for whom Christ has also died. And then I went to bed, and to sleep, and slept soundly.'[58]

Inspiration from God as the basis for foreign policy and colonial expansion: should we use this as an argument to question the secular nature of the USA or Western states as a whole? Probably not. But this does raise serious doubts about that comfortable pair of opposites – Western / secular / pragmatic on the one hand and Middle Eastern / religious / ideological on the other. We should remind ourselves that, while some politicians in all countries are genuinely motivated by personal religious conviction in the execution of their political office, religious vocabulary uttered by politicians should not automatically be taken at face value, but is often used simply to give legitimacy to their actions. While this may appear obvious to us where our own leaders are concerned, we do tend to take the religious utterances of other leaders literally – as if they were not political pronouncements but actual religious ones. How Christian, for example, are the Christian Democratic parties of Europe?

John Esposito, an American student of the Arab world, believes that there are lessons to be learned from the Cold War:

> Viewing the Soviet Union through the prism of the 'evil empire' was ideologically reassuring and emotionally satisfying, justifying the expenditure of enormous resources and the support of a vast military-industrial complex. However, our easy stereotypes of the enemy and the monolithic nature of the communist threat also proved costly in other respects. Despite an enormous amount of intelligence and analysis, few seemed to know until the end that the emperor had no clothes. Neither government agencies nor academic think tanks predicted the extent and speed of the disintegration of the Soviet empire. The exaggerated fears and static vision which drove us to take Herculean steps against a monolithic enemy blinded us to the diversity within the Soviet Union and the profound changes that were taking place.[59]

A mutual challenge

In conclusion, I offer the following suggestions as a way forward from the present morass of confusion.

First, we should try to avoid using religious categories such as 'Muslim', 'Christian', 'Buddhist' or 'Hindu' to describe an ethnic or cultural group. It could be argued that all cultures have religious underpinnings; and that even secular nationalism has all the characteristics of a religious faith (a theme that I shall pursue in a later chapter). But none of the major world faiths can be encapsulated within any particular culture. Writers such as Huntington muddy the waters by occasionally referring to the West as 'Christendom', when Christian missions long ago liberated Christianity from its identification with any one culture, let alone a geographical territory. He is oblivious to the fact that the bulk of the world's Christians live in Asia, Africa and Latin America; or that there are over 15 million Christians in the Middle East, most of whom are members of ancient Christian communities that pre-date the rise of Islam.

No doubt the Islamic world is far more homogeneous than the Christian church; and this reflects the untranslatability of the Qur'an in comparison with what Andrew Walls has called the 'infinite translatability of the Christian faith'. We shall return to this theme in a later chapter.

Secondly, whatever religious traditions we belong to and whatever religious convictions we hold, we should apply the same standards to political phenomena in other societies that we apply to our own. Thus, just as Christians living in Europe would not wish to associate National Socialism, Fascism or Stalinism with Christianity or even with some enduring, transhistorical entity called 'Western culture', so most Muslims would not identify Shi'ite terrorism in the Middle East with Shi'a Islam. As Esposito observes, in a relatively recent American context:

> Many failed to make the same distinctions with regard to Islam and Islamic organizations between the actions of a radical minority and the mainstream majority that were made so easily when ... the world watched the Branch Davidian sect, an extremist 'Christian' group in Waco, Texas, kill FBI agents and, protected by an astonishing arsenal of weapons, hold off federal authorities for weeks.[60]

What this would also entail is that we seek to understand the rise of any political movement against the backdrop of the specific social, economic and political situation of the country or cultural group in question. Invoking sweeping generalizations about religion or culture can often be not only inaccurate, but also dangerously misleading. For example, the militancy of Arab Palestinian youth on the West Bank is not caused by 'the return of Islam' or 'traditional Islamic hatred of non-Islamic peoples', but by the cynical manipulation of some Arab states and acts of naked aggression by Israeli governments to which American and other governments have often turned a blind eye. Such religious rhetoric only plays into the hands of all who want to perpetuate oppression by diverting attention away from the real causes of suffering.

To say this is not to surrender to the secularism of those Western commentators who take it for granted that 'religion' is a well-defined area that belongs to the realm of the private individual, and that it can only enter the realm of the political by betraying its original vision. None of the major world faiths would accept this version of post-Enlightenment reductionism. Religions are total worldviews; and, like other worldviews, they embody themselves in distinctive socio-ethical practices. It is natural to suppose that what a community believes about the character of Ultimate Reality *will* shape its collective behaviour.

However, what I want to suggest is that, while religious beliefs and visions may inspire a Hamas terrorist to sacrifice his own life in an act of violence, the way he interprets his past religious inheritance is not divorced from the particular economic and political context in which he and his community find themselves. All traditions are the site of constant renegotiations and re-appropriations. We have seen that much that passes for 'tradition' in Islam is also recent innovation, and we shall see that the same is true for other faiths.

My third suggestion is addressed to those Muslims who live in countries where they enjoy freedoms denied to non-Muslims in most majority Muslim societies. I have pointed out that it is hypocritical for governments to subscribe to the UN Declaration of Human Rights and to prohibit freedom of religious worship and conversion among their citizens. It is doubly hypocritical for their citizens to enjoy those rights when they are living in a foreign country, but to deny those rights to foreigners living in their own country. Thus there is a moral onus laid on those members of the Muslim *ummah* who are 'in exile' in Europe and elsewhere to put pressure on their governments and intellectual communities back home. If, as I have suggested, there is surely no *necessary* connection between Islamic theology and the suppression of democracy and human rights, then this needs to be demonstrated first of all by those Muslim thinkers who have been beneficiaries of liberal democracies abroad. Are they capable of a self-criticism which enables them to denounce those Islamist movements and states which practise repression and terror in the name of Islam? Are those writers who are most vocal about 'Islamophobia' in the West willing to promote the same measure of legal and social tolerance for non-Muslim minorities in Islamic states that they demand for Muslims in, say, the United Kingdom?

Consequently, serious questions are raised for thoughtful and compassionate Muslims by the savage repression of women in Afghanistan, the prohibition of Christian worship in Saudi Arabia, the imposition of Islamic law on non-Muslims in Sudan and Pakistan, the discrimination against non-Muslims in government employment and development programmes in all states which claim to be 'Islamic', and the persecution and withdrawal of civic rights of converts from Islam in every country where Muslims are the majority. Religious tolerance and political pluralism are challenges which call for a rethinking of the dominant tradition within Islam.

Finally, we must take seriously the challenge to explore the faiths and cultures of other people, especially those who live in our own neighbourhood. What a German journalist complained of concerning education in her own country is true all over Europe and America:

> Hardly anything on the Middle East, or on historical clashes or points of contact between East and West, is learned in schools. Instead of knowledge or at least an unbiased examination of Islamic societies, we have clichés and stereotypes, which apparently make it easier to deal with the phenomenon of Islam. The Western image of Islam is characterised by ideas of aggression and brutality, fanaticism, irrationality, medieval backwardness and antipathy towards women.[61]

We have seen that such stereotypical imaging is also widespread in Islamic circles. One feeds off the other. Patrick Bannerman, a former diplomat and analyst for the British Foreign Office, reminds us, 'How non-Muslims think of Islam conditions the manner in which they deal with Muslims, which in turn conditions how Muslims think of and deal with non-Muslims.'[62] This is why I view with some concern the demand in Europe by some Islamist associations for separate Muslim schools for their children. If Muslim children are segregated from non-Muslims and not exposed to the best in other faiths and cultures, such schooling will only reinforce prejudice and stereotyping.

I have mentioned the *Islamophobia* report of the Runnymede Trust in Britain, which focuses far too narrowly on the negative stereotypes of Islam in the Western media and cases of discrimination against Muslims in the West. 'Islamophobia' is too loose a word, being used to cover everything from the unfair dismissal of a Muslim woman for wearing a *hejab* (head covering) at work to any criticism of particular Islamic teachings or practices. The Report dangerously fuses terms such as 'racism', 'stereotyping' and 'Islamophobia', even suggesting that any opposition to large-scale immigration is tantamount to racism. If that were the case, then every country, including all Islamic states, are guilty of widespread racism.

In brief, the Runnymede Report runs the risk of exacerbating the very phenomenon it wants to eliminate. For, in painting with too broad a brush, it encourages paranoia among Muslims in Britain, deflects valid criticisms that may lead to better community relations, and fails to condemn those Muslim organizations, such as the Muslim Parliament and Hizb ut-Tahrir, which justify the harsh images of Islam that are prevalent among many British people. Many Muslim organizations practise both a militant 'Westophobia' and what Peter Riddell has called a 'Christophobia': namely, the perverse highlighting of caricatures of Christians and the Christian faith in Muslim journals in Britain. Moreover, what Christians would have appreciated in the Runnymede Report would have been an equally vigorous denunciation of the way Christian doctrines and values are routinely and openly ridiculed and denigrated in the schools and mass media of all Muslim-majority countries, including the more 'enlightened' states such as Malaysia. The Report also fails to acknowledge the contribution that many churches and Christian groups have made towards the social upliftment of poor Muslim neighbours in cities such as Bradford, and the examples of Christians and Muslims in local neighbourhoods quietly working together to fight discrimination of all kinds.

Islamophobia, Westophobia, 'Christophobia' – these are ugly words, but they draw our attention, however unsatisfactorily, to ugly realities. All phobias are the result of ignorance and the inability to look critically at oneself and one's own community. Good relations can be established between Christians and Muslims in the West only if Christians are forthright in exposing and condemning all expressions of anti-Muslim bigotry in the West, and if Muslim leaders condemn, with equal fervour, similar bigotry and discrimination by their own ranks both in the West and in what they regard as the *dar-ul-Islam*.

What would it mean for Muslims to rid themselves of caricatures and to study empathetically the faiths of others? Islamic apologetics in the West is concerned to stress the essential unity of all theistic faiths, while claiming for Muhammad the role of the final Messenger of God. The basic message of Islam that was given to the first Prophet, who was also the first man, was the same as that given to the last Prophet. The Qur'an confirms what they had been given rather than repudiates it, and clears it of accretions and distortions rather than throws it away. Thus, Khurram Murad from the Islamic Foundation in Britain argues as follows:

> We do not invite people to a 'new' religion, we invite them to the oldest religion, indeed to their 'own' religion, the religion of living in total surrender to their Creator, in accordance with the guidance brought by all His Messengers … Islam is not a new or rival religion among the

many competing for human allegiance; it is the natural and primordial religion. All nature lives in submission to its Creator; all Messengers – Adam to Muhammad – brought the same religion.[63]

The question that disturbs me is whether this axiom of Islamic apologetics is a major obstacle to any serious exploration of other faiths and their Scriptures. If it is simply assumed that, for instance, we already know what Jesus taught and did, because what he taught and did was not significantly different from what other prophets taught and did, then there is little room for listening, humility and respect – all the qualities necessary for genuine dialogue with others in a pluralist world. This is all the more tragic given the copious references to Jesus in the Qur'an itself. There are references to Jesus in fifteen different surahs of the Qur'an, and he is mentioned ninety-seven times in ninety-three verses, as compared with Muhammad who is mentioned only twenty-five times. Jesus is also addressed with respect as Ibn Maryam (Son of Mary), Masih (Messiah), Abd-Ullah (Servant of God) and Rasul-Ullah (Messenger of God). Even more remarkably, he is spoken of as 'The Word of God', 'a Spirit from God', as being 'highly honoured in this world and the next' and being 'near stationed to God' (3:40), and numerous other epithets of honour.

Muslims are discouraged from reading the Bible on the unquestioned assumption that the Bible teaches nothing that the Qur'an itself does not teach, and that wherever there is real divergence this is due to distortion and corruption of the original message by Christians. Little evidence is ever offered in support of this assertion. In the last two hundred years Muslims have come to rely more on the account of Jesus given in a spurious sixteenth-century document called the *Gospel of Barnabas* than they do on the Qur'an itself.[64] For instance, in *Jesus, a Prophet of Islam*, Muhammad 'Ata ur-Rahim goes so far as to describe the so-called *Gospel of Barnabas* as the 'only surviving Gospel written by a disciple of Jesus, that is, by a man who spent most of his time in the actual company of Jesus during the three years in which he was delivering his message'.[65] Naturally, he does not attempt to marshall any evidence for these incredible assertions, for there is none.

This new-found glee over the so-called *Gospel of Barnabas* not only brings Islamic apologetics into disrepute, but it is also quite remarkable, given that it blatantly contradicts what the Qur'an itself teaches. Thus, whereas the Qur'an acknowledges Jesus as the one and only Messiah explicitly in eleven different places, the *Gospel of Barnabas* not only makes Jesus deny that he was the Messiah but even makes him claim that Muhammad was the Messiah.[66]

Muslim writings on Christianity, whether polemical or scholarly, tend to follow a predictable pattern. They rely on outdated works of liberal theological scholarship which apply historico-critical methods to Christian origins, but naturally refuse to apply the same approach to the Qur'an and the early Muslim community. They portray the political ethic of Christianity as essentially passive in contrast to the activism of Islam, and draw invidious comparisons between an ideal Islamic state on the one hand and the worst examples from 'Christian states' on the other. Even the more scholarly among them tend to be poorly informed on the complex relations between Christian mission and European imperialism.[67]

There has been a wealth of European and American scholarship on Islamic teaching and history, and Christians have often been in the forefront of such scholarship. The writings of Richard Bell, Arthur Jeffrey, Montgomery Watt, Constance Padwick, Sir Norman Anderson, Kenneth Cragg and Vivienne Stacy (among many others) have greatly enriched our understanding of many important topics, from the calling and preaching of Muhammad to folk Islamic practices in Asian villages. In contrast, it is extremely rare to meet a Muslim who has made a serious study of the New Testament, and no-one among the nearly one billion professing Muslims in the world has been recognized as having made a contribution to the study of the Bible or of early Christian history. As long as this situation continues, the claim of Islamic apologists to be well read, respectful and tolerant in their dealings with Christians and Jews must be treated with considerable scepticism.

For the Christian living among Muslim neighbours, the poignancy of this situation is well caught by that oft-quoted passage from Kenneth Cragg's work, *The Call of the Minaret*, written over forty years ago but still timely:

> This is the inward tragedy, from the Christian angle, of the rise of Islam, the genesis and dissemination of a new belief which claimed to displace what it had never effectively known. The state of being a stranger to the Christian's Christ has been intensified by further failures of love and loyalty on the part of institutional Christianity in the long and bitter external relations of the two faiths through the centuries.
>
> It is for these reasons that the call of the minaret must always seem to the Christian a call to retrieval. He yearns to undo the alienation and to make amends for the past by as full a restitution as he can achieve of the Christ to Whom Islam is a stranger. The objective is not, as the Crusaders believed, the repossession of what Christendom had lost, but the restoration to Muslims of the Christ Whom they have missed.[68]

2
Hinduism and the search for identity

Modern India: A tale of two cities

On the plains of the Punjab in northwest India, with the towering Himalayan peaks in the distance, stands the city of Chandigarh. It is the newest, cleanest and most orderly city in India. It was conceived by Jawaharlal Nehru, prime minister at the time of the birth of post-imperial India, who invited the famous French architect Le Corbusier to design a modern city 'symbolic of the freedom of India, unfettered by the traditions of the past ... and expression of the nation's faith in the future'.[1] Nehru wanted India 'to move forward by one decisive act that broke both with its ancient and its more recent history'.[2]

None of the existing architectural styles in India (traditional Hindu, the Mogul style of Muslim rulers, or the Indo-Gothic creations of the British Raj) were considered appropriate for what Chandigarh was to represent: namely, a modern, secular, democratic state. Modern India had to free itself from both the colonial imagery of the Raj and nostalgia for its pre-colonial past. So the city was built in the rationalist, International style, on an empty plain. The few hundred villagers who lived on the site were forcibly evicted.

Chandigarh is the modern capital of the states of Haryana and Punjab, but it was meant to symbolize so much more. The showcase government buildings, huge and geometrical, were Nehru's 'temples of democracy'. Sunil Khilnani, an Indian political scientist at the University of London, has argued that Nehru had an unshakeable faith in constitutional democracy as a power to forge an

47

Indian identity and to effect deep-seated social transformation. Nehru, how-ever, was no mere imitator of the West. Educated at Harrow and Cambridge, and nurtured in the Fabian socialism of post-Great-War Britain, he saw himself as a benevolent father-figure who would skilfully insert the Indian nation into its rightful place in the flow of international history. Nehru saw universal significance in the West's historical trajectory. This new image of a secular, pluralistic, interventionist Indian state would unite a diffuse, diverse and deeply divided country.

Khilnani expresses Nehru's vision for Chandigarh thus: 'In celebrating a wholly alien form, style and material, it aspired to a neutrality, a zero-degree condition that would make it equally resistant to the claims upon it of any and all cultural or religious groups.'[3] Just as the use in matters of state of an unfamiliar language, English, would, it was believed, place all Indians at an equal disadvantage, so too Chandigarh's deliberate renunciation of a national style meant that it could not be identified with and possessed by any one group.

Chandigarh, then, was Nehru's St Petersburg. Just as Peter the Great (1672–1725) tried to raise Russia to greatness by importing modern European civilization, and brought the most celebrated architects from Western Europe to show Russians how to build a modern city, so Le Corbusier was Nehru's herald of modernity. His buildings would forge new attitudes to politics and to progress.

Khilnani regards Chandigarh as a failure. It never produced 'a society of secular individuals or a modernist politics'.[4] Today it is a comfortable haven for civil servants and retired army officers who despise the squalor and anarchy of urban India. Chandigarh's much-vaunted 'temples of democracy' are surrounded by a steel fence and barbed wire, guarded by policemen with machine guns, following the car-bomb killing of Punjab's chief minister by Sikh separatists in 1995. For much of the late 1980s and early 1990s, the citizens of Chandigarh did not even vote for their local government, because the city came under direct rule from New Delhi. The city was caught up in the bloody vortex of Sikh separatism and remained a museum to a remarkable, if somewhat bizarre, dream.

Perhaps the real temples of democracy in Chandigarh, and a fulfilment of Nehru's ideals in a somewhat ambivalent way, are the 'colonies' of the poor on the fringes of the city. The men and women who laboured on Le Corbusier's monuments were paid a pittance and not given permanent housing. They were expected to disappear to wherever they had come from, once the buildings and roads were completed. However, as the poor are wont, they stayed, in illegal squatter settlements which are really displaced villages. After the repeated failure of attempts by the police to chase the people away by burning down their dwellings, local politicians began to see personal profit in the situation. They would burn down the slums and then promise to rebuild them, and even to legalize the whole colony, if the colonists would vote for them. In this way the poor have been drawn into Indian politics, and the idea of the state as a patron has taken hold of the Indian imagination, but not quite in the way that Nehru intended.

Four hundred miles to the southeast of Chandigarh stands the city of Ayodhya. In stark contrast to Le Corbusier's city, Ayodhya is ancient, filthy, and full of dilapidated temples, dedicated not to the modern gods of secularism and democracy, but to the ancient gods of Hindu sects, particularly Ram. It is located in the middle of Uttar Pradesh, the most populous state in the Indian Union and the one which has produced most of India's prime ministers since independence, including Nehru himself.

Nehru's vision of a secular, pluralist state was formally buried on 6 December 1992. Over several years Indian politics had become increasingly chauvinistic, but, on that day, a mob of Hindu activists, gathered from all over the country, tore down an unused sixteenth-century mosque in Ayodhya, called the Babri Masjid, claiming that it had been constructed by Babur, founder of the Mogul dynasty, on the birth site of Ram, the mythical Hindu king. An earlier attempt to storm the mosque had ended in violence, and the Hindu nationalists had been driven into a frenzy by politicians on videos and cassette tapes screaming for Muslim blood, by TV soap operas about Ram and other Hindu heroes, and by stories in the press of Hindu 'martyrdoms'. L. K. Advani, a former movie journalist and current leader of the Hindu nationalist Bharatiya Janata Party (BJP), was driven like a god-king from Gujarat to Ayodhya in a Nissan pick-up truck adorned as a chariot from a Hindu epic.

For all their contrasts, Chandigarh and Ayodhya are both products of modernity. If Chandigarh represents the optimism of India's first prime minister and the rationalism of a French modernist architect, Ayodhya represents the modern reconfiguration of 'Hindu' religion. Hindu nationalism is as modern as Nehru's secular idea of India. Its ideological roots are usually traced to the 1920s, when Indian intellectuals were grappling with ideas of the Indian nation. An influential text was V. D. Savarkar's *Hindutva: Who is a Hindu?*, published in 1923. Savarkar was greatly impressed by Mazzini, Darwin and Herbert Spencer, but he was mainly inspired by fear – fear that the disunited Hindus, who lacked an ideology, a Mecca or a universal church, would be overwhelmed by Muslims and Christians.

Savarkar was not a practising Hindu himself. Like many European thinkers who used religion to fashion new national identities, he thought Hindu rituals and pilgrimages were useful 'from a national and racial point of view'. Ram, the focus of worship in Ayodhya, is not worshipped by all Hindus, but only by Vaishnavites, devotees of Vishnu of whom Ram is a manifestation. To Savarkar and his modern followers Ram is the symbolic king of the Hindus, the father of the nation. 'Some of us', he wrote, 'worship Ram as an incarnation, some admire him as a hero and a warrior, all love him as the most illustrious representative monarch of our race.'[5] Hindus are given a territorial identity: they are all those in India who claim their 'Fatherland' as a 'holy land'. This was intended to include Buddhists, Jains and Sikhs within the fold of Hindutva, and to exclude Muslims and Christians.

A new mythology

The project of Hindutva, Hindu revival or, more accurately, the political assertion of 'Hinduness', carries its own mythic historiography. India is now referred to as Bharat, the name of one of the mythical brothers of the equally mythical Ram. Muslim rulers, far more than the British, are demonized. The pre-Muslim period of Indian history is represented as a golden age of progress, of high cultural, intellectual and economic achievement. The land was studded with temples. Then came the Muslim hordes, bringing destruction and catastrophe in their wake. This was the age of barbarity, forced conversion, cultural decay, religious repression and economic collapse. Temples were destroyed throughout the land. The regeneration of Bharat required a restoration of Hindu unity and the glories of the pre-Muslim age. Most Hindu nationalists were from the higher castes. Their idea of India was as a powerful, upper-caste Hindu nation, although the emphasis on caste was often muted to attract a wider following. They saw the Congress movement for Indian independence as dangerously egalitarian, a betrayer of Hindu ideals.

Thus, M. S. Golwalkar, the leading intellectual inspiration behind Hindutva until well into the 1960s, gave this advice to Indian Muslims and other minorities:

> The non-Hindu peoples in Hindustan must either adopt the Hindu culture and language, must learn to respect and hold in reverence Hindu religion, must entertain no ideas but those of glorification of the Hindu race and culture, i.e. they must not only give up their attitude of intolerance and ungratefulness towards this land and its age-long traditions but must also cultivate the positive attitude of love and devotion instead – in one word, they must cease to be foreigners, or may stay in the country, wholly subordinated to the Hindu nation,

claiming nothing, deserving no privileges, far less any preferential treatment – not even citizen's rights.[6]

Hindu nationalists mimicked the symbols of British power, unlike Gandhi who invoked romantic symbols of rural India to challenge the power of the Raj. The RSS (*Rashtrya Swayamseval Sangh* – National Volunteer Association), founded in 1925 as a paramilitary Hindu cultural organization, dressed its youth in khaki shorts and drilled to British martial music. It drew on a well-established culture of martial asceticism in north India, and was a cross between a Boy Scouts movement and the pre-war Fascist youth organizations of Germany and Italy. The ideology of *rashtra* (nation) that was promoted by the RSS was based on the application of nineteenth-century European conceptions of nation and religion to India. It stressed the supposedly common Aryan ethnic and linguistic heritage of those opposed to Muslim expansion. It gave European Fascism one potent symbol, the swastika, the symbol of good fortune (*suasti* in Sanskrit).[7]

The RSS was a social organization and stayed out of active politics, but most of the Indian political parties today have been infiltrated by its members. It remained on the margins of cultural life in the first two decades following its banning in 1948 after the Congress Party had alleged that the assassin of Gandhi had been one of its members. Another Hindu cultural front, the World Hindu Council, or VHP (*Vishwa Hindu Parishad*) was founded in Bombay in 1964. The BJP was formed in 1980 out of the earlier nationalist party, the Jan Sangh, which itself had been an upgraded version of the pre-independence Hindu Mahasabha.

The VHP goes beyond both the RSS and BJP in articulating a vision of Hindutva or modern Hinduism. Unlike the RSS, its core is made up of religious specialists – often celibate monks (*sadhus*) – who act as spiritual leaders (*gurus*) to the community of lay followers. The VHP seeks to 'reconvert' backward caste and tribal groups to Hinduism, sometimes through force, and to reach out to middle-class Hindus both in urban India and in the Western diaspora. It has set up centres in several European countries and in the USA. It has lists of ethnic Indian students studying in American universities and raises funds abroad for its activities in India, presenting itself as a global pan-Hindu movement.[8] Linked to the RSS, with its disciplined and lightly armed youth squads, and the *Shiv Sena* (Army of Shiva), an even more militant group founded in 1966 in the state of Maharashtra, these movements acquired a major influence in Indian politics both at the electoral level and in mass actions, culminating in the seizure and rededication of the Babri Masjid. The BJP reached its zenith in the February 1998 national elections, when, by virtue of being the largest single party in Parliament, it was invited by the President to form a coalition government with smaller, regional parties.

Nehru's secular idea of India prevailed for at least thirty years after Independence. The social and communal problems begotten by India's long and complex history were confronted at the outset of independence, first through the anguish of Partition, and then through rights and safeguards written into the Indian Constitution. A principle of positive discrimination, or affirmative action, in compensation for past injuries was introduced. This took the form of a policy of 'reservation' of government jobs and educational places, for those excluded from the system of caste. (These were the so-called 'untouchable' castes and tribes which the British administrators had earlier listed in a special 'schedule', hence the terms 'scheduled castes' and 'scheduled tribes'.) It was forbidden by law to use religious symbols for electoral purposes. By securing the support for his Congress Party of most high-caste Hindus and also of the Muslims, whose interests he tried to protect, Nehru pushed the Hindu chauvinists to the extreme fringes of political activity. The socialists and communists in opposition shared his secular views.

It would not be an exaggeration, however, to say that it was the Nehru dynasty that also paved the way for the regeneration of Hindu nationalism. As India's electoral population burgeoned and threats to Congress rule emerged from Sikh separatists, Indira Gandhi made dubious deals with Hindutva political parties and offered state patronage in exchange for votes. In order to woo Hindu minorities in Punjab and Kashmir she began to frequent Hindu places of worship and to include mysterious holy men (*sadhus*) in her retinue.

Her son Rajiv continued the process. In 1948, the Constituent Assembly had refused to accept that Muslim personal law was an inseparable part of the Islamic religion, and rejected attempts to exempt it from the Directive Principle regarding a uniform civil code. However, in 1986, in a celebrated case involving an appeal for alimony by a Muslim woman (Shah Bano) the government overruled a Supreme Court decision and allowed Muslims to retain special marriage laws – to the advantage of Muslim men but not of Muslim women, whose rights, after a divorce, are limited. This angered the Hindu nationalists. As though to restore the balance and to mollify the latter, Rajiv launched his 1989 election campaign near Ayodhya, because, he declared, it was 'the land of Ram, the holy land'. And it was Rajiv who gave the instruction to unlock the gates of the disputed but defunct Ayodhya mosque, as the first step to a Hindu restoration.

The 1948 Indian Constitution abolished 'untouchability' and said that citizens should not be denied access to shops, restaurants and other public places on grounds of caste and religion. In Indian law the caste system does not exist, but in practice caste-consciousness has proved to be remarkably intransigent. Caste Hindus resent the efforts by governments to reserve specific quotas of government jobs (22.5%) and seats (85) in the legislature for members of 'scheduled' castes and tribes. On 7 August 1990, the then prime minister, V. P. Singh, announced that his government would honour the ten-year-old recommendations of the official Mandal Commission that 27% of all federal government jobs should be reserved for 'other backward castes'. Within hours of the announcement, government buses were burned, trains were attacked, public property was extensively damaged, and some upper-caste youths immolated themselves. The government fell.

The Hindutva argument, which rapidly gathered momentum from the mid-1980s, was simple: secularism has led to a civilizational crisis in India; the Congress Party leadership (the dominant party in post-Independence politics) was rife with corruption; Muslim immigration and population growth threaten the survival of the true inhabitants of the land; Hindutva alone can provide the possibility of the nation's survival. Secularism, so runs the charge, 'is draining away the nation's *élan vital* of Hindu spirit'. Secularists are 'Trojan horses' who 'weaken Hindu strength from within'.[9] These 'traitors' have to be attacked to defend the Hindu nation. Thus the rhetoric is directed more strongly against secular Hindus who believe in religious tolerance than against Muslims and people of other faiths. In fact, all the latter are assumed originally to have been Hindus who were converted forcibly or by financial inducement; thus, given a Hindu state, they will all naturally revert to the Hindu fold without any need for coercion.

This is how one Indian observer sums up the recent rise of Hindu nationalism:

> One major objective of the VHP is to forge a national and international unity amongst all those it defines as Hindu. Hindus, they feel, have been fragmented and divided into groups and castes in conflict with each other. This weakness has allowed foreigners to invade and rule over India, and the minority communities to become defiant. To reassert their power, the Hindus have to become conscious of their underlying common identity, rediscover and forge the unity which lies submerged ... This project of forming a Hindu Community, united at the national and international levels, marks a major effort at restructuring religious traditions within India. The diversity and differences within religious traditions, considered by religious reformers a sign of the strength and vitality of tradition, now acquires a new meaning: it becomes a sign of weakness of the community. To

overcome the weakness the Hindus must unite, they must act together, they must speak with one voice.[10]

In April 1984 the VHP convened a large gathering of Hindu religious leaders in Delhi, calling it the *Dharma Sansad* (Assembly of the Faith). This meeting issued a unanimous resolution for the 'liberation' of three temple sites in north India, at Mathura, Varanasi and Ayodhya, and chose to focus initial efforts on the *Ramjanmabhoomi* in Ayodhya. The choice of site is interesting. There is far more evidence for the existence of pre-Mogul shrines in these other locations than in Ayodhya. But Ayodhya juxtaposes two figures well known to most people in north India – Ram and Babur. God and human, they are made to stand for two religions – 'Hinduism' and 'Islam' – in a lopsided manner.

Ram is a manifestation (*avatara*) of Vishnu, who entered into the world to preserve moral order (*dharma*). Ram is often depicted in VHP literature as striding forward with bow ready for combat, a vigorous slayer of demons who defeats evil to stabilize the world order. Ram is 'the Hindu god most amenable to utopian projects', for in the epic *Ramayana* he created the state (*rajya*) that most completely instantiates righteousness on earth, *Rama-rajya*. As an interventionist, this-worldly, human deity, 'Ram serves the rhetorical purposes of the VHP better than any other deity of the Hindu pantheon, certainly better than the lovable-but-untrustworthy Krishna or the often-remote and non-human Shiva'.[11]

The *Ramayana* is perhaps the best-known of the Indian epics. It has been adapted over the centuries to numerous local contexts and read in a variety of ways. Heterodox traditions like Buddhism and Jainism had their own versions of the *Ramayana*. In some provincial versions Rama is the personification of the ideal *Kshatrya*, the perfect man, while in others he is the embodiment of treachery. The *Dalits* (those outside the caste system) in south India contest the interpretation of Rama as a virtuous king. The twelfth-century Vaishnava cults in north India read the story of Rama as an incarnation of the god Vishnu, and transformed the *Ramayana* from a cultural idiom to a sacred scripture. It is this reading of the *Ramayana* that has been adopted by the VHP and BJP. It was serialized into a mega-TV production and shown all over India and to Indian immigrant communities in Europe and North America a few years ago. It is the culmination of what one writer has called the 'adoption of militant devotionalism by a middle-class laity' – one generated by modern media rather than by traditional instruction in beliefs and practices.[12]

What this represents, then, is an organized, systematic effort to erase the diversity and conflict within Indian tradition. It represses all those voices which question the dominant myths, and instead produces a homogeneous, universalist Hindu tradition that will generate a new Hindu identity and legitimate a Hindu-centred politics.

This project of reconstructing Hinduism is not new, of course. However, unlike earlier nineteenth- and twentieth-century Hindu reform movements, which sought to cull the ancient texts for religious ideas that were in tune with the modern age, the VHP does not appear to engage in scriptural exegesis to define the 'essence' of 'Hinduness' or Hinduism. Like the RSS ideology of the 1920s, it tends to define 'Hinduness' geographically and genealogically, rather than through a shared creed or texts. Its rhetoric emphasizes the notion of family, and its collective rituals have centred on activities such as pilgrimage, brick-building and the waving of saffron flags. It is the nearest equivalent to a global Hindu 'church', and its major feat has been to bring a large number of competitive ascetic orders and religious leaders (*gurus*) under the banner of Hindu nationalism.

Muslims constitute about 12% of the Indian population, and for the most part form a poor, despised, and politically insignificant, religious minority. The VHP, however, required a worthy adversary to justify its strategy of confrontation, and accordingly it reified and mythologized all Indian Muslims as the children of Babur, Akbar and Aurangzeb, all formidable and aggressive Mogul conquerors. As far as Indian Muslims and Christians are concerned, it is not so much their beliefs or practices that invite the VHP's denunciation as their allegiance to supposedly foreign religions which were instruments of foreign powers. Underscoring the 'foreignness' of Islam, Christianity and secularism to India is part of the project of making India Hindu that is pursued by the supporters of Hindutva.[13]

Religious nationalism

What can we learn from the rise of religious nationalisms, as illustrated by the Indian context?

First, they are not atavistic, anti-modern forms of religious affirmation. The VHP and BJP do not want a return to a medieval India. They want a strong India that will embrace the scientific and technological fruits of modernity. They are anti-secularist, anti-pluralist, but not anti-democratic. Their understanding of democracy is of 'majority rule'. They want both God and nuclear warheads. They draw their political strength from those who benefited from traditional social structures but who feel that their privileges have been restricted under the new secularist regimes. The majority of their most enthusiastic advocates are to be found among the educated, urban middle classes; there were many, even in the bureaucracies of Congress-led governments, who supported Hindutva.

Secondly, religious nationalisms represent the creation of a homogeneous religion which is projected as the revival of an ancient tradition, adapted to meet the needs of the modern age. The eminent historian of ancient India, Romila Thapar, has written of the 'semitization' of Indian religious traditions. Characteristics of the Semitic religions, such as a historically attested prophet, a sacred book, a geographically identifiable location for its beginnings, an ecclesiastical community – all these were largely irrelevant to the various manifestations of Hinduism until recent times. 'Thus instead of emphasizing the fact that the religious experience of Indian civilization and of religious sects which are bunched together under the label of "Hindu" are distinctively different from that of the Semitic, attempts are being made to find parallels with the Semitic religions as if these parallels are necessary to the future of Hinduism.'[14]

Thirdly, much of this religious discourse has been encouraged by modern European writings on Asia. Ever since the 1960s it has become fashionable to term as 'orientalist' , 'communalist' or 'ethnocentric' those European works of scholarship which seem to have reinforced stereotypes of native peoples which have then served, wittingly or unwittingly, to justify colonial domination. Even the all-embracing term 'Hinduism' came into general usage in the nineteenth century in British writings on India as a way of conceptualizing the religious landscape of India. But the term 'Hindu' did not begin its career as a religious category, but rather as a term used by outsiders and by state officials to designate people who lived east of the Indus river. From the days of Alexander the Great, people east of the Indus were called 'Hindus' and their territory became 'India'. The word 'Hindu' is of Arabic / Persian origin and has exactly the same meaning etymologically as the word 'India', which is of Greco-Roman origin. None of the Hindu sacred texts even once mentions the word 'Hindu'. It is doubtful if the word 'Hindu', before the nineteenth century, excluded the ancient Christian communities of the present-day Kerala, the Zoroastrians, and the Jewish communities of Maharashtra and Kerala, and even many of the Muslim communities of the subcontinent.

Hindu India was first defined not by the religious traditions of the subcontinent, but by modern state institutions. Under British rule, 'Hindu' became a category for people in India who were not Muslims, Christians, Sikhs, Jains, Parsis or Buddhists. *Adivasis*, or native tribal peoples, were included within this all-encompassing 'Hinduism'. 'Hindu' became an official term for counting people, and this gave the statistical impression that India was a majority Hindu country. This division of the population by religious categories was used to create the descriptions of India that we inherit.

The term 'communalism' in the Indian context is often used by social scientists and historians to describe the assumption that Hindus and Muslims form well-defined and totally separate communities whose economic, social and political interests are mutually and essentially opposed. This assumption is then used to explain and justify whatever antagonisms are observed. Thus, colonial writing, by both administrators and historians, statistical surveys, etc., consistently used religious and caste categories to measure the distribution of people in jobs and in general cultural and economic activity, even when religion or caste was not the most relevant category, and to neglect more meaningful criteria in this context, such as income, educational level, ethnicity and language, ownership of land or other means of production, regional cultural traditions, etc.[15]

Histories of Indian civilization, art, politics and culture conventionally separate Hindu, Muslim, British and National epochs. Permanent galleries in the British Museum and the New York Metropolitan Museum of Art are organized on these lines, with museum exhibits often presenting Hindu ritual, texts and art to depict Indian culture. 'India' and 'Hindu' are often equated when defining Indian culture, while Islamic artefacts are equally used to describe a Muslim culture that originated in the Middle East and then expanded into India. Ancient Christian communities and the considerable impact of Christian missions on the modern transformation of India are usually downplayed. Indian Islam and Indian Christianity are portrayed as being foreign and derivative, alien to India. Thus, the dominant Western perception of India since the nineteenth century has served to reinforce the modern VHP ideology.

Such readings of Indian society and history are still widespread in the West. For instance, with regard to the Ayodhya destruction of 1992, *Newsweek* reported that the 'battle over a mosque refuels the ancient conflict between Hindus and Muslims', while *The Washington Post* attributed the violence to 'centuries-old religious hatreds and modern-day economic deprivation'.[16] Following the retaliatory nuclear tests in Pakistan on 31 May 1998, Britain's *The Independent* newspaper proclaimed: 'India's bomb was a *Hindu bomb*. Pakistan's bomb was a *Muslim bomb*.'[17] Yet it is unlikely to have made similar assertions about other faiths; for instance, if the writer had gone on to state that Israel's nuclear programme is capable of delivering a *Jewish bomb*, he would, no doubt, have been charged with anti-Semitism!

The irony, then, is that Hindutva nationalists (as well as their Hindu critics) have borrowed from naïve orientalist constructions of 'Hindu tolerance' and 'Hindu spirituality' as the defining markers of Hindu civilization, in contrast to the iconoclastic fanaticism of Muslim civilization. All nationalist discourse, whether religious or secular, is selective and homogenizing. It tends to demarcate social boundaries sharply and to downplay the diversity and ambiguities of everyday life. It is important to note that the 'Hindu' and 'Muslim' nations are not the products of transhistorical religious beliefs and practices, but of specific discourses, which are always contested by others.

The legacy of Empire[18]

There is some evidence that British colonial administrators were impressed by James Mill's *The History of British India* (1826) and perceived India and Indian history according to the views expressed in his book. Mill saw Indian society as divided into two strict compartments: Hindus and Muslims. The Muslims had lived in India as rulers and had oppressed and persecuted the Hindus. Mill saw both Hindus and Muslims as obsessed with religion, and while the Hindus were by nature submissive, Islam made Muslims aggressive. He was convinced that the two communities were so radically incompatible that peaceful co-existence was impossible. Islam and Hinduism were incompatible because, while the Hindus worshipped idols, the Muslims destroyed idols. Mill argued that British rule was a boon for the Hindus because it liberated them from the intolerant rule of the Muslims. He made the point indirectly that the British Empire was better than the earlier Mogul Empire. British officials and writers influenced by Mill saw themselves as the liberators of the Hindu spirit. For them the British Empire was also justified as the way of keeping the peace between religious communities that were eternally and implacably at each other's throats. Similar arguments were used to legitimize the British presence in India right up to 1947. Britain was forced reluctantly to stay in the defence of minority interests and to prevent a communal civil war.

The first Muslims came to India in the eighth century, long before the advent of Mogul rule. Moreover, apart from some of the medieval sultans of Delhi and the Mogul emperor Aurangzeb (1618–1707), who had a reputation for fanatical brutality, Muslim rulers did not generally embark on widespread destruction of temples or the forcible conversion of Hindus and tribal peoples. The Nawabs of eighteenth-century Avadh (the province where Ayodhya was situated) sought the collaboration of Hindus, particularly the Kayasthas and Rajput *zamindars* both in administration and military affairs. The Nawabs and their officials contributed to the development of Hindu places of worship, while Muslim officials also patronized Hindu institutions and priests. This was the normal manner in which power was exercised in Avadh, which had a large Hindu population. Ayodhya's development into a pilgrimage centre in the eighteenth century was due largely to the patronage of the Nawabi court. Indeed, the real conflicts in Ayodhya were between two Hindu sects, the Bairagis (Vaishnavites, associated with the *bhakti* of Ram) and the Shaivites, worshippers of Shiva. They fought each other for control of the places of worship, and these conflicts were more fundamental than those which surfaced in the middle years of the nineteenth century between Hindus and Muslims.[19]

Among the social élites, social intermingling and co-operation among Muslims and caste Hindus was fairly common, well into the post-Independence epoch. Muslims and Hindus from the same class or locality seem to have had more in common with each other than their co-religionists in other sections of society.[20] Poor Muslim converts from low-caste families continued to live as they had before, participating in Hindu festivals and rituals, even as Hindus gathered round the shrines of local Sufi saints to pray against calamity, procure children and improve the circumstances of the dead. While there were certainly localized and sporadic outbreaks of violence involving Hindus and Muslims, the real divergences and conflicts in Indian society were not fundamentally between Hindu and Muslim. As one historian observes about communalistic agitation among Muslims in India:

> No amount of pious exhortation could bridge the wide gulf separating, say, a Muslim peasant in Mymensingh from a Muslim *taluqdar* in Avadh ... The Ahmadiyas and the Ahl-I Hadith had a running battle over this or that doctrinal matter. And the Shias and the Sunnis were estranged, especially in Lucknow, with separate mosques, religious endowments and educational establshments ... If anything, the lines of cleavage in north India were more sharply drawn between the Sunnis and the Shias than between Hindus and Muslims.[21]

Following what British historians refer to as the Indian Mutiny of 1857 (Indians tend to call it the Revolt of 1857 or their first War of Independence), the British became hostile to Muslims, whom they believed had instigated the violence. For the next twenty years, the number of Muslims employed in the colonial administration dropped sharply in many areas. There were other unintentioned factors which also contributed to the Muslim middle classes lagging behind their Hindu counterparts. British rule came first to Bengal, where the Muslims belonged largely to the poorer sector of the population. It was only much later that British rule spread to the northwest provinces where a significant section of the upper classes was Muslim. Thus Muslims were unable to take advantage of modern Western education and thereby enter government service or other middle-class occupations. The shift from Persian to English as the official language of the Raj further aggravated the imbalances, as the English-educated Hindus had a distinct advantage.

The colonial restructuring of the Indian economy, and the economic stagnation that followed the suppression of indigenous entrepreneurship, meant that by the time modern education had spread substantially among the Muslims, employment opportunities had shrunk even further. The social and religious reform movements of the nineteenth century (the so-called 'Hindu Renaissance') were confined to upper-caste Hindus. The Muslim ruling classes tended to be more hostile towards modern education and social change.

Thus the end of the nineteenth century witnessed the emergence of conditions favourable to the growth of communal ideologies. Middle-class Muslims and Hindus saw themselves as now forced to compete with one another in the new climate of social and economic insecurity. Colonial intervention had dismantled the traditional economic and moral order in Indian society without replacing it with an adequate modern structure. The British had also codified Hindu and Muslim law so as to provide themselves with instruments for ruling India. In so doing, they had inadvertently defined the arena of cultural debate. The legal orientalism of the colonial state challenged the somewhat ambiguous boundaries of Muslim and Hindu communities.

However, it would be misleading to suggest that, prior to the colonial period, there were no attempts by Hindu or Muslim rulers to carve out religious communities, or that Hindu expansionism was only a product of colonial intervention. We shall examine the myths of pre-colonial Hindu 'tolerance' and 'non-violence' later in this chapter. But with regard to state-induced constructions of communalism, mention should be made (on the Muslim side) of the Mogul emperor Aurangzeb's destruction of the Vishwanath temple in Banares and his imposition of taxes on Hindus; while (on the Hindu side) one well-known example would be the attempts of the Rajput king Jai Singh II of Jaipur (1688–1743) to create a society based on Hindu ideology (*varnasrama-dharma*). It is, of course, not the case that the religious nationalisms of the present day are a linear development from these state attempts to create Muslim and Hindu societies. However, the point is that, prior to the colonial intervention, there were constructions of religious community in which state institutions were involved.

Moreover, the Cow Protection Movement of the late nineteenth century (initiated by the Hindu reformists, the Arya Samaj, but taken up by many anti-reformist, revivalist Hindu organizations) was particularly directed at defining the Hindu community against Muslim beef-eaters and British rulers. Muslims bore the brunt of the ensuing violence and reacted by asserting their own identity in distinction from that of Hindus.[22]

The Indian National Congress, founded in 1885, arrested those communal tendencies by adopting an anti-colonial discourse of India as 'one nation'. It tried to meet the identity crisis of a society moving out of a pre-capitalist and largely feudal system into the modern era by forging broad secular identities such as nationhood. In the latter years of the nineteenth century the British colonial government sought to woo Muslims away from political agitation and support for Congress by offering them special concessions. When the Indian national movement became more militant in its opposition to the Raj, the policy was changed from that of keeping Muslims out of politics to promoting the loyalist, communal politics of the Muslim League in order to create a countervailing force to Congress. As is well known, the British, in all their imperial domains, were masters at the art of exploiting local cultural or religious differences and divisions to further their economic and strategic interests![23]

British India's administrative provinces were arbitrarily demarcated territories. When elections were introduced, the units of representation in these provincial legislatures were not territorial constituencies comprising individual voters (as in Britain) but communities defined by religion. As the independence movement gathered momentum in the early years of the twentieth century, the Muslim League, founded in 1906, was promoted by the colonial government as the voice of the Muslims. The League, however, did not have the allegiance of more than a tiny proportion of the Muslim population. As late as 1937, the Muslim League received only 4.8% of the total Muslim vote in provincial elections, despite communal electorates and the franchise being restricted to the upper and middle classes (11% of the population), among whom the League had a greater following. The Hindu nationalist Mahasabha Party fared even worse among the Hindu voters.

The Congress could easily claim far greater support among the Muslim population. Nevertheless, the government branded a secular, broad-based party like the Congress as a Hindu organization, and the communalistic Muslim League was projected as the real and sole representative of the Muslims. In the 1940s the Muslim League was given a virtual veto on all constitutional proposals, effectively thwarting all Congress moves. This posture on the part of the British naturally enhanced the prestige of the League among the Muslims, and demoralized those Muslims who wanted to stay away from communalist politics. (The sense of political alienation among Muslims was compounded by their experience of Congress rule after 1937 in the provinces where Hindus were a majority. Congress-led provincial governments, increasingly under the sway of Hindu nationalists, lost the trust of many Muslims and so helped to kindle support for the Muslim League.)

Furthermore, the colonial government, after cynically exploiting Muslim communalism for well over half a century, finally abandoned both Hindus and Muslims. Until 1945, 'the British had worked on the assumption that the empire must survive'. Muslim communalism and its ultimate demand for a separate state (Pakistan) were a 'useful counterpoise to the Congress demand for independence'.[24] However, in 1946, once the decision to leave was clear, the British preferred to transfer power to an undivided, independent India, since that was perceived to serve British economic and military strategic interests better in the post-war world.

However, the Pandora's box of religious communalism, Hindu and Muslim, had by now been well and truly opened. For various reasons, still disputed by historians, Congress finally acquiesced in the demand by Jinnah, the leader of the Muslim League, for a sovereign Muslim territory. The holocaust following the Partition of 1947 was the result. The final boundaries were announced by Lord Mountbatten only after the transfer of power had taken place, so that the British could wash their hands of what was now an 'Indian problem'. British civil and military officials adopted, for the most part, a laid-back attitude while one of the most horrific massacres in modern times unravelled in front of them. Again, the British made no attempt to insist on safeguards for the minorities in the newly independent states. It became clear that communalism was promoted because it had served to 'prop up' the colonial regime, and not because of any concern for the protection of any community. In the words of one historian, 'Never before in South Asian history did so few decide the fate of so many.'[25]

As late as 1946 the British Viceroy of India, Lord Wavell, confessed privately:

> Though I agree as to the contrast between the Muslim and Hindu outlook on life and that the masses can be worked on mainly by the appeal of religion, I think that the root of the political conflict, so far as the leaders are concerned, lies in the fear of economic determination rather than differences of religion. It has been found that Hindus and Muslims can live together without conflict where there is no fear of economic and social domination, e.g. in the army.[26]

But, whatever their private views, the British continued to work on the assumption that the deepest rifts in Indian society were those caused by religion. The result was Partition and the formation of Pakistan on the grounds

that Hindus and Muslims in India formed two separate nations.
Hindu–Muslim riots continued after Partition, although on a very limited
scale under the Nehru regime. However, the Indo–Pakistan conflicts of the
1960s and 1970s, the rise of Kashmiri militancy and Sikh separatism in the
1980s, the formation of the VHP, the perceived threat to high-caste Hindus
posed by the state's policy of affirmative action on behalf of low-caste groups
in job placements and support for minority interests, and the increased
hardships faced by the lower middle classes in the face of growing economic
globalization since the late 1980s have all revitalized Hindu–Muslim antagonisms on a scale comparable to the years immediately preceding Partition.
Hindu political activism is now a formidable phenomenon on the Indian
political scene. It is this modern context of Hindutva which explains part of the
enthusiasm for the idea among urban, middle-class Indians and expatriate
Indians in the West; they see their secular interests as well as private hopes,
anxieties and fears well reflected in the ideology.

Another glance at 'Hinduism'

For many Indian intellectuals, any critique of Hindutva can only take the form
of presenting it as a Western or modern distortion of a basically pure and
problem-free pre-colonial Hindu world. Thus, for the social critic and
psychologist Ashis Nandy, 'the ideologues of religious violence represent the
disowned other self of South Asia's modernized middle classes'.[27] In this view,
the conflict is part and parcel of the legacy of Western imperialism and its
'assault' on the 'core organizing principles of Hinduism'. It is 'one more
desperate attempt to make the two communities deserving citizens of a global
order built on the values of the European Enlightenment'.[28] In an earlier,
much-acclaimed work, Nandy clearly declared his scholarly intent as being 'to
justify and defend the innocence which confronted modern Western
colonialism'.[29]

The 'innocence' proclaimed here involves a deeply disturbing re-reading of
Indian history and religious traditions. What is ironic is the sight of anti-
orientalist writers such as Nandy joining hands with early orientalist
scholarship, Hindu 'New Age' gurus in the West, and some Hindutva
ideologues, in depicting a 'Hindu spirituality' which, unlike Muslim and
Christian spiritualities, is tolerant, non-violent, egalitarian and ecologically
sensitive.

As Peter van der Veer, a student of Indian religions, observes, 'There is
strong consensus from, say, people like Nehru to people like Advani that Hindu
civilization is basically tolerant. The radical Gandhian thinker Ashis Nandy

argues about Gandhi that "traditional Hinduism, or rather *sanatan dharma* ['eternal religion'] was the source of his religious tolerance", and the VHP tells us that Hinduism is "a parliament of religions and the very antithesis of violence, terrorism and intolerance".[30] In other words, 'Hindus have a pluralistic, tolerant "civilization" and Muslims have a fanatic "religion" and the problem is that Hindus are becoming like Muslims instead of the other way around.'[31]

What is often not appreciated in these anti-Western, anti-colonial discourses, is that the very condition of being oppressed is likely to produce its own distorted forms of perception, collective as well as individual: mythical histories, conspiracy theories, prejudice and self-righteous denunciation of others, unreal fantasies of liberation, etc. The move from the 'global' to the 'local' and 'indigenous' is not necessarily a move from tyranny to freedom. These may conceal and distort as much as the ideologies of oppression. They may even be as coercive as the structures they claim to challenge.

Fred Halliday has made the unpopular but perceptive observation, in the context of a critique of anti-orientalist writings about the Middle East as typified by Edward Said, that 'the very fact of trying to subjugate a country would to some degree involve producing an accurate picture of it.' He continues:

> If you want to dominate a country, you need to know where its mines and oases are, to have a good map, to be aware of its ethnic and linguistic composition and so forth. The experts who came with Napoleon to Egypt in 1798 were part of an imperial project, but the knowledge they produced, whatever its motives, financing and use, had objective value ... To put it bluntly: if you plan to rob a bank, you would be well advised to have a pretty accurate blueprint of its layout, know what the routines and administrative practices of its employees are, and, preferably, have some idea of who you can suborn from within the organization ... those outside the region [the Middle East] who try to overcome the myths of the orient rather too quickly end up colluding with, or accepting, the myths of the dominated within the region.[32]

It is to some of those abiding myths of pre-modern Hindu 'innocence' that we now turn.

Hindu social harmony

Central to any understanding of Hindu society and history is the concept of *dharma*. The term has no direct semantic equivalent in English, and though it has often been translated as 'religion', its connotations are much wider than those normally expressed by that word. It has also been translated as 'law', 'duty', 'order', 'morality', 'principle' or 'right'. Even within the various Hindu schools of thought *dharma* enjoys a range of inter-connected meanings. Historically, it first referred to the right performance of Vedic ritual, particularly sacrifice, by the Brahman in early Aryan culture. This eternal and unchanging *dharma*, the performance of which sustained the cosmos, was revealed to the ancient sages (*risi*) in that large body of texts known as the Vedas, in the sacred language of Sanskrit.

Dharma, by natural extension, however, came to be understood as the principle of cosmic harmony that pervaded all things; and the idea of right ritual was taken beyond the Vedic sacrifice to denote all right action within a harmonious social order. It thus becomes an all-embracing ideology, encompassing ritual and moral behaviour, whose neglect would have not only personal and social, but also cosmic, consequences. The cosmic, the social and the individual all blend in the concept of *dharma*. As Gavin Flood writes: '*Dharma* is identified with Vedic obligation, which is eternal, and with action which is particular: the transcendent *dharma* is expressed, or manifested at a human level, in ritual action in order to produce that which is good.'[33]

One striking feature of Hinduism is that practice takes precedence over belief. What a Hindu does is more important than what a Hindu believes. Hinduism is not credal. Adherence to *dharma* is therefore not an acceptance of certain beliefs, but the practice or performance of certain duties, which are defined in accordance with *dharmic* social stratification. The boundaries of what a Hindu can and cannot do have been largely determined by his particular endogamous social group, or caste, stratified in a hierarchical social order, and, of course, by gender … As Frits Staal says, a Hindu 'may be a theist, pantheist, atheist, communist and believe whatever he likes, but what makes him into a Hindu are the ritual practices he performs and the rules to which he adheres, in short, what he *does*.'[34]

Consequently, 'A Hindu is someone born within an Indian social group, a caste, who adheres to its rules with regard to purity and marriage, and who performs its prescribed rituals which usually focus on one of the many Hindu deities such as Shiva or Vishnu.[35] These ritual and social rules are revealed both in the Vedas and in the sources of secondary revelation, books such as the *Dharmasutras* and *Dharmasastras*, one of the earliest and best-known of which (in the West) is the so-called Laws of Manu. The members of the Brahman class are the guardians and reciters of the Veda, and, as such, have played the dominant role in the definition and dissemination of the Hindu ethos and worldview, and the structuring of Hindu society. It is their self-understanding and self-representation that has shaped not only Indian history but non-Indian perceptions of Hinduism.

Within this worldview, *dharma* refers to the duty of high-caste Hindus with regard to social position (*varna*), and the stage of life one is at (*asrama*). All this is incorporated by the term *varnasrama-dharma*. The historical connection between the idea of caste (*jati*, literally 'birth') and *varna* (literally 'colour') is not exactly clear, but an association with slavery cannot be ruled out. Vedic society was divided into four classes, the Brahmans, the Nobles or Warriors (*kshatrya*), the Commoners (*vaisya*) and the Serfs (*sudra*), the top three classes being called the 'twice-born' because boys in these classes underwent an initiation. Only the twice-born males were allowed to hear the Veda, as recited by the Brahmans at ritual events. Many scholars believe that the term *varna*, 'colour', usually translated as 'class', refers to a system of colour symbolism reflecting the social hierarchy as well as the particular qualities (*guna*) which are present in varying degrees in all things. The Brahmans were associated with white, the colour of purity and lightness, the Kshatrya with red, the colour of passion and energy, the Vaisya with yellow, the colour of the earth, and the Sudras with black, the colour of darkness and inertia.[36]

The sacred texts emphasize that the origin of the four-fold division of the society is divine, not human, and rooted in the structure of the cosmos. Thus the right ordering of human society is a religious, and not merely political, concern. Hierarchy and interdependence are the fundamental features of a society conceived as an extension of the cosmic order. According to the *Rg Veda*, the society modelled on the cosmic Brahman is a giant organism, in the image of the human body: the Brahman is the head, the Kshatrya its arms, the Vaisya its trunk, the Sudra its feet.[37]

Collaboration and exchange of services define this organic view of society. The Brahman priest is the microcosm of the cosmic Brahman, and all exchange of services revolves around his pivotal role. The king, however, is the guardian of all material wealth, and it is he who legitimizes the Brahman's status through his patronage. 'Hierarchy culminates in the Brahman, or priest; it is the Brahman who consecrates the king's power, which otherwise depends on force ... From very early times, the relationships between Brahman and kings or Kshatrya are fixed. While the Brahman is spiritually or absolutely supreme, he is materially dependent; while the king is materially the master, he is spiritually subordinate.'[38]

Thus Brahmanical religion was concerned with the ritual status of kingship, the maintaining of strict boundaries between the diverse social groups, and the regulation of social behaviour through the overarching principle of *varnasrama-dharma*. It reached its zenith in the Gupta period of Indian history (c. 320–600 AD), often described as 'the Golden Age' by modern Hindus. In the *Dharmasastra* tradition developed in this period, the Brahman authors of these texts depict the *varna* system as the ideal social order. The Brahman priest is described as the preserver and protector of the universe by means of sacrifice. The *Vishnu Smrti* states clearly that the Brahmans' duties are to study and teach the Veda and to perform the ritual sacrifice for others; the Kshatrya's duties are to protect the people with arms and to give gifts to Brahmans in the royal courts; the Vaisya should tend cattle, practise agriculture and money-lending; and the Sudra exist to serve the other classes and to practise art (*Vs. Smrt.* 2.4–14).

The pivotal role of Brahmans in Indian history ensured that the *varna* system would become virtually universal throughout the land. The social hierarchy conceived as the *varna* system was legitimated by the law of *karma* (action). The Brahmans were born into the highest class on account of *karma* accumulated over their past lives. Lesser *karma* resulted in lower births. Birth as a Sudra was designed to atone for past sins.

While the term *varna* refers to the four classes of Vedic society, the term *jati* (birth) refers to those endogamous sections of Hindu society which we know as 'castes'. The human *jatis* are a highly complex social reality which incorporates many occupational groups whose relative ranking can change in a region over time. The Brahman and Kshatrya *varnas* are also taken to be *jatis*. The term *jati* refers not only to social classes, but to all categories of beings. 'Insects, plants, domestic animals, wild animals and celestial beings are all *jatis*, which show that differences between human castes might be regarded as being as great as differences between different species.'[39]

While the *varna* system centres on the distinction between ritual status and political power, the core of the caste system is the distinction between purity and impurity. The ideas of purity and pollution are extensively treated in the scriptures and the law books. Pollution rules are linked to caste gradations. Pollution permeates all of life: no person, no thing, no act, is exempt from it, and so the avoidance of pollution is a major preoccupation in Hindu social life. Concern over who may receive food and water from whom, without incurring pollution, reflects a view that to share food with another is to share, to a degree, in the other's nature. Hindu social space has thus been organized around the principle of purity and pollution, with the Brahmans – as the most pure of human beings – at the summit, and the Untouchables (or *Dalits* as they prefer to call themselves) – as the least pure, even non-human – at the bottom.

Although 'untouchability' is now legally prohibited in India, Untouchable groups constitute about a fifth of Indian's population. In a typical Indian village, the Brahman (as 'god on earth') lives in the centre of the village while the Untouchable lives outside. The Untouchable is excluded from the religious life. The murder of a Brahman is as serious a crime as the murder of a cow, while the Untouchable is the scavenger and the eater of dead cows. The Brahman purifies himself in order to approach the gods, and thus mediates between man and god. The Untouchable makes personal purity possible for the 'twice-born' castes by removing human excrement and corpses, the strongest sources of religious impurity. The impurity of the Untouchable is conceptually inseparable from the purity of the Brahman. For the execution of impure tasks by some is necessary to the maintenance of purity for others. In other words, without the Untouchables to take upon themselves the society's impurities there can be no Brahman, and therefore no purity.

Such a caste society has proved remarkably resilient, but its ongoing stability requires the suppression by violence of all dissent from below. Thus, not only in the past, but also in more recent Indian history, local or regional movements by *Dalits* and tribal groups have often been brutally attacked by police and thugs bought off by landowners belonging to the dominant caste in the area. Caste itself, however, representing as it does a socio-ethical ideal, is an institutionalization of violence, a denial of any concept of individual freedom.

Although *dharma* is, in principle, universal and timeless, there is no universal morality equally applicable to all human groups. Caste morality is based on the assumption that what others call 'humanity' is really composed of groups of different natures (*guna*) who thus inhabit different locations in ritual space. Moral conduct permissible for members of one caste can be wrong for those of another. Thus the well-known saying in the *Bhagavad Gita*: 'Better to do one's [caste] duty, though devoid of merit, than to do another's, however well performed. By doing the works prescribed by his own nature a man meets with no defilement' (18.47).

This leads to a moral relativism among many Hindus. This acceptance of the contextual relativity of moral ideas, however, is nothing like its counterparts in the postmodern West. For it goes hand in hand with a denial of any freedom of choice on the part of the individual or the group to which he or she belongs. As no-one can choose the caste in which one belongs, there is also no possibility of preferring one or another set of caste rules for one's personal conduct. As one writer has observed, 'The caste system requires the co-existence of two opposing attitudes: one of extreme intolerance regarding any deviant behaviour on the part of the members of one's own in-group, and great tolerance in regard to the conduct of members of other castes.'[40]

Hindu tolerance

The early Gupta period, which witnessed a revival of Brahmanical religion, has bequeathed to us much of what is universally recognized as the cultural glory of Hinduism. It is in this period that the first Hindu temples, including sculptured icons, were built. It was the epoch of great literary works, such as the poetry of Kalidasa, the greatest of all Sanskrit authors. The *Kamasutra* of Vatsyayana reflected the leisurely ambience not only of the royal courts but also the new class of sophisticated, urban men and women. This was the age in which the great Epics, most notably the *Mahabharatha* (the world's longest epic poem, comprising more than 100,000 verses) and Valmiki's *Ramayana*, were given their final forms. The *Puranas*, mythic narratives dealing with the realm of the gods, reflected a growing devotional theism, principally focused on the great deities Vishnu and Shiva. It is these epics and *puranas* that have shaped the worldview and formed the emotional heartbeat of most Hindu men and women down to the present day.

Yet there is another, darker, face to this period which cannot be described as an Indian 'golden age' for all its people. The Chinese pilgrim Fa-Hsien, reporting on his visit to the holy places of Buddhism around AD 400, was shocked by the fact that the Candalas, or Untouchables, were compelled to strike a wooden clapper whenever they entered a city, for fear of polluting their betters.[41] It is also possible to sense a violent reaction against the 'heretics' (often dubbed 'foreigners', *mlecchas*) among the instigators of the Hindu revival. The heretics – the Buddhists, Jains and Carvakas, or Materialists – are referred to as *nastikas* because they deny the authority of the Veda, and, by implication, the ritual sacrifice of the Brahmans. In one of these revivalist works, the *Vishnu Purana*, which first appeared between AD 400 and 500, the Buddha is depicted as deluded and destructive, an *avatara* (manifestation) of Vishnu designed to lead the wicked and demons astray, and so hasten the end of the present evil age (the *Kali Yuga*). The Jain and Buddhist texts are contemptuously denounced as scriptures of delusion.[42]

The classical scholar Wendy O'Flaherty has noted that the *puranic* and *dharmasastra* texts of the Gupta period were 'weapons in a battle between the instigators of the Hindu revival and the still thriving establishments of Jainism and Buddhism'.[43] By the tenth century AD, heresy was so 'widespread and so abhorred' that Shiva himself was said 'to have become incarnate as the philosopher Shankara in order to explain the Vedas, destroy the temples and books of the Jains, and massacre all who oppose him, particularly the Jains'.[44] Later, when Buddhists were waning in India, the Hindus could afford to be generous, and the Buddha is depicted in a more favourable light:

> To the Hindus as a whole, Buddhist and Jains (and Carvakas or Materialists, with whom the former two are often confused) are heretics. To many Vaishnavas, Shaivas are heretics, and to many Shaivas, Vaishnavas are heretics. To many North Indians, South Indians were regarded as heretics. And just to round things out, the Jains regarded the Hindus as heretics ... Hindus came to use the term 'heretic' as a useful swear word to indicate anyone who disagreed with them, much as the late Senator Joseph McCarthy used the term 'communist'.[45]

The later Gupta period saw the rise of monastic orders modelled on those of Buddhists and Jains, first among Shaivites and later among the Vaishnavites. This later led to the phenomenon of 'soldier monks' (*sadhus*) and the emergence of a powerful martial tradition within Hindu monasticism. Hindu monks (*sadhus*) have always been soldiers as well as traders, and fighting societies (*nagas*) form important military sections of most Hindu monastic orders. Their organization into regiments and armies is probably a development of the eighteenth century, but these *nagas* represent a long tradition within asceticism.

The greatest pilgrimage festival in India is the *kumbh mela*, which is held in rotation every twelve years in the north Indian cities of Hardwar, Allahabad, Ujjain and Nasik. Millions of pilgrims from all over India gather on the banks of the sacred Ganges, in the hope that a dip in the river on this auspicious occasion will wash away their sins. The *kumbh mela* gained prominence as the main arena for resolving monastic rivalries. Every festival was the scene of considerable sectarian violence between Shaivites and Vaishnavites.

William Pinch, a social historian of India, writes as follows about these militant *sadhus*:

> Whatever the origins of armed monasticism, by the eighteenth century,

soldier monks had evolved into major players in north Indian political and economic affairs, and were involved in activities that extended well beyond the defence of religious property. The major soldiering orders were, as financiers and traders, central to the expanding economic integration of the subcontinent, making up for the decay of Mughal political unity. Soldier monks ... combined their command of sub-continental pilgrimage routes and privileged status in society with a formidable martial tradition to extend and diversify their institutional (monasterial) savings into urban land ownership, money lending, and luxury goods in a variety of urban centres.[46]

Religious conflict involving soldier monks was usually enacted in a circumscribed setting – the *kumbh* festival – where the supremacy of these religious orders was negotiated continually. But soldier monks also signed on as mercenaries for local kingdoms, and as often as not the rulers for whom they fought were Muslims. The army of the Nawabs of Awadh, the greatest Muslim power in the eighteenth century, depended on Shaivite ascetics. With the emergence in nineteenth-century India of the modern state, first embodied in the East India Company and later in the British Raj, which demanded a monopolistic control of armed force, the countryside was demilitarized. The *kumbh*, which by the eighteenth century had become 'a popular occasion for audacious displays of monastic military prowess', became a religious theatre, closely supervised by colonial officials alert to any outbreak of sectarian violence.[47] The result is that militant monks did not play a significant role in political violence any more – at least, not until the resurgence of the VHP in the 1980s.

The VHP/RSS propaganda romanticizes the militant *sadhus* of the eighteenth century, depicting them as forerunners of modern-day nationalists, fighting to liberate their Hindu motherland from foreign slavery. This is flatly contradicted by the evidence: 'In fact, the resistance to company rule on the part of the various bands of soldier monks in Bengal – both Hindu and Muslim – in the last three decades of the eighteenth century was not grounded in a patriotic vision of India, but, rather, in a monastic desire to retain a right to carry arms, levy contributions from the countryside while on pilgrimage, and serve as mercenaries for local notables in the province.'[48]

Peter van der Veer observes that 'the great shift in the nineteenth century is the laicization of institutionalized religion. A lay Hindu and Muslim public had come to occupy a sphere that was previously the domain of sacred specialists. To put it very crudely, warfare between religious specialists was replaced by civil warfare between lay communities.'[49]

A young Hindu scholar, Rajmohan Ramanathapillai, from Jaffna in northern Sri Lanka, has argued that the effectiveness of the Tamil 'Tiger' guerrillas in gaining the support of the majority of Hindu Tamils in that country lies in their manipulation of religious symbols and themes drawn from the medieval *Puranas* and epics.[50] These stories are disseminated widely through school textbooks, cinemas and songs, as well as through ritual enactments and recitations at public festivals. A dominant theme in all the myths and epics is that coercion and violence are necessary for the protection of cosmic and social *dharma.* In the politically volatile atmosphere of northern Sri Lanka, the *puranic* association of evildoers with 'heretics' (*nastikas*) and 'barbarians' (*mlecchas*) has easily lent itself to the extermination by the Tamil Tigers of all those Tamils who publicly express disagreement with their methods and ideology. Ramanathapillai points out that, contrary to popular Western belief, there is no Hindu tradition among Tamils of non-violent resistance to evil. He writes: 'The LTTE's success would not have been possible had the sacred symbols of Tamil religion not already shaped the people's ethos and worldview toward accepting and legitimizing coercion and violence as norms for the protection of society during times of chaos.'[51]

I give these examples not to portray the pre-colonial period as being rife with religious violence and intolerance, but, rather, in order to dispel the persistent myth that violence and persecution were 'foreign' to the Hindu religious ethos in India and solely the work of Moguls and the British. Many Western writers, including Christian theologians and teachers of 'religious studies' who write about 'Hindu tolerance' and 'Hindu other-worldliness' have drunk deeply from an orientalist discourse that identifies Hinduism with a few selected texts. Hence the puzzlement with which Westerners read of militant speech and violent actions performed by religious monks, whether in India or Sri Lanka.

Hindu inclusivism

It has become a truism to speak of Hinduism as an inclusivist faith. Over the centuries, several Western students of Indian society have marvelled at the 'genius' of Indian thought which is able to assimilate contradictory philosophical positions, seemingly without inner conflict. It is this inclusiveness that has also been commended by such eloquent apologists for neo-Vedanta in the modern West as Swami Vivekananda and Sarvapalli Radhakrishnan. It constitutes part of the appeal of Hinduism to young Western men and women disillusioned with consumerism and sensitive to the terrible pain that religious conflicts have brought in the past.

Religious pluralism, it is held, poses a problem only for Semitic faiths with their narrow, exclusivist categories of thinking. The Hindu tradition, particularly that school of thought known as *advaita Vedanta*, readily accounts for the diversity of religious conceptions and forms of religious practice. They should be seen as movements, not from falsehood to truth, but from a lower to a higher truth, and the highest truth is non-duality (*advaita*), or the knowledge of that undifferentiated reality that underlies all diversity and is one with the essential human self. For Vivekananda, the world of religions is 'only a travelling, a coming up of different men and women, through various conditions and circumstances, to the same goal.'[52]

Consequently, many modern Hindus, especially the Western-educated, like to speak of their religion as *sanatana dharma*, or 'eternal religion'. It provides the umbrella under which adherents of all religions (and none) can find shade. This neo-Vedanta way of dealing with diversity reminds me of the story of the man who was asked if the word 'trousers' was singular or plural. He deliberated awhile and then replied, 'They are singular at the top and plural at the bottom.'

Sarvepalli Gopal, a well-known Indian historian and ardent defender of secularism against the advocates of Hindutva, expresses the oft-heard view that 'to the person moved by the religious impulse, the ultimate truth is one, every religion shows some traces of it and it is a matter of indifference to which religion one adheres'. For Gopal, 'devotion to truth and respect for all human beings, a deepening of inner awareness and a commitment to compassion, form the essence of the Hindu religion.'[53]

Gopal's father, Sarvepalli Radhakrishnan, former Professor of Eastern Religions at Oxford University and the first president of the post-colonial Indian state, summed up the vision with customary eloquence:

> We cannot have religious unity and peace so long as we assert that we are in possession of the light and all others are grasping in the darkness. That very assertion is a challenge to a fight ... We can do so only if we accept something like the Hindu solution, which seeks the unity of religion not in a common creed but in a common quest ... God wills a rich harmony and not a colourless conformity. The comprehensive and synthetic spirit of Hinduism has made it a mighty forest with a thousand waving arms each fulfilling its function and all directed by the Spirit of God.[54]

Radhakrishnan's 'comprehensive and synthetic spirit of Hinduism' does on the level of thought what the ranking of caste distinctions does on the level of

Indian society. 'Hinduism', he writes, 'insists on our working steadily upwards and improving our knowledge of God. The worshippers of the Absolute are the highest in rank, second to them are the worshippers of the personal God, then come the worshippers of the incarnations like Rama, Krishna, Buddha, below them are those who worship ancestors, deities and sages, and lowest of all are the worshippers of the petty forces and spirits.'[55]

This is simply religious imperialism masquerading as tolerance. Pluralism is ultimately undermined, because the 'Other' is never taken seriously as a challenge to the entire framework of discourse. Radical differences can never become the occasion for debate and self-questioning, because it is assumed at the outset that such differences do not affect our final destination. Some of us (the *advaitins*) get there quicker than others, that's all. The *advaitin*, free of dogmatic blinkers, has achieved a superior vantage-point from which he can survey the whole world of religion and see that all religions are but partial glimpses of that unfathomable mystery which the Vedanta discloses.

There are forms of ecumenical 'dialogue' today which share in this subtle arrogance. It is roundly asserted that, unless we are willing to recognize the salvific validity of all religious traditions, our encounter with others is not authentic. As a representative example of this very common notion, let me quote from a statement on Christian–Hindu dialogue in a World Council of Churches publication, *Current Dialogue*:

> Religions as they are manifested in history are complementary perceptions of the ineffable divine mystery, the God-beyond-God. All religions are visions of the divine Mystery. No particular religion can raise the claim of being the norm for all others. We religious believers are co-pilgrims, who share intimate spiritual experiences and reflections with one another with concern and compassion, with genuine openness to truth and the freedom of spiritual seekers.[56]

This is essentially the neo-Vedanta worldview. Religion is one, grounded in 'intimate spiritual experiences'. Thus the boundary-markers are already pre-defined. All those religious faiths which centre not on some impersonal Absolute, but on a personal God who speaks and reveals himself in historical events, are automatically ruled out of court. For that would challenge the assumption that we all start our quest for the divine Mystery from where we are, that every individual has equal access to Truth. Since the Christian Scriptures question the naïve belief that we are all seekers after Truth, the Christian Scriptures – and those who take them seriously – become an embarrassment in this kind of dialogue. It seems, then, that all who participate in dialogue must give up the convictions of their own faiths and embrace this particular worldview as the condition for dialogue.

This is a very bizarre way to enter into a conversation. If we cannot be challenged where our most basic assumptions are concerned, then what we have is not dialogue but a monologue. That is why this kind of ecumenical dialogue becomes an exercise in mutual 'back-scratching' rather than genuine understanding. Far from being dishonest and unethical, the possibility of conversion is what makes dialogue real and exciting.

In this context, Anantanand Rambachan, a Hindu scholar from Trinidad who teaches at a Christian college in the United States, makes the interesting observation that 'Communities where differences are real, but where they are minimized or downplayed, are more likely to suffer violence and traumatic upheavals when, in times of tension and conflict, such differences become prominent'. He continues:

> Communities, on the other hand, which engage each other in a deep search for mutual understanding and which honestly acknowledge differences and cultivate respect are less likely to explode in times of conflict. Such communities are less likely to cite difference as a basis for hostility towards the other. I often wonder about this matter when we witness neighbours, in many recent conflicts, suddenly turning upon each other with ferocity and violence, shattering the veneer of civility and harmony.[57]

The renouncers

Traditionally, the only way a Hindu can abandon caste society and caste status is by becoming a *sannyasin* or homeless, wandering ascetic. By wearing the *sannyasin*'s ochre robe and divorcing himself from the conventional ties of family and society, he is freed from the need to observe caste rules. The *sannyasin*'s quest is for *moksa*, or liberation from the endless rhythms of births and rebirths, of samsaric existence. The result is an opposition and tension between the Brahman householder, 'the man-in the-world, who is not an individual' and the *sannyasin* 'who is an individual-outside-the-world'.[58] Despite his opting out of society, the *sannyasin* acquires great social prestige because he is believed to be the possessor of extraordinary magical and spiritual powers.

Brahmanical religion had little difficulty in containing the challenge of individual ascetics, since some of the early philosophical texts had reinterpreted the Vedic rituals in terms of psychic self-disciplines. The *sannyasin*'s vocation of spiritual liberation was simply absorbed into the *varnasrama-dharma* scheme by locating it as the final stage in the ideal life-cycle of the Brahman householder. But the communal renouncers, those like the 'heretical' Buddhist and Jain monks, who not only 'dropped out' of society but formed an alternative or 'parallel society'[59] in which caste distinctions were considered irrelevant, posed a serious threat to Brahmanical Hinduism. For here, in Buddhist and Jain monasteries, a common disciplinary code (often in contradiction to caste rules) and new institutional structures based on ascetic goals, marked the renouncers off from other groups in society.

The eminent social anthropologist Louis Dumont has argued the provocative thesis that 'the agent of development in Indian religion and speculation, the creator of values, has been the renouncer'; and that 'not only the founding of sects ... but the major ideas, the "inventions", are due to the renouncer whose unique position gave him a sort of monopoly for putting everything in question'.[60] Brahmanical religion, with its genius for absorbing and adapting, took over the values of *ahimsa* (non-violence) and vegetarianism, which were originally renouncer values (particularly from Jain mendicants). In the seventh to the ninth centuries when religious controversy was intense, Shaiva monasteries modelled on heterodox monasteries were established as agents of a 'missionary' Brahmanism.

The great Brahman theologian Shankara (c. 788–820 AD), the founder of Hindu monasticism, created the renunciate order of Shaiva *Dasanamis*, with centres in the four corners of the land, to combat these rival schools. He borrowed from Buddhist monks elements of their organizational structure and the same broad rules of discipline – 'permanent residence in the monasteries, austerity, celibacy, subsistence on alms and the study and teaching of the prescribed texts'.[61] The *bhakti* cults that developed about the same period could be understood as responses to the appeal of Buddhist *bodhisattva* cults that were a feature of popular Buddhist religiosity. But all these features were incorporated into a religious framework that kept intact the dominance of the Brahman householder and the caste system.

In more recent times, reformers such as Dayananda Sarasvati (1824–83), the founder of the Arya Samaj, Swami Vivekananda (1863–1902), and Mohandas Gandhi (1869–1948) were all 'renouncers', and paradoxically left their mark on Hindu society by stepping outside it.

It is illuminating to view the impact of Christian missions in this perspective of the 'renouncer tradition' in Indian history. Most of the early Protestant missionaries came from the lower-middle classes of European society and practised a sacrificial, almost ascetic, lifestyle. For instance, contrast William Carey (1761–1834), the cobbler from Northampton who made India his home, with Robert Clive (1725–74), the arch-imperialist of the East India Company. Carey gave away his earnings from printing and translating for the missionary cause in India, where he died; whereas Clive salted away a massive personal fortune through his ruthless exploits in India, and retired to England to enjoy it.

A cursory study of the lives of the early Christian missionaries to India, beginning with the sixteenth-century Jesuits right through to the middle years of the nineteenth century, reveals the incredible hardships they were willing to endure. Theirs is, more often than not, a tale of debilitating illness, personal tragedy and premature death. There is a well-known portrait of Carey at his desk, working on a translation of the Bible, with a pundit beside him to offer advice and correction. What is not often realized is that Carey's wife was in the next room suffering from a state of psychic collapse. She had already shown signs of mental instability before the couple sailed from England with their young children. The death of their eldest son within a few weeks of setting foot in India seems to have pushed her over the edge into complete insanity. Several times during their life in India she attempted to kill her husband and children. There were no psychiatric care or mental hospitals for her and people like her.

Moreover, far from seeking to adapt to the values of caste-*dharma*, the early nineteenth-century missionaries sought to create an alternative, parallel society, one that would in time act like leaven in transforming the values and structures of the wider society. They built on the pioneering efforts of Bartholomew Ziegenbalg (1682–1719) and others from the early eighteenth century onwards, in offering education to all who aspired to it, irrespective of caste or class or gender. If all men and women were created in the image of God, and if the Son of God himself had stooped to take our humanity into his own being, then that message imparted a new vision of humanness. It gave to every individual human being an intrinsic dignity, transcending the particular community to which he or she belonged. Egalitarian education was a radical innovation in Indian society and led to agrarian reform, a greater sense of social responsibility, and a new appreciation for vernacular languages.

The concern of men like Carey to educate Indians in the vernacular languages of India was opposed both by the orientalists, who championed the classical languages of Sanskrit, Persian and Arabic for Indian learning, and by the Anglicists, who wanted to transform India through an English education. Carey's printing of Matthew's Gospel was the first prose literature in Bengali. By compiling Bengali grammars, and translating the Indian classics from Sanskrit into Bengali so that ordinary men and women, and not just the pundits or scholars, could read them, the Serampore missionaries paved the way for the mid-nineteenth century 'Bengal Renaissance'. Carey's breadth of vision was rooted in the global reach of the gospel. He provided schools for women and *Dalits*, an asylum for lepers, persuaded the British officials to outlaw such social evils as infanticide and widow-burning, pioneered forestry projects in Bengal and became one of the founding members of the Agricultural and Horticultural Society of India. Little wonder that Rabindranath Tagore called Carey the 'Father of Modern Bengal'.[62]

The impact of Christians on Indian society, whether indigenous disciples of Jesus or missionaries from Western lands, cannot be assessed by numbers alone. The radical and unprecedented social and religious changes witnessed in nineteenth-century India were quite out of proportion to the number of converts made or churches established. The ideal of disinterested service which missionaries and indigenous Christians provided was unique. Charity for the sake of achieving religious merit or as an inducement to religious conversion – these are readily grasped. But that charity and social betterment should have no other motive than love itself – this was an alien notion. Hence the suspicion with which any Christian initiatives in social welfare and social action are viewed even today by intelligent Hindus and Buddhists. As Richard Young, a historian of nineteenth-century missions in South Asia, notes:

> ... historically it can be argued that until Protestant Christianity arrived in South Asia the organizational infrastructure for expressing disinterested benevolence was almost entirely lacking ... it might be said that the wheel of social change in South Asia has a Christian hub and a Buddhist-Hindu rim.[63]

Christian missions in India are routinely dismissed in contemporary Indian scholarship as simply an adjunct to colonialism. But, in fact, they were the soil from which both modern Hindu reform movements and Indian nationalism sprang. Most of the Indian intellectual and political leadership of the late nineteenth and early twentieth century emerged from Christian schools and colleges. Gandhi may have claimed to have been nurtured in the spiritual atmosphere of the *Bhagavad Gita*, but it was not from this text that he derived his philosophy of *ahimsa* (non-violence) and *satyagraha* ('truth-force'). The deepest influences on Gandhi came from the 'renouncer' traditions of Jainism and the New Testament, particularly the Sermon on the Mount as mediated through the works of Tolstoy.

Christians in India have long been in the forefront of movements for the emancipation of women, with missionary societies from Britain and the United States often giving the lead where the colonial government was hesitant to tread for fear of upsetting local sensibilities. Some of the finest medical hospitals and training schools in India owe their existence to Christian missions. Many Hindus would rather go to a Christian hospital than to a government hospital because they know the quality of personal care in the former is so much better. In areas such as leprosy, tuberculosis, mental illness and eye diseases, Christian missionary doctors and nurses pioneered new methods of management and surgery. Moreover, the training of women doctors and nurses was first introduced into India by Christian missionaries. For many years the entire nursing profession was filled with Anglo-Indians and Indian Christians, as other communities regarded nursing as menial work fit only for uneducated girls and widows. It has been estimated that, as late as the beginning of the Second World War, 90% of all the nurses in the country, male and female, were Christians, and that about 80% of these had been trained in mission hospitals.[64]

However, apart from the transformation of the social order, Protestant Christianity had a significant impact on the traditional religions of the Indian subcontinent. Once again, it was from a position of 'renunciation', of ruthless criticism of the indigenous traditions rather than from an uncritical attempt to 'enreligionize' the gospel within the thought-forms of these religions, that the most interesting transformations were effected. The first level at which this process began was through changes in indigenous religious beliefs and concepts.[65] For example, most books on Hinduism written today in the English language translate *murti* as 'icon' rather than 'idol' or 'image', and most educated Hindus assume that the image in the temple is indeed a representation of the deity rather than the deity itself. It is an aid to contemplation, but this was not the traditional understanding. The *murti* was alive because the 'breath' of the deity had been infused into it in a special ceremony called *pranapratishta*. Such a change in understanding came about through Christian (and perhaps earlier Muslim) criticism. A second level of change involved religious practices such as *sati* (the immolation of widows), temple prostitution, and the exclusion of *Dalits* from temple premises. The gospel acted as a catalyst in mobilizing Hindus, especially those educated in Christian mission schools, to spearhead such changes within Hindu society.

The highest level of religious influence is sometimes referred to as the 'Protestantization' of religion in South Asia. Protestant Christians, more so than their Catholic brethren, have been what the Qur'an dubs 'a people of the book'. Protestant Christian identity is defined by reference to a corpus of authoritative texts. Any belief, custom or practice is evaluated in terms of conformity or nonconformity to these texts. Protestant missionaries in South

Asia brought this textual understanding of religion to their encounter with 'Hinduism' and 'Buddhism'. Missionary scholars, along with other orientalists, set up the Royal Asiatic Society, unearthed many ancient texts and wrote extensive commentaries on them. It could be said, ironically but truly, that it was the missionaries who often gave to the Hindus and Buddhists their own sacred texts. The first work on Buddhism to appear in the English language (by a British Buddhist scholar, Rhys Davids) was published by the SPCK in 1860. I know of no Christian work that has been published by a Hindu, Buddhist or Muslim publishing house to the present day!

To return to the story, assuming that 'Hinduism' and 'Buddhism' were to be identified with the philosophical teaching found in these texts, the early missionaries mounted a relentless critique of the superstitious and inhuman practices of what they called 'folk' or 'popular' religion. Not only did they show that much of what went on in South Asian societies had no foundation in these texts, but they also raised awkward moral and intellectual problems with the texts themselves. This forced educated Hindus and Buddhists to return to the Buddhist *Tripitaka* or the Hindu *Agamas*, for instance, determined to counter the Christian criticisms with their own apologetic. This led to the gradual identification of these religions with a certain corpus of canonical texts. Another aspect of Protestant practice, the formulation of credal summaries of belief and short catechisms to create an informed laity, was also taken over by Buddhist and Hindu reformers in the late nineteenth century to make their religions more like that of the missionaries.

There are several interesting ironies here. The 'Protestantization' of Hindu and Buddhist religious traditions, and the greater exposure of educated Hindus and Buddhists to both Semitic faiths and Western secular humanism, meant that the exegesis of sacred texts became central both to religious instruction and to interreligious dialogue. Hindus and Buddhists often read their own scriptures through Christian (missionary or native) eyes; and this paved the way for many internal critiques and reforms of tradition and practice. It led, eventually, to a renewed intellectual confidence on the part of the educated Hindu and Buddhist laity and a strong resistance, in the name of nationalism or 'protecting our ancient heritage', to Christian mission.

Indian Christians have also developed a consciousness that is critical of any attempt to 'contextualize' the gospel within the dominant religious traditions of Indian society. For, as we have seen, these traditions have over many centuries legitimated an oppressive social order and the degradation of millions of men and women as well as their cultural inheritances. Between 50% and 80% of Christians in India today are of *Dalit* origins. Not only have Christian *Dalits* suffered deprivation common to all *Dalits*, but the Indian state does not allow them to receive economic assistance or to benefit from the 'affirmative action' programmes introduced for scheduled-caste communities. Indian Christian theology as taught in seminaries in the past came from converts to Christianity from the upper castes. Many of these theologies sought to make the gospel congenial to the worldview of Brahmanical Hinduism. The latter is also the discourse that is still invoked by many Western writers on religious pluralism as embodying the 'lofty spirituality' of the 'Hindu religion'. *Dalit* Christians have rightly seen this as a 'sell-out' of the gospel and a betrayal of their own identity. They seek to develop a theology, in radical discontinuity from a classical Indian Christian theology, that would challenge the religious and philosophical perspectives under which *Dalit* oppression is legitimized.

With Hindu militancy on the rise and the lower castes increasingly trying to assert their rights, Christian congregations and missionaries are caught in a political maelstrom. 'For priests and nuns striving to bring about change in the lives of India's poor', says Delhi's (Roman Catholic) Auxiliary Bishop Vincent Concessao, 'the journey ahead may involve more than the usual quota of sacrifices.'[66]

Concluding reflections

For Nehru and many of the early Indian nationalists, the West's present defined the image of India's future. Yet 'the odd twist', as Sunil Khilnani notes, is that India's present may actually be a window into the West's own future.

> The themes and conflicts that animate India's politics today have a surprisingly wide resonance – the assertion of community and group rights and the use of democracy to affirm collective identities; the difficulties of maintaining large-scale, multi-cultural political unions; the compulsion to make democracy work despite economic adversity, to sustain democracy without prosperity. The older democracies might recognize that each of these stands uncomfortably close to their own doorsteps.[67]

Indian political culture today seems to be the site of contention between two modernities expounded by two modernizing élites. One either ignores religious traditions or shunts them to the realm of the purely private; and the other adopts an instrumental, sometimes manipulative, stance towards religious narratives, symbols and piety. Nationalist religion may sound like a 'return to tradition' to those who equate 'secular' with 'modern' and 'religious' with 'tradition'. But nationalism has been the dominant discourse of modernity since the nineteenth century, and a 'secular nationalism' is no less religious than a Hindu or Buddhist one. (We shall return to this myth of the secular in the last chapter.)

Many Indian intellectuals treat Hindu nationalism as an aberrant form of Indian religion, representing a modern rupture with 'indigenous' Hindu practices. In this perspective, Hindu nationalism is not a return to an ancient 'tradition', but a reconfiguration of Hinduism as a modern political religion. It is designed to unite a diverse polity in the face of perceived danger, just as Hinduism has been so reshaped and re-enacted many times in India's long history. The aim of Hindu nationalists is to bring the complex of Indian religious and cultural activities under the command of the state, to 'tidy up the compromises and accommodations that litter Indian life'[68] by bringing them under a single legal system. Hindu identity, however, is multiple, by definition, and India consists of many other religious identities. We have noted that the 'core' beliefs and rituals that comprise what has been called 'Hinduism' deeply discourage the formation of a collective religious identity among its practitioners.

I have argued that, while this reading is true to a large extent, it fails to acknowledge the depth to which Hindu nationalism is nurtured by major strands in the dominant Brahmanical Hindu ethos: namely, the relegation of those outside the 'twice-born' to a less than human status, let alone a voice in the public sphere; organized violence as a time-honoured, legitimate way of resolving religious disputes and restoring the rule of *dharma*; the suppression of genuine 'otherness' in a misleading form of religious inclusiveness; the assimilation of tribal groups and other religious communities into a pan-Hindu identity, and so on.

Moreover, both Indian secularists and Hindu nationalists share a conception of 'traditional Hinduism' that is, ironically, heavily indebted to orientalist discourses on Indian religion. Elements of Hindu culture, such as yoga, *bhakti*, gurus, some Vedanta writings, dance and music, were exported to the West from the late nineteenth century onwards as representations of 'Hindu spirituality', and their popularity among the jaded upper-middle classes stimulated a new-found popularity among English-educated Hindus in India. One writer has, somewhat playfully, dubbed this process of re-enculturation, common in global Hinduism, the 'Pizza Effect'.[69] The original pizza was a hot baked bread which was exported to America from Italy, embellished, and returned to Italy where it became a national dish. The VHP, with its support drawn from Indian immigrants in the West and the urban middle classes in India, has built on orientalist understandings of Indian religions and presented a modern Hinduism through the mirror of the West. On the level of discourse, as Peter van der Veer has observed, there is very little difference between VHP propaganda and the sayings of the founder of the Ramakrishna Mission, Swami Vivekananda. 'Moreover, Vivekananda had the same audience as the VHP. The difference lies in the historical development of that audience, the modern middle class.'[70] Van der Veer continues:

> This is reflected in VHP discourse on 'individual growth', 'social concerns', and religion as a 'code of conduct' whereby every man can make a success of life, which sounds like the credo of the success-oriented Western middle-class. If there is a 'mainstream' constituency for the VHP's discourse on spiritual Hinduism as India's 'national identity', then it is the middle class, together with those who aspire to that status.[71]

Sunil Khilnani notes that from being a society where the state played a marginal role, India has today become 'the most intensely political society in the world'. Indians have 'poured their faith into politics, pinning their hopes to once-great movements like the Congress Party or to its current challengers like Hindu nationalism or the surging movements of India's lower-caste or Dalit parties'.[72]

The post-colonial Indian state grew to monstrous proportions, and was heralded as the saviour and creator of the modern nation. It was transformed from 'a distant, alien object into one that aspired to infiltrate the everyday lives of Indians, proclaiming itself responsible for everything they could desire: jobs, ration cards, educational places, security, cultural recognition'.[73] However, this state regularly failed to protect its citizens against physical violence, was unable to end oppression and reduce economic inequities, and has not fulfilled its ambitions to rejuvenate Indian society. Yet this hope in the modern state continues to inspire secular nationalists and Hindu nationalists alike.

The Indian people's faith in state-directed social transformation, understandable as it is, is always bound to end in disillusionment. For democracy to blossom in India, the nurturing of civil society is the need of the hour. By a civil society I mean that realm which is neither the private sphere of the individual citizen nor the public sphere that is totally absorbed into the state; but one that overlaps both, the dimension of social life where debate is encouraged on matters of common concern. Indian society has splintered into a sea of politicized minorities competing against each other for state benefits. While democracy in the form of electoral participation has become indelibly inscribed in the popular imagination, democracy as the rule of law, the recognition of individual rights, and of constraints on the use of power by the state, is still struggling to take root in Indian soil.

Governments can encourage the cultivation of a civil space, where peoples of all communities and classes can articulate their worldviews and fulfil their aspirations to contribute to public life. But is it the case that only some worldviews encourage and sustain a genuine culture of respect and, consequently, the creation of this type of government in the first place? This is a vital issue to which we shall return in the final chapter.

Both secular and Hindu intellectuals in India, as much as its political leaders, routinely ignore the historic and ongoing contribution of Christians to the public life of the nation. So the discursive space is further restricted in this kind of society. What makes this ignorance, whether genuine or intentional, so ironically anti-nationalist is that it refuses to face the paradoxical nature of Indian social transformation highlighted by Dumont and others: namely, that it is those individuals and communities which have self-consciously stood 'outside' Hindu society (and its dominant social values) which have been the agents of renewal and vitality in Indian society. India, perhaps more than any other nation, owes a special debt to the people who have constituted its 'periphery'.

The late M. M. Thomas, an influential theologian and former governor of the Indian state of Nagaland, was probably guilty of some exaggeration when, a few years before his death, he wrote that the leaders of the nineteenth-century Indian Renaissance and the political thinkers in the ideological leadership of twentieth-century Indian Nationalism 'grappled with the person and teachings of Jesus Christ and assimilated the essence of Christian humanism into the religious and secular thought of modern India'.

Thomas, however, is more on track when he claims that it was not only professional thinkers, Hindu, secular and Christian, who have contributed to the 'Christianization / Humanization of Indian religion, ideology and philosophy', but also

> the local Christian congregations, which in their worship and sacramental life, demonstrated a pattern of corporate life of fellowship, transcending caste-division impelled by their new sense of being made brethren through the death of Christ on the cross. The Lord's table open to people of different castes and tribes and sexes challenged the traditional spirituality that divided peoples into the ritually pure and impure and thereby supported social structures of caste, sex and other discriminations. It does not mean that the church congregations did not make compromises with such structures themselves. They did. But

they also promoted a spiritual vision and practice that challenged them, thereby acting as a transforming ferment in the larger society.[74]

Christians on the social periphery lived the way they did, and posed the challenges that they did, because of specific beliefs concerning the centrality of Jesus of Nazareth in God's dealings with God's world. Are those beliefs still credible? Is the Christian movement founded on a gigantic misunderstanding, even a hoax? Conversely, if those beliefs are true, do they not call into question much of what we take for granted concerning politics, culture and the world of 'religion'? It is to these questions that we now turn.

3

The Jesus enigma

[Inspector Morse's] favourite Gibbon quotation flashed across his mind, the one concerning the fifteenth-century Pope John XXIII, which had so impressed him as a boy and which he had committed to memory those many years ago: 'the most scandalous charges were suppressed: the vicar of Christ was only accused of piracy, murder, rape, sodomy, and incest.' It was no new thing to realise that the Christian church had a great deal to answer for, with so much blood on the hands of its temporal administrators, and so much hatred and bitterness in the hearts of its spiritual lords. But, behind it all, as Morse knew – and transcending it all – stood the simple, historical, unpalatable figure of its founder – an enigma with which Morse's mind had wrestled so earnestly as a youth, and which even now troubled his pervasive scepticism.[1]

A controversial figure

The fictional detective Inspector Morse is not alone in his wrestling. Jesus of Nazareth continues to fascinate men and women of all cultures. Many are attracted by the power of his teaching, others by the way he ruthlessly exposed the barrenness and hypocrisy of the religious establishment. His witty aphorisms and devastating parables are continuing sources of delight and admiration to professional communicators and literary critics. Many women see in him a man who was liberated from the pervasive chauvinism of his society, at ease in the company of women. Many social reformers and political revolutionaries have found in Jesus an inspiring model in the struggle for social justice. He was not reluctant to trample upon oppressive social conventions and taboos. More books, plays and films have been made of him – and more music and art inspired by him – than of any other figure in human history. And a good deal of this was by people who would not consider themselves Christians.

But Jesus was also – and continues to be – a controversial figure. First in Jewish Palestine, and then in the pagan Greco-Roman world, Jesus evoked attitudes of bewilderment, scorn and indignation. Crucifixion, though widespread in the Roman empire, was viewed with universal horror and disgust. It was cruel and degrading, the victim often being flogged and tortured before being strung up on a cross. It was the most humiliating form of death in the ancient world: the penalty reserved for rebellious slaves, dangerous criminals of the lower classes and (what today would be called) 'terrorists' against the state. No Roman citizen could be crucified. Crosses with their gory exhibits were set up in busy, crowded road junctions to act as a deterrent to the masses. It was Rome's way of preserving the imperial status quo.

It is in such a world that we meet a group of men and women, first called 'Christians' by the curious citizens of the Roman city of Antioch, moving from Jerusalem to other parts of the empire and eventually forming a community in Rome itself. What they announced as they travelled was not a new religion or a new morality, but a message which they called 'good news' (*euangelion* in Greek, later to become 'gospel' in English): namely, that among those forgotten 'nobodies', those degraded victims of crucifixion, there had been one who was no less than the Son of God, the Saviour of the world.

The foolishness of such a message cannot be overemphasized. If you wanted to convert the educated and pious people of the empire to your cause, the worst thing you could ever do would be to link that cause to a recently crucified man. To put it mildly, that would have been a public-relations disaster. To associate God, the source of all life, with this crucified criminal was to invite mockery and sheer stupefaction! This was indeed the experience of the first Christians. And the mockery turned to hatred and eventually to active persecution when Christians, in the name of that crucified criminal, began to practise a radical social inclusiveness in their gatherings, rescued infants abandoned on city dung-heaps, cared for prisoners of war from enemy armies, and refused to burn incense at the city shrines in honour of local deities and the Roman emperor himself.

The more intelligent of the scoffers realized that this was a message which, in the unlikely event of its being true, would lead to the subversion of all religion. For it claimed that God was to be found, not in the lofty speculations of the philosophers or the esoteric rituals taking place in the countless religious temples that dotted the empire, but rather among those forgotten victims of crucifixion. To know what God is like, and to understand God's purposes for God's world, said the early Christians, one had to come to the foot of the cross of Jesus of Nazareth.

This message was also political dynamite. To say that 'Jesus is Lord' (the earliest confession of faith that made a man or woman a Christian) was to say that the emperor, in Rome or anywhere else, was not Lord, however powerful he imagined himself to be. Indeed, it was to say that Caesar himself would have to bow the knee to this crucified Jew. It implied that by crucifying the Lord of the cosmos and of human history, the much-vaunted civilization of Rome stood radically condemned.

Little wonder that the Christians' 'good news' was labelled a 'dangerous superstition' by educated Romans of the day.[2] It ran counter not only to Roman political convictions but to all the religious assumptions of pagans as well as of Jews. For the Jews, a crucified Messiah or Saviour was a contradiction in terms, for it expressed not God's power but God's inability to liberate the people of Israel from Roman rule. For pagans, the idea that a god or son of a god should die as a state criminal, and that human salvation should depend on that particular historical event, was not only offensive, it was sheer *madness*. As a second-century Christian writer, Justin, summed it up: 'They say that our madness consists in the fact that we put a crucified man in second place after the unchangeable and eternal God, the creator of the world.'[3]

It is the madness of this 'word of the cross' that compels thoughtful men and women to take it seriously. I would want to argue that it is the very absurdity of the Christian message, then and now, that makes it *ring true*. And if true, then it changes *everything*. It turns upside down (or is it right way up?) our views of God and the world, of suffering and death, of the meaning of what we call 'religion' and 'politics', and so much else.

Answering the sceptics

There are many who assume, often without any argument, that the claims of Christians regarding Jesus of Nazareth bear no relation whatsoever to what Jesus himself thought about his life and aims. Jesus, it is often said, had no pretensions about himself, other than perhaps as some kind of social reformer or travelling 'guru'. The New Testament gospel narratives are embellished propaganda. After all, they are the products of 'faith', and 'faith', surely, can have nothing to do with historical fact or the arguments of reason. The 'real Jesus' (sometimes called the 'historical Jesus') has to be reconstructed from this unpromising material by painstaking historical-critical methods.

Often the Jesus who emerges from such reconstructions is a mirror-image of the supposedly unbiased scholar. The best-known examples of this have been provided by the school of Rudolf Bultmann in the 1950s and 1960s when Jesus was introduced to the world as a Franco-German existentialist philosopher. More recently the notorious Jesus Seminar, a floating conference of mostly North American scholars, which uses a system of coloured beads to vote on the authenticity of the sayings of Jesus in the New Testament narratives, has come up with a bland, egalitarian, 'politically correct' Jesus. So harmless and uninspiring is this figure that one is left wondering why on earth people bothered to have him crucified! Here is a Jesus clearly reconstructed in the image of the American liberal academy.[4]

Even more bizarre reconstructions of 'the real Jesus' have turned up from time to time in the name of scholarship: for instance, those that depict him as an other-worldly visionary influenced by Tibetan Buddhism, as a wandering hippie railing against the establishment, as a New Age *shaman*, as a disillusioned seer, or as a proto-Marxist with a purely political programme of social revolution.

Generally, the more outlandish the picture of Jesus that is conjured up, the more the media publicity. In the secular academy, where theologians and Bible scholars are perhaps hard pressed to demonstrate their intellectual credibility, it seems that novelty and fashion are coveted at the expense of historical accuracy. This is the only explanation I can find for the naïve enthusiasm with which, for example, some of the Jesus Seminar scholars seize on hypothetical sources such as a 'Q community' (a yet-to-be-discovered Christian group which allegedly had knowledge of Jesus' sayings only, and no knowledge of his life and sufferings) or a second-century Gnostic document called the *Gospel of Thomas*, while subjecting the biblical gospels to ruthless vivisection.

We can, of course, choose to be totally sceptical about the historical value of the biblical narratives. But, if so, the only logically consistent position would be to have nothing at all to do with Jesus of Nazareth, since no claim concerning his worth as a leader, moral guide, visionary, etc., would have any historical credibility. The sceptic, however, has still to account for the picture the biblical narratives present of Jesus of Nazareth, and these remain the principal source of testimony concerning him. That he was a real historical figure who was crucified in Judea in the reign of Tiberias is attested by first-century Roman and Jewish writers. Speculations drawn from dubious sources, such as claims in the mass media about new teachings of Jesus in the Dead Sea (Qumran)

Scrolls or the Ahmadiyya sect's belief that Jesus died peacefully in Kashmir, must be treated as what they are: namely, pure speculation, with no basis in fact.

Even the most sceptical of scholars accepts that the four New Testament gospels were complete by the end of the first century, while a great many would bring that date forward to a little over one generation after the crucifixion. This small time gap between the events reported and the writing down of the tradition (parts of which were, of course, circulating orally and even in written form well before their final compilations) is itself unique in the history of religious movements. We search in vain for parallels for such rapid developments among followers of other significant leaders. Contrast, for instance, Gautama the Buddha, whose life and teachings were first written down by Buddhist monks between AD 100 and 400, i.e. six to nine hundred years after his death. We are not, in the case of Jesus of Nazareth, dealing with long folk-traditions or collective mythologies.

Therefore any glib talk of 'creative innovation' on the part of the four evangelists must be treated with caution. Theological creativity there was, and no-one reading through the books of the New Testament can fail to be impressed by the extraordinarily rich variety of graphic expressions, metaphors and pictorial representations used by the writers to expound and proclaim the significance of Jesus within God's purpose for the world. But it is very difficult to imagine such a range and depth of expressions of faith being attached, say, at the date of publication of the present book, to someone who had died around 1970.

I suggest that we need to ask, instead: what was it about Jesus, compared to other influential figures in both contemporary Judaism and Greco-Roman religions, that he should become the object of extraordinary truth-claims and personal allegiance within a generation after his death? If we invoke a 'faith-experience' of a Christ who transcends space and time, why were such an experience and such a 'Christ' associated exclusively with Jesus of Nazareth and not with the other prophets, revolutionaries, miracle-workers, itinerant cynics, charismatic healers and exorcists who dotted the Palestinian landscape? Also, unless it was Jesus who was raised from the dead, the very existence of the Jesus movement and its growth beyond the confines of Judaism become hugely problematic. We shall return to these issues.

The present consensus among biblical scholars seems to be that Mark was the first written gospel, and that Matthew and Luke make use of Mark's account but also have access to other sources, oral and written (cf. Luke's description of his approach in the opening section of his gospel). John witnesses to an independent tradition of Jesus' teachings and deeds, though familiarity with Mark, and even with Matthew and Luke, is likely but difficult to demonstrate. All four narratives were written both to satisfy the natural curiosity of Christian converts eager to know about Jesus, and to evangelize Greco-Roman and Jewish audiences (hence the term 'gospels') in the surrounding culture.

We should remember that the gospels were written in a literate society. Recent scholarship has pointed to many similarities between all four gospels and the widespread and ancient Greco-Roman literary genre known as *bioi* ('lives', biographical reminiscences of public figures, but a more flexible category than what we would expect from a modern 'biography'). For instance, the *bios* writer displayed 'a certain freedom and licence, greater than that of the historiographer, to select and edit his oral and written sources, to deal with episodes in greater or lesser detail, or even to include or omit them when composing his portrait of the subject'.[5] This would account for the apparent indifference they show to exact chronological order in the events of Jesus' life, and also for the large amount of space given to the events surrounding his death. However, 'because this is a Life of an historical person written within the lifetime of his contemporaries, there are limits on free composition'.[6]

Thus the gospel narratives combine historical faithfulness with theological creativity. To suppose that the former was lacking is to be left with the impression that, throughout the first Christian generation, there were no eyewitnesses to the original events who could act as a control on their fertile imaginations, nothing about Jesus' sayings or actions that stuck in his hearers' memories. When a saying of Jesus is dismissed as 'unauthentic' without adequate reasons, or simply because it 'fits the post-Easter situation' of the early Christian communities, the assumption seems to be that the disciples' experience of the presence of the risen Lord not only transformed their recollection of Jesus' teaching but *inevitably* led to changes in the content of that teaching.

This is contradicted by the evidence of the narratives themselves. Given that they were mostly written in the context of vigorous Gentile (non-Jewish) outreach, it is very surprising (in the light of the above assumption) to find relatively scanty evidence in the words and actions of Jesus for any Gentile mission, and no teaching at all on the most pressing issue, namely, circumcision for Gentile converts. All the disciples, and especially those who were highly respected leaders of the early church, are depicted in a less than flattering light as cowardly, ambitious and so slow to understand what Jesus was saying. They are often chided by Jesus for their behaviour.

Furthermore, we also note that Jesus' style of teaching made much of figurative language in the manner of the Jewish sages. He uses forms of speech (e.g. aphorisms, beatitudes, parables or narrative *meshalim)* that would have placed him squarely within the ancient Wisdom tradition in Israel. This tradition, found in the Hebrew Bible in works such as Proverbs, Job and Ecclesiastes, reaches its fullest development before the era of Jesus in the books of Sirach and the Wisdom of Solomon. The Wisdom tradition is a form of creation theology, celebrating Wisdom both as a personified attribute of God (e.g. Proverbs 8) and as permeating the created order, thus giving a moral structure to the universe.

It is highly likely that Jesus was perceived as a teacher of Wisdom and, like other sages such as the Preacher of Ecclesiastes and Sirach, attracted disciples to himself and transmitted his teaching in forms that would have been both memorable and memorizable.[7] Indeed, the Jewish historian Josephus, born a few years after the death of Jesus, is reported to have written of him: 'Now at this time there lived ... a wise man ... He was one who performed surprising feats and was a teacher of the sort of people who accept the truth gladly. He won over many Jews.'[8]

In view of the similarities with earlier sages in Israel, coupled with the evidence that Jesus apparently went beyond them in actively gathering his own disciples, Jesus' words would have been seen as examples of godly Wisdom, and were learned and transmitted accordingly. The American biblical scholar Ben Witherington III has argued plausibly that 'Both the character of Jesus' teaching (normally given in poetic and / or some sort of memorizable form), and the evidence of the approach to learning by the disciples of earlier sages encourage one to think of rote learning as not merely possible but likely among Jesus' inner circle.'[9] This is not to say that there was no editorial shaping of the Jesus tradition (the variations in the synoptic gospels and elsewhere make it plain that there was), but, nevertheless, Witherington insists that 'the techniques used in the early transmission of Jesus' sayings would have placed more stress on *conservation* than on innovation ... Conservation rather than innovation was the order of the day in the Wisdom tradition of teaching and learning especially since "a disciple is not above his teacher" ...'[10]

The gospel writers, then, offer us trustworthy *portraits* of Jesus, intended to show us what sort of person he was and what was really happening in his life and death. And can anyone who has studied, say, the seventeenth-century Dutch Masters, doubt that there can often be more truth in a portrait of a living person than in a photograph?

It seems to me that any *plausible* reconstruction of the 'real Jesus' must satisfy the following three conditions:

(a) It must present a Jesus who is recognizably Jewish. He should make sense within his historical and cultural context, although he must certainly have stood apart from his contemporaries in many ways. What this means is that his aims and 'agenda' must have some grounding in the Hebrew Scriptures and the world of contemporary Judaism.

(b) It must explain satisfactorily why Jesus was rejected and eventually crucified. An innocuous sage, relating edifying fables or uttering Zen-type riddles, would have been a threat to nobody. If, on the other hand, he was fomenting revolution against Rome, the Roman authorities would have intervened directly and got rid of this troublemaker. Neither would they have left his followers alone, but would have wiped them out along with the leader.

(c) It must explain satisfactorily why and how the early Christians, all from Jewish backgrounds, came to worship the crucified Jesus as a risen Lord in the language they had used for the God of the universe. There must, in other words, be some reasonable continuity between what Jesus thought about himself and what the early church came to think and say about him. Ben Witherington III puts it like this:

> ... one must ask what is more likely, that an anonymous Jewish Christian or group of Jewish Christians somewhere in the 30s and 40s AD came up with this christological modification of Jewish mono-theism, or that Jesus himself, in the way he presented himself, suggested such a revolutionary notion, and then his disciples teased out the implications of this seminal idea?[11]

The calling of Israel

Jesus was a Jew, born around 6 BC, who spent the last years of his life mostly as an itinerant preacher in Galilee, probably with a 'home base' in the town of Capernaum. Much scholarship in recent years has rightly emphasized the importance of understanding Jesus against both the self-understanding of Israel given in the Hebrew Bible and the social, political and religious worlds of Judaism in the early first century.

Fundamental to every Israelite's identity was the sense of belonging to a 'called out' people, called by the living God to be a *priestly nation* that would mediate the purposes of God to the rest of creation (cf. Exod. 19:4–6; Deut. 7:6; 4:6–8, 32ff.; Josh. 4:24). Israel was a rabble of nomadic tribes, forged into a nation after the experience of redemption from slavery and genocide in ancient Egypt. The God who revealed himself to them as their liberator, and who entered into covenant with them, did so not because of any achievement or superiority on their part but because of God's unmerited and unconditioned love (cf. Deut. 7:7–8; 9:4–6). Their existence as a people, and their receiving a land for which they had not laboured, stood as testimony to divine grace. They knew this God who had redeemed them by his covenant name Yahweh (from YHWH, the third-person form of the Hebrew verb 'He is' or 'He will be', cf. Exod. 3:13–15),[12] not simply another tribal deity in the West Asian pantheon but no less than the creator and sustainer of the entire universe (cf. Pss. 24:1; 47:7–9; 95:4ff., 148:4ff.; Deut. 10:14–15; Jer. 10:10–13; 27:5ff.).

The emergence of the people of Israel is set, in the Hebrew Bible, against the dramatic background of the story of creation and the alienation of all humankind from its Creator. All human beings share in sin and death. Sin is the attempt to shake off one's creatureliness in the futile quest to be 'like God' (cf. Gen. 3 and 11). Human sin has disfigured and corrupted all human relationships – with God, with the earth, between men and women, within families and between families. It is on the heels of a depressing narrative about collective human rebellion (Gen. 11) that we read of God's call to Abraham: to distance himself from Babylon, the archetypal city of human arrogance and wickedness, and to begin an adventure in the wilderness alone with God. The covenant that God makes with him (Gen. 12:1–3) is ultimately for the blessing of 'all the families of the earth'. The effects of sin are universal, but God's redemptive purpose is equally universal. God works with the one man and his family while his gaze, so to speak, is on all the families of the earth. God's final word on even Babylon itself is one not of judgment but of hope – but a hope that is to be mediated through the heirs of Abraham.

The God of the biblical revelation, then, is the God of universal history. Yet he brings that history to its goal (*shalom*, translated as 'salvation' or 'peace') through the particular history of a particular people. This interplay between the universal and the unique runs right through the biblical narrative. One striking example is given in the early chapters of the book of Deuteronomy. There it is repeatedly stressed that Yahweh is not Israel's private possession but the sovereign God of the whole earth. He is actively involved in the histories of nations other than Israel, and this is the axiomatic framework within which the calling of Israel is understood. For instance, Moses tells the people of Israel of Yahweh's sovereignty in the migrations and conquests that marked the pre-Israelite history of Canaan (Deut. 2:9–12, 20–23).[13] It is only within Israel, however, that Yahweh works in terms of a redemptive covenant, begun and preserved by his grace. The people of Israel had experienced something unparalleled 'from the day God created man on the earth' and 'from one end of the heavens to the other' (Deut. 4:32): namely, a unique revelation of Yahweh and a unique experience of his redemptive power (Deut. 4:7–8, 32–38). This was all of sheer mercy, never to be construed as favouritism (e.g. Deut. 7:7–8), to which the only appropriate response was to imitate Yahweh's awesome love towards the poor, the weak, and the alien (e.g. Deut. 10:14ff.).

'You were shown these things so that you might know that the LORD [Yahweh] is God; besides him there is no other' (Deut. 4:35). This is the heart of the monotheism of Israel. It had little to do with mathematical unity, even less with a new-found conviction of a single Supreme Being beyond (or underlying) the multiplicity of gods (real or imagined) – a belief by no means confined to ancient Israel. Israel had been entrusted with a unique historical experience of Yahweh's character and purpose for his creation. It is this that enabled them to bear witness to *his* uniqueness as the living God (e.g. Is. 43:8–13). Israel existed as a nation at all only because of Yahweh's intention to redeem people from every nation. While Yahweh works in all nations, in no nation other than Israel did he act *for the sake of* all nations.

Israel's unique experience of Yahweh issued in a unique socio-ethical witness to Yahweh among the nations. Their obedience to Yahweh was now to take the form of imitating Yahweh's own dealings with them. Their national life was to mirror what Yahweh was like to the rest of the nations. The distinctiveness of Israel's social, political and economic structures were an integral part of their theological significance in God's saving purpose for his world.[14] Israel was defined not only by ethnicity and land, but supremely by the Law (Torah) given to them by God as a witness to his character. Covenantal obedience to the Torah was the appropriate response to grace. To choose the true God was to choose the truly human as well. Living out the requirements of the Torah among the nations would be their priestly witness (e.g. Exod. 19:4–6; Deut. 4:5–8). Their distinctiveness was the means by which God would attract the nations to himself, so that ultimately all the earth would acknowledge and experience the gracious rule of Yahweh as the only true and living God.

However, the Hebrew Bible testifies to numerous occasions in Israel's life when they abandoned this global vision and calling. The great temptation Israel faced, and to which they repeatedly succumbed, was to think of Yahweh too as simply another tribal deity and to worship him in terms derived from an alien religious framework, thus betraying the revelation entrusted to them for the sake of the nations. Idolatry went hand in hand with social injustice. Once the vision of Yahweh's justice and compassion was lost and the Torah neglected, Israel descended to the customs and practices of their neighbours. Such betrayal robbed Israel of their self-identity and any claim to uniqueness.

The call of the prophets was to speak God's word to a wayward people, to expose the poverty of their idolatry:

The whole OT (and the NT as well) is filled with descriptions of how Yahweh-Adonai, the covenant God of Israel, is waging war against those forces which try to thwart and subvert his plans for his creation. He battles against those false gods which human beings have fashioned from the created world, idolized, and used for their own purpose. Think, for example, of the Baals and the Ashteroth, whose worshippers elevated nature, the tribe, the state and the nation to a divine status. God fights against magic and idolatry which ... bend the line between God and his creation. He contends against every form of social injustice and pulls off every cloak under which it seeks to hide.[15]

As the Old Testament scholar Christopher Wright perceptively reminds us, the calling of Israel to bear faithful witness to the revelation of the living God entrusted to them was not 'a matter of Israel's flaunting their privilege in an attitude of "our religion is better than yours" – as if Israel's faith was one among many brands of a commodity, "human religion". Rather, what was at stake, what was so threatened by Israel compromising with the gods and worship of other nations, was the continuity of the redemptive work of the Creator God of all mankind within the unique historical and social context which he himself had chosen.'[16]

It is precisely this biblical stress on the historical 'particularity' (or 'situatedness') of human life, a particularity that God takes seriously in his dealings with his creatures, that challenges both the ancient Indian and the post-Enlightenment Western worldviews. Thinkers nurtured in either tradition find the biblical teaching on divine choice troublesome, if not downright offensive. Why does God not reveal himself directly to every individual human soul?

The biblical answer is simply that human beings are not spiritual or rational 'essences', abstracted from their location within social and material relationships that develop through space and time. Biblical teaching about election can be grasped only when seen as part of the characteristically biblical way of understanding human reality. Human life consists in mutual relationships: a mutual interdependence that is not simply a temporary phase in the *journey* towards salvation but one that is intrinsic to the *goal* of salvation itself. If God's way of blessing 'all the families of the earth' is to be addressed to those families in their concrete situations, and not to unreal abstractions such as 'immortal souls' or 'autonomous selves', then it must be accomplished through election – calling and sending *some* as vehicles of that blessing for *all* – so that human community may be freed from fragmentation and re-created in communion with God.

Israel's continued existence in the land depended on their obedience to the Torah (e.g. Deut. 8:19–20). The prophets were men (occasionally women) called by Yahweh and commissioned to speak in his name to the people, especially at times when the nation was on the brink of total apostasy and the betrayal of their vocation. They warned of imminent disaster, that Yahweh in his sovereignty would use even the cruel rapaciousness of pagan empires to discipline Israel. In 722 BC, the marauding Assyrians destroyed the northern capital of Samaria and dispersed the Israelites far and wide. In 587 BC, Jerusalem fell to the armies of Nebuchadnezzar, the new world-ruler, and most of the people of the southern kingdom of Judah were taken captive to Babylon. But the prophets also brought a message of ultimate hope: that the exile would not be for ever, that the temple would be rebuilt as the focus and symbol of Yahweh's abiding presence in Israel, and that Yahweh would fulfil his promise to Abraham in the blessing of the nations and the final defeat of evil.

Although the temple was rebuilt and many who were taken into exile eventually made their way back to the land of their forebears, Israel's troubles were far from over. They were always at the mercy of the power-politics of the great empires of the Mediterranean world. They enjoyed a brief period of self-rule under the Maccabean freedom-fighters[17] in the second century BC, but soon came under the governance of the new imperial power, Rome. As was its custom, Rome ruled its far-flung provinces through local client-kings who were given some measure of autonomy as long as they swore allegiance to Rome and provided funds for the Roman treasury through local taxation. The more effective these puppets were, the less any need for the deployment of Roman legions in the province in question.

The Jewish-Nabatean King Herod was such a puppet ruler till his death in 4 BC. Herod was a despot and did not shrink from murdering members of his own family to maintain his hold on power. Like all such despots, he launched several massive building projects in a vain attempt to impress both his subjects and his Roman overlords. After his death, Palestine was divided among his sons; but owing to the incompetence of one them, Archelaus, the province of Judea (which included Jerusalem) soon came under direct rule from Rome through Roman prefects or governors. Throughout Jesus' adult life Judea was a Roman province, with Pontius Pilate as its prefect from AD 26 to 36. Galilee, which was predominantly the scene of Jesus' activities, continued to be ruled by client-kings, in particular Herod Antipas.

Hostility among the common people would have been directed not only at Rome but also towards collaborators: local toll-collectors, Gentile residents, and the Herodian regime and its retainers who sought to establish a form of Greco-Roman society in Galilee. There was no obvious military presence in

Galilee, unlike in Judea, however, so the hostility for the most part simmered under the surface and did not break out in violent attempts at rebellion. This changed after Jesus' lifetime, culminating in the violent uprising throughout Galilee and Judea that is referred to as the First Jewish War, AD 66–70. The first-century Jewish historian Josephus chronicles several incidents of local sabotage and banditry, and also brutal insensitivity to local religious sentiments on the part of Pontius Pilate.[18]

For most devout Jews, it seemed as if the exile of Israel was still continuing. For, though they were physically living in the land of their forebears, the land of promise, it seemed as if Yahweh, the God of their forebears, had abandoned them. They were strangers in their own land, ruled by men who did not worship Yahweh. They longed for the day when Yahweh would act in power to cleanse the land of these idolaters and re-establish his own rule (Yahweh's kingdom) through his own anointed priest or king (*messiah* in Hebrew, *christos* in Greek, lit. 'anointed one').

Most New Testament scholars believe that there was no single, all-encompassing messianic hope during or immediately preceding the era of Jesus. There was a variety of hopes, including different expectations of a coming Messiah. But they all involved the expectation of the restoration of the holy land to its rightful owners, the restoration of God's people Israel to right observance of the law, and the restoration of the temple under the right priesthood to its proper role of offering right sacrifices.

The lifestyle of Jesus

It was in such a seething hotbed of political and religious fervour that the 'Jesus movement' emerged and grew eventually into a 'third race' that embraced both Jew and non-Jew. The popular image of an innocuous, inoffensive Jesus who went around telling entertaining stories (called 'parables') and engaging in purely academic controversy with the religious parties of his day fails to read Jesus in the context of the volatile atmosphere of early first-century Palestine. All his claims and actions would have been understood in a political light, as either bolstering or threatening the status quo. His words and deeds were fraught with political as much as religious overtones: was he, for instance, leading a revolt against the state in taking groups of people out into the wilderness with him, as Judas the Galilean had done a few years before?

One of the most revolutionary of Jesus' actions, as far as the Jewish leaders were concerned, was his invitation to 'sinners' to share in table-fellowship with him. His habit of associating with the outcasts of Palestinian society drew hostile criticism from the religious authorities. The Jewish scholar Geza Vermes sees this aspect of the lifestyle of Jesus as what served to differentiate him 'more than any other' from 'both his contemporaries and even his prophetic predecessors'. He writes:

> The prophets spoke on behalf of the honest poor, and defended the widows and the fatherless, those oppressed and exploited by the wicked, the rich and powerful. Jesus went further. In addition to proclaiming these blessed, he actually took his stand among the pariahs of his world, those despised by the respectable. Sinners were his table companions and the ostracized tax collectors and prostitutes his friends.[19]

Following the Maccabean crisis, the covenantal heritage of Israel had become the subject of heated dispute. Different groups came into being, each denouncing other Jews for their disloyalty to Yahweh. Each lay claim to be the true custodians of the Torah and thus the true members of the covenant. The best-known of such groups are the Pharisees and the Essenes. The term 'Pharisees' is probably a nickname, meaning 'separated ones'. Out of their zeal for God they separated themselves by their lifestyle from their fellow Jews in order to observe more scrupulously the religious traditions of their forebears. They themselves were laymen, scholars rather than priests, but they tried to live at the level of holiness and purity required of priests in the Jerusalem temple. From early rabbinic traditions we learn that they desired to treat the whole land as sacred, as sharing in the holiness of the temple where God had located his presence in Israel. Thus they sought to maintain at the level of everyday life the purity laws designed originally for worship in the temple.

The Essenes, such as the famous community at Qumran, took such separation even further. They physically withdrew into the Judean wilderness, there to await God's imminent judgment on wayward Israel. They attacked their political and religious opponents, particularly the Pharisees, as the wicked who had departed from the paths of righteousness and transgressed the covenant.

What is at issue here is: what behaviour is appropriate to the covenant and who has the authority to determine it? Jesus' mission to sinners embraced those traditionally identified as outside the fold of the religiously orthodox: Samaritans, lepers, women and children, tax-collectors. By cutting across social conventions he attracted the critical fire of those who saw themselves as the defenders of covenant loyalty.

In the Middle East, as in most Asian societies, the sharing of a meal takes on a quasi-religious character: it is an act of hospitality, a mark of acceptance and fellowship. When the head of a Jewish household breaks the bread and distributes it to those with him at table, he invites them to share in the blessing spoken over the bread. Eating together is an expression of solidarity. So, naturally, the scope of table-fellowship has to be restricted to those considered acceptable. Sinners are, by definition, excluded.

Jesus not only disregarded ritual observances when it came to meals with his disciples (e.g. Mark 7:1ff.; Luke 11:37ff.), but also angered many in the religious establishment by his festal sharing of food and drink with 'sinners' (e.g. Mark 2:15–16; cf. Matt. 9:10–11 and Luke 5:29–30; Matt. 11:19). Sometimes he was their guest, but more often he invited himself (e.g. Luke 19:1–11), thus demonstrating the good news of the kingdom of God. Life with Jesus seemed, for those who followed him, a continuous round of partying!

Jesus broke down social barriers in forming around himself an alternative community drawn from the marginalized peoples of Palestinian society. What the Pharisees saw as sinful disregard of covenant ideals, Jesus saw as the birth of a new covenant, the visible expression of God's liberating reign. In the table-fellowship that he and his disciples celebrated, and to which the 'tax-collectors and sinners' were invited unconditionally, Jesus was enacting a parable. Here was a foretaste of the messianic banquet, when 'many will come from the east and the west, and will take their places at the feast with Abraham, Isaac and Jacob in the kingdom of heaven' (Matt. 8:11; cf. Luke 13:29).

Indeed, one could see the festal meals of Jesus and his disciples as the social context for many of his teaching parables. Three of his most famous parables – the lost coin, the lost sheep, and the lost son – are said by Luke to have been Jesus' rejoinder to the charge that he ate with sinners (Luke 15:1–32). Other parables also defend, implicitly or explicitly, his friendship with outcasts: the unmerciful servant (Matt. 18:23–35), the two sons (Matt. 21:28–32), and the wedding banquet (Matt. 22:1–10; cf. Luke 14:15–24).

Both the feasting of Jesus with sinners and the parables taught in that context would have been especially meaningful to those familiar with the Wisdom traditions in Israel. We saw earlier that this tradition is thoroughly 'this-worldly' in its celebration of God's creation and the creational blessings of food, health and friends. Even more pointedly, passages such as Proverbs 9:1–6 in the Hebrew Bible depict Wisdom (in personified female imagery) inviting the most unlikely guests – the simple, the foolish, the immature – to a feast that she has prepared, in order that they may learn from her how to be wise. So Jesus presents himself as embodying Wisdom in Wisdom's search for the least and the lost in society. While dining with them he would impart a wisdom that would 'save' (cf. Wisdom of Solomon 9:18). Thus, when accused by the religious leaders of being a 'drunkard and a friend of tax-collectors and sinners', Jesus could respond with the confident assurance that 'wisdom will be vindicated by her deeds' – in other words, that many who had been given up as 'lost' would be saved and incorporated into a new people of God as a result of his mission (Matt. 11:16–19).

Thus it is sinners, not the righteous, who are the beneficiaries of God's liberating rule. The righteous, like the rich and powerful, are secure in the confidence of their status and acceptability and have little sense of need, and their pride thus blinds them to what God is doing in their midst through Jesus of Nazareth. The outcasts whom Jesus befriended and to whom he gave a new identity as members of his disciple-community were caught completely unawares by the shattering generosity of God's acceptance, experienced through Jesus. Many of these people were virtually 'untouchables', not very different from the lowest castes of the Hindu social system, though the status of outcast was not hereditary in the Judaism of Jesus' day.

The distinction between pure and impure lies at the base of all religious cultures and is probably the greatest single source of *fear*. This is especially true of the Brahmanical tradition in Indian religion. An ethos of fear permeates Hindu society: the fear of ritual defilement by things, persons and events. Men fear women as sources of moral impurity and spiritual debilitation. Women fear the sexual violence and social dominance of men, the latter often sanctioned by religious decree. Eating, drinking, sleeping, travelling, working, copulating, touching – all become potential sources of pollution. Moreover, extending beyond the system of caste to embrace tribal people and the popular Buddhism and folk Islam of the subcontinent, there lurks the all-pervading fear of evil spirits, threatening illness, misfortune and death. As Richard Gombrich, Boden Professor of Sanskrit at Oxford University and a student of South Asian Buddhism, has observed:

> For the moment, what strikes the observer is the widespread flight from the rational and interest in every form of the occult: palmistry, table-tapping, hypnotism, astrology. Astrology is a pseudo-science traditionally of great importance in Indian culture, traditionally not unknown in Sinhalese culture and considered compatible with Buddhist cosmology. But like all forms of divination it has greatly increased, a product no doubt of the widespread anxiety which there seem to be few rational means to allay.[20]

To such cultures of fear, Jesus' lifestyle, particularly his repudiation of the religious-social distinctions between pure and impure, his authoritative offer of divine forgiveness, and the demonstration of his absolute power over the spirit-realm are perceived as joyfully liberating. But, as in the Judea of Jesus' day, it is also perceived as threatening by the defenders of the status quo. In religious cultures, such as the traditional villages and towns of Asia, the monk or holy man wields considerable social power while living a life of economic poverty. And, as the Bengali writer Nirad Chaudhuri has acutely observed, even the most world-denying tradition of Hindu spirituality is, in reality, 'a pursuit, not of beatitude, but of power'[21] – a quest not only for mastery of body and mind, but also mastery of the spirit world through the magic arts. 'This kind of power has as its complement, or rather fulfilment, the power to dominate other men. Actually, an appearance of indifference to things that the world has to offer, even without occult powers, has by itself created a moral authority for those who have shown it.'[22]

The self-giving lifestyle of Jesus, reflected in his modern disciples who are found cleaning the sores of leprous beggars, providing free nursing care for terminal AIDS victims or building half-way homes for 'degraded' heroin addicts, offers a radically different conception of spiritual power for cultures where fear and spirituality are often but two sides of the same coin.

The self-understanding of Jesus

While all the gospel narratives testify to the extraordinary behaviour of Jesus, they also depict another side, what we may call the 'unobtrusiveness' of his life, namely his relative social obscurity and the initial sense of puzzlement he generated among his hearers ('Isn't this the carpenter? Isn't this Mary's son and the brother of James, Joseph, Judas and Simon?', Mark 6:3). This is significant when we read the gospels from the perspective of the myths and folk tales of the Asian religious traditions. Here is no superhuman *avatar*, no handsome prince or ascetic recluse in total mastery of his bodily reactions, but a man who sheds tears, feels hunger and pain, experiences anger at the evil he encounters, and overflows with humour and the joy of life.

However, along with the servant posture that Jesus demonstrates in his relationships with other people, especially the infirm and the outcast, there are also the remarkable and often shocking claims he made, both implicitly and explicitly, concerning his vocation. It is these that eventually prompted the progression from puzzlement to hostility and then to outright rage on the part of his contemporaries.

Jesus' implicit claims

We saw that the 'good news' that Jesus announced and embodied in his actions was addressed not to a religious élite but to the non-religious, the moral failures and the social outcasts. The kingdom of God – the great hope of Israel for God's saving presence – was breaking into the world. For Jesus, it was taking shape in and through his words and deeds. In his presence, men and women were offered unconditional forgiveness for their sins, and given new identities in new relationships based on mutual service rather than on domination. Jesus reconstituted Israel, the people of God, around himself. In choosing and commissioning twelve of his disciples to be his 'apostles' (the term refers to authorized representatives), he was deliberately creating an alternative community to the twelve tribes of Israel, even setting them up as future judges of Israel. The most significant point about this act was that he did not include himself among the twelve but stands above them, implying that he understood himself to be sent by God to gather the true Israel and to free her to fulfil her calling in the world.[23] Moreover, as the Sermon on the Mount (Matt. 5 – 7) makes clear, it is no longer the Torah per se that defines the covenantal response of the people of God, but the Torah as interpreted and elaborated by Jesus.

In declaring the unconditional forgiveness of sin, Jesus bypasses the temple with its divinely-instituted priesthood and sacrificial system. If we keep in mind that the temple represented the very identity of Israel as a nation, serving as the focus of its political, cultural and religious uniqueness, then the radical nature of Jesus' acts of forgiveness become apparent. Even more provocative was the act of driving out the money-changers from the court of the Gentiles in the temple precincts (Mark 11:15–19; Matt. 21:12–16; Luke 19:45–47). Many scholars believe that this was the act that precipitated the plot against Jesus by the chief priests.

That this was not an attempt at social reform but a symbolic act (a dramatized parable?) of divine judgment on Israel is made clear by the way, in Mark's account, it is sandwiched between another symbolic act, the 'cursing' of the fig tree outside the city, and Jesus' pronouncement of doom on the city (Mark 13:1ff.). Far from offering liberation from their Roman overlords, Jesus angers his contemporaries by pronouncing the destruction of the city and its temple by Yahweh himself, with the pagans as Yahweh's agents! In other words, Jesus saw that Israel had failed in its calling to be God's agent of healing for the nations. The temple had become an object of national idolatry and religious power-mania. Far from siding with the Jewish nationalists in their fanatical violence against Rome, Jesus saw the present Roman occupation and the impending destruction of Jerusalem by the Roman armies as God's just punishment on a people who had forsaken the very God whose name was constantly on their lips. Jesus then returns to the temple courts as a teacher whose authority was both unmatched and unnerving (11:27ff.). His teaching was based neither on the invocation of rabbinic authority (the 'teaching of the elders', as in the case of the Pharisees) nor on the classical Old Testament prophetic formula, 'Thus says Yahweh'. He spoke on his own authority or lay claim to an independent authority.

In the triple tradition common to Mark, Matthew and Luke, we are given in the early chapters several examples of what linguistic philosophers call 'speech-actions' or 'performative utterances' on the part of Jesus: namely, the performance of an action *by way of* saying something. Making a promise, issuing a command or giving a warning are common examples. Jesus says to a paralytic, 'Son, your sins are [hereby] forgiven' (Mark 2:5; Matt. 9:2; Luke 5:20).[24] Jesus' effective words of exorcism ('Be silent, and come out of him!', Mark 1:25) are seen in the triple tradition not simply as a miracle as such, but as a messianic word-deed which in its utterance constitutes the binding of the evil powers and the plundering of their kingdom (Mark 3:23–27; Matt. 12:22–30; Luke 11:14–23).[25] On all such occasions, the response of the crowds and of the disciples is one of shock and amazement: who then is this? ... what sort of person is this? ... with what authority does he do these things? ... why does this fellow talk like this? He is blaspheming!

The narratives make room for the reader to reflect on the all-important question: for such speech-actions to function effectively, what is implied about the competence of the one who utters them? Only a judge can pronounce a man 'guilty' or 'not guilty'; only the Chairman of the Board can declare a meeting adjourned; only a clergyman or registrar can pronounce a couple married; only my employer can tell me that I am 'fired', and so on. To use language that is associated with the later work of the famous Austrian philosopher Ludwig Wittgenstein (1889–1951), these speech-acts 'show' rather than directly 'say' the status and role that Jesus believed he enjoyed in the purposes of God for the world.

Even to call men and women to a personal loyalty to himself, expressed in costly discipleship, was to make implicitly an outstanding claim: 'Follow me, and let the dead bury their own dead' (Matt. 8:22); 'Whoever loves father or mother more than me is not worthy of me; and whoever loves son or daughter more than me is not worthy of me; and whoever does not take the cross and follow me is not worthy of me' (Matt. 10:37–39; cf. Luke 14:25–27; Mark 8:34–35).

How high a self-understanding is involved here can be seen when such words are read in their monotheistic, Jewish context.[26] The words of Jesus reinterpret the Old Testament traditions which shaped the pattern of Jewish national and individual life for centuries. His word is set above the law of Moses and the tradition of the elders as the means to life (e.g. Matt. 5:21–37; 8:24ff.). He calls people to put himself before every other relationship in life and to be willing even to give their lives away for his sake. All this in a culture imbued with the passionate conviction that God the Creator was the source, owner and Judge of the whole world, and that allegiance to this God came before everything and everybody else.

We have already seen how Jesus assumes authority to declare to men and women the forgiveness of sins in anticipation of the eschatological judgment of God, and thereby circumvents the God-given temple cultus (e.g. Mark 2:1–12; Luke 7:48). Remember, too, that there was no Jewish tradition that the Messiah had the right to forgive sins. The Messiah would exterminate the godless in Israel, crush demonic power and protect his people from the rule of sin, but the forgiveness of sin was never attributed to him. Jesus does not speak as an agent, priestly or prophetic or angelic, assuring the other of God's forgiveness on the day of final judgment, nor does he offer a provisional pardon to be later ratified by a higher court.

Moreover, Jesus assumes the role of being not only Israel's judge but also the one to whom *all nations* will give account at the end of history (e.g. Matt. 25:31ff.). Even more remarkably, the basis of judgment will be the nations' response to *him* – expressed in their response to those with whom he has identified himself. He proclaims the arrival of God's reign, inaugurating the new age of Old Testament promise. We need to bear in mind that, within the background of Jewish thought, this 'in-breaking' of the reign of God in the works and words of Jesus constitutes a cosmic, and not simply a national, turning-point (e.g. Mark 1:15; 2:21–22). The matter-of-fact way in which Jesus assumes the rights and prerogatives of Yahweh startled his contemporaries and often provoked the indignation of the scribal authorities.

Thus we cannot separate the teaching of Jesus (about what was involved in following him) from how Jesus saw himself in relation to God, Israel and God's world. Jesus' pronouncements on discipleship imply a profound self-understanding. If the implied self-understanding is mistaken, then the whole series of speech-actions depicted in the narratives (the promises of forgiveness, the commanding of evil powers, the invitation of outcasts to the banquet of the kingdom, the call to discipleship, the warnings of judgment, the commissioning to mission, and so on) have no proper basis. They must be dismissed as nothing more than constructs of a wild imagination, or deliberate deception.

Jesus' explicit claims

We could briefly classify the more explicit claims that Jesus made concerning himself under the following separate, but overlapping, headings:

A claim to enjoy a unique filial relationship to God

We find the term '*Abba*, Father' for God some fifty-one times on the lips of Jesus in the synoptic gospels (excluding parallels), of which on seven occasions it is in the direct address of prayer. Perhaps there was nothing very startling in a Jew referring to God as Father, although it was extremely rare, but the way Jesus used that term was nothing less than extraordinary. There is no suggestion that all human beings are sons of God by virtue of the fact that God is their Creator. Rather, the relationship of which Jesus spoke was not one shared by all people, or even by all Jews. God was always 'my Father' and he himself was never 'a son' but always '*the* son' of God. Jesus never linked the disciples with himself so that together they could say 'our Father'. The prayer of Matthew 6:9 is for the disciple community to use, and it is a privilege made possible through their faith in Jesus. Every use of 'Father' in Jesus' teaching is found in sayings addressed specifically to his disciples. And if the evidence of John 20:17 be allowed, Jesus distinguishes between 'my Father' and 'your Father', making explicit what is implicit elsewhere.[27]

In the most startling passage of all, Jesus announces that the Father has entrusted 'all things' to him and that 'no one knows the Father except the Son and anyone to whom the Son chooses to reveal him' (Matt. 11:27; Luke 10:22).[28] In other words, Jesus claims a unique intimacy with God and a unique authority, born of that intimacy, to reveal the heart of God to humankind. It is on the basis of this authority to make known the Father that he proceeds to issue his celebrated appeal to all the 'weary and burdened' to come to him for rest (Matt. 11:28). The promise of rest echoes the Hebrew text of Jeremiah 6:16, where it is the offer of God to those who follow his way. Here it is grounded in a disciple-relationship with *Jesus* ('learn from me'): a relationship that frees men and women from the oppressive 'yoke' of religious legalism. In an amazingly casual way these claims to a unique relationship with God and a unique offer of freedom and rest are accompanied, in almost the same breath, by a claim to be 'gentle and humble in heart' (11:29)![29]

A claim to be the unique climax of God's self-disclosure

We have seen how another prominent feature of Jesus' teaching is the manner in which he understands his life and ministry as bringing into focus various strands of Jewish hope. He not only proclaims the approach of God's kingdom but is the one through whom that kingdom takes shape (e.g. Mark 1:14–15; Matt. 12:28). His disciples are blessed because they, unlike the prophets of old, are actually able to taste the powers of God's kingdom through their association with him. 'Blessed are the eyes that see what you see. For I tell you that many prophets and kings desired to see what you see, but did not see it, and to hear what you hear, but did not hear it' (Luke 10:23).

The cities of Nineveh, Tyre and Sidon, Sodom and Gomorrah, all bywords of pagan idolatry in the Old Testament prophetic writings, now become witnesses against the unbelief of Israel, for now 'something greater than Solomon … greater than Jonah is here!' (Luke 11:29ff.; Matt. 11:20ff.). He is the one of whom Moses wrote, the one whose day Abraham rejoiced to see, the one who is even David's Lord (cf. Mark 12:35–37; John 5:46; 8:56). In other words, he is not so much a prophet as *the object of all prophecy.* On him converge the Old Testament imagery of the Isaianic Servant of Yahweh, bearing the wrath of God for the healing of the nations, and Daniel's Son of Man, receiving an everlasting kingdom which embraces all peoples. He sets his face to Jerusalem, convinced that what is written of him *must* be fulfilled.[30]

We saw earlier how Jesus' table-fellowship with sinners and outcasts mirrored the call of Wisdom to the simple and foolish. The reference to 'something greater than Solomon' being here prompts us to look for Wisdom allusions in many undisputed sayings of Jesus. Thus Matthew 11:28–30, which we discussed earlier ('Come to me, all you that are weary and are carrying heavy burdens, and I will give you rest. Take my yoke upon you … for my yoke is easy, and my burden is light') would also have been taken as an allusion to the invitation of Wisdom in Sirach 51:23, 26–27: 'Draw near to me, you who are untaught … why are your souls very thirsty? … Put your neck under the yoke, and let your souls receive instruction …' (RSV). Here the yoke of Wisdom becomes, on the lips of Jesus, 'my yoke'.

Similarly, Jesus' lament over Jerusalem, in the wake of the personal rejection he experienced ('Jerusalem, Jerusalem, the city that kills the prophets … How often have I desired to gather your children together as a hen gathers her brood under her wings, and you were not willing!', Luke 13:34; Matt. 23:37) echoes the trajectory of Wisdom herself in the inter-testamental Jewish work 1 Enoch. In 1 Enoch 42, Wisdom goes to Jerusalem, the heart of Israel, is rejected there and, finding no resting-place, returns to the side of God. It seems likely, as Ben Witherington has pointed out, that Jesus saw in such Wisdom hymns as Proverbs 8, Sirach 24 and Wisdom of Solomon 8 – 9 the clue to his own career: he had come from God and would return to God by way of his rejection in Jerusalem.

If the king-sage Solomon was the pre-eminent 'Son of David' and the one with whom the entire corpus of Wisdom literature was later identified, what could Jesus have meant in speaking of 'something greater than Solomon' being present in his own person and ministry? Witherington points us to the logical conclusion, exemplified in the passages above as well as several others: that Jesus presented himself in Israel not only as a prophetic sage, drawing on all the Jewish sacred traditions, and not even as the greatest in a long line of sages; but, rather, as the *embodiment* of Wisdom, indeed as Wisdom come in the flesh.[31]

Although Jesus anticipated the suffering and death that had befallen other prophets in Jerusalem, unlike theirs his death was the climax of his God-given vocation, having redemptive significance for Israel: it was a 'ransom for many' (Mark 10:45; Matt. 20:28),[32] the inauguration of a new covenant between God and his people through the forgiveness of their sins (Matt. 26:27–28; cf. Is. 53:12 and Jer. 31:31–34). Whether or not the Last Supper was the regular Passover meal, the sacrificial language and the rich Old Testament allusions are unmistakable, and Jesus uses the traditional Passover 'this is that' language ('this is my body', 'this is my blood of the covenant') to announce the redemptive character of his impending death.[33] Under the old covenant he would bear the judgment of God on sinful Israel, so that the true Israel may emerge as a new people of God. He would thus himself *bring the story of Israel to its climax*: bear her judgment at the hands of pagan powers, demonstrate perfect filial obedience to her God, reveal the glory of God by making atonement for the sin of the nations, and so draw them into the light of the knowledge of God.

Thus, right here, in the public world of historical action and transformation, and not in some interior, private world of 'religious experience', does Jesus of Nazareth stake his claims. His many utterances of what he has come to do presuppose an authority to put into operative effect the promises of God concerning his world. Jesus claims to do what prophets, sages and others failed to do.

True, false or deluded?

What, then, are we to make of Jesus Christ? The one thing we cannot say is that he was *merely* a wise religious teacher, for we have already seen that it is impossible to separate the content of his moral instruction from the self-conscious authority that is *presupposed* by that instruction – an authority that surpasses that of any Jewish prophet or ancient sage. If what he believed about himself was not true, then he can hardly be a moral exemplar for the rest of us. If one hesitates to acknowledge the truth of his claims, then logically one is compelled to dismiss him either as a liar and charlatan, thus claiming that the whole edifice of Christianity is built on a gigantic hoax, or as a megalomaniac, a self-deceived fool.

(I have also indicated that attributing all such truth-claims to the pious imagination of the Christian faith-community does not get us very far. For it still leaves the question: what was it about Jesus of Nazareth, compared to other messianic claimants and charismatic figures in Palestine and elsewhere, that led to such outrageous claims about him being made – and believed – within a generation of his death? We are also faced with the same choice – true, false, or deluded – but this time with regard to the Christian church. *Someone* said the things attributed to Jesus, and that someone was true, false or deluded.)

Why is the charge of megalomania so difficult to stick on Jesus? Simply because the lifestyle of Jesus and the values he embodied strike even the most hardened sceptic as eminently sane, indeed deeply attractive. Here is a man who describes himself as 'gentle and humble in heart' and stoops to wash the feet of his disciples in an act of menial service. In his betrayal and suffering, he refuses to answer violence with violence, but prays for the forgiveness of his torturers. No contemporary of Jesus, or any serious thinker since, has accused Jesus of being insincere or hypocritical in his relationships with either friend or enemy. Gandhi and Martin Luther King both drew their inspiration for how to deal with those who opposed them from the example and teaching of Jesus. Jesus' lifestyle of lowly, compassionate service towards the sick, the vulnerable and the oppressed continues to attract many people to him from diverse cultural backgrounds. I would like to suggest that *this combination of an other-oriented lifestyle with self-directed claims* is what makes Jesus of Nazareth unique.

Let me elaborate. When we explore the great religious traditions of the world, we come across many great figures who impressed their contemporaries with the other-centredness of their way of life. They lived lives of exemplary courage, compassion and sacrifice. Gautama the Buddha would be an out-standing example from the Asian context. But such people make no grand claims for themselves, other than to be pointers to the truth. One noted authority on Buddhism observes that the Buddha 'saw himself as simply preaching the Dharma'[34] (that account of the world which presents the possibility of liberation from its coils). In the Mahayana tradition, Buddha-hood is an ideal state open, in principle, to all life-forms. Likewise, in Islam, Muhammad is simply a prophet, albeit the final Prophet, in a long tradition of prophets and messengers commissioned by God to turn people away from idols. In all these cases there is no call to personal allegiance, no claim to be communicating anything other than a word from God or an insight into ultimate reality.

On the other side we come across people who do make self-centred claims, but these claims do not impress us for very long. Not only have the Caesars, the Hitlers and Idi Amins of the world disappeared into the mists of history, but their megalomania led them into forms of brutality and self-aggrandizement which seemed to fit quite naturally with the claims they made for themselves. It is here that Jesus stands out as unique. One may search all the religious traditions of humankind, and indeed all the great literature of humankind, and still fail to find one like Jesus, who makes seemingly the most arrogant claims concerning himself and yet lives in the most humble and selfless manner conceivable. Jesus of Nazareth simply boggles our imagination.

Jesus: resurrection?

Jesus was not *remembered* by the early disciples the way martyrs and sages from the past live on in the collective memory of a people. They did not make pilgrimages to the hill on which he was crucified or to the tomb in which his corpse was laid. Something had happened soon after Jesus' death that transformed a situation of defeat and desolation into one in which a new movement came into being, a movement that was characterized not by nostalgia but by 'hope'.

At the heart of early Christian faith and preaching lies the claim that Jesus was *resurrected* by God: that over a period of forty days after his crucifixion he encountered the disciples in a physical body that was recognizable as that of the man they knew before, and that after that period he continued to communicate with them, 'indwell' them and empower them by this Holy Spirit. All the earliest accounts of Christian origins are agreed that what distinguished the new 'Jesus movement' in its Jewish and Greco-Roman environment was that it proclaimed not a new religion or ethic, but rather a new *event*, namely the resurrection by God of the crucified Jesus, and the implications of that event for the world.

It is impossible to discuss here in detail the traditional arguments in support of the empty-tomb tradition and the reality of the post-Easter appearances of Jesus. However, the evidence, though circumstantial, is far more impressive than is commonly assumed. For example, although we have much evidence of anti-Christian polemic from Jewish and Roman sources in the early years of the Jesus movement, we find no-one disputing the claim that the tomb was empty. What reasonable hypothesis, other than the early Christian proclamation, can account for this? There is something prima facie unlikely that a story concocted in a Jewish milieu should have as its principal eyewitnesses a group of women (and some of dubious moral character at that!) whose testimony would not have been permissible in a Jewish court of law. As fabrications, these accounts lack historical plausibility. *Something* happened to compel the early disciples of Jesus to break with a centuries-old tradition and to meet to worship God on the first day of the week. *Something* happened to make these Jews, within a few years of the death of Jesus, ascribe to him titles and honorifics that they traditionally ascribed to Yahweh, the covenant God of Israel, and to address prayers and worship to him as they did to Yahweh.

It simply will not do to say, as many in the liberal Western theological tradition (including Asian writers influenced by this tradition) have said, that the disciples had such a wonderful inner experience of the love and grace of God mediated through Jesus that the 'mythical' language of 'resurrection' was the only way they could express the abiding significance of this experience. The Jewish people had experienced God's love and grace in many fresh and illuminating ways after catastrophic experiences of humiliation and suffering. They had several ways of describing this experience, but the language of 'resurrection' – least of all applied to an individual leader, however inspirational – was simply never one of them.

The more natural way of highlighting the importance of Jesus would have been to continue the traditional language Jews used of their great heroes Moses (whose body was never found) or of Enoch and Elijah, that God 'received them' by way of direct translation into his presence. Or they could have done what the followers of John the Baptist did with their dead master who had been beheaded by Herod Antipas. They could have revered him as a dead and martyred prophet lying in his grave. This would have been considered normal by the Jews. But by choosing to speak of Jesus' 'resurrection' they suffered the ridicule and persecution of the religious establishment.

Nor does it make any historical sense to assume that because the disciples of Jesus were so crushed by his death and the failure of their dreams that they projected the latter into a fantasy about Jesus' being raised from death as a way of coping with their painful situation. The Jewish world of the first century was awash with revolutionaries with messianic pretensions, most of whom were put to death in a violent way by the authorities. Nowhere do we hear of their disappointed and dispersed followers projecting their broken dreams into claims about their hero being raised from the dead. That option was not available to them. For Jewish language about 'resurrection' was not about a private spiritual experience: it was about a physical and public event. The followers of the failed revolutionary had either to give up the revolution or else to find another leader. The question that cannot be evaded, therefore, is simply this: why did the earliest disciples use the language of 'resurrection' in relation to Jesus?

It cannot be stressed too strongly that contemporary Jewish belief in resurrection had nothing to do with the resuscitation of a body or with the immortality of a disembodied soul or spirit. It is about the conquest of death, of going through death into a new world of *physically embodied* existence, and the birth of a new creation. Recent scholarship has shown how it is expressed in the desire of the Maccabean martyrs of the second century BC that the God of Israel would vindicate their cause by restoring the limbs and bodies they would lose through horrible torture and death.[35] It was a late development of Israelite faith, and is clearly evidenced in only a handful of Old Testament texts (such as Is. 26:19; Ps. 49:15 and Dan. 12:2). Resurrection, for all first-century Jews, was bound up with the hope of the kingdom of God, of God's vindication of his people Israel before their pagan enemies and the renewal of his disfigured world.

Resurrection, then, was corporate, as well as public and physical. It was not something that happened to isolated individuals, here and there. The age to come would be a renewed space-time world in which the righteous dead would be given new bodies in order to inhabit a renewed earth. Thus, the resurrection of the dead – the righteous to eternal life and the wicked to destruction – marked the consummation of the human drama. It spelt the triumph of Israel's God who was also the universal Creator and Judge of all humanity. Resurrection marked the dawn of a new world order, the final and supreme manifestation of God's justice, mercy and power in history.[36]

Herein lies the basic difference between theories of the immortality of the soul and the biblical hope of *resurrection*: it is the difference between believing in some immanent power within oneself to survive death, and recognizing oneself to be given by God and so entrusting oneself to him even in death. There is no natural orientation of human life to resurrection. The latter becomes a possibility only through radical faith in a trustworthy Creator who graciously gives life to us as his gift.

Early Christian faith in resurrection shares this Old Testament and first-century Pharisaic perspective (Acts 23:6). But with this *revolutionary and decisive difference*: the early Christians proclaimed that the resurrection had occurred in Jesus *before* the day of resurrection for all. Here was a real anticipation of the end of history. In the resurrection of Jesus, God not only gives a glimpse and pledge of the new creation, but he announces the dawn of that new creation before its promised fulfilment. Here is a foretaste of the future age in the present.

In the ancient Jewish world, as in our modern one, for someone who had been certifiably dead to become visibly alive again would not at all justify a claim that the person to whom this odd event had happened was therefore the Saviour of the world, the Son of God, or anything else in particular. More than two hundred years ago, the sceptical Scottish philosopher David Hume (1711– 76) pointed out that, faced with an anomaly in our experience, we are more likely to explain it away than label it a 'miracle'. If, say, one of the two brigands crucified along with Jesus had appeared to his friends a few days later, we may suppose it very unlikely that he would have been hailed in any such way, or that anyone would deduce from that event that Israel's salvation had dawned. This forces us to ask: could the belief that someone had been raised from the dead, whatever precisely was understood by that, have produced the results it did – unless it was also known that the one who had been crucified and raised had lived in such a manner and made such extraordinary claims concerning himself that resurrection was actually remarkably consistent with all that had occurred before?

In summary, we have seen that the Jewish hope of resurrection expressed, at one and the same moment, hope in the Creator God's reaffirmation of his covenant with Israel and the reaffirmation of his whole creation. Resurrection is a fresh creative act of God in which he displays his faithfulness to his creation by raising it to new life in his presence beyond death and decay. Resurrection, then, is the Creator's final act of faithfulness to his creation, and the uniqueness of the resurrection of Jesus *within* history is consistent with Jesus' *self-consciously unique role* in God's saving purpose for his world.

By speaking of Jesus, Spirit and God in the same breath, the early disciple-community not only makes remarkable claims about Jesus within the monotheistic framework of Jewish thought, but, at the same time, makes staggering claims about God. The claim is not that Jesus is like God, but that God is like Jesus. Jesus, and especially Jesus in his crucifixion, is in some way the fullness of deity in human personhood. It is this claim that gave birth to the uniquely Christian belief that at the centre of all things there is a love that suffers.

An eminent patristic historian sums up the extraordinary challenge that the first followers of Jesus faced, and out of which a radically new conception of God as Tri-unity emerged:

> From the beginning Christianity carried within its bosom two convictions: that there is only one God, and that Jesus Christ is divine. It had for three hundred years refused to compromise on the question of monotheism; it had steadfastly refused to make any concessions to

the tolerant polytheism of the culture of the late Roman empire in which it lived, and thousands of Christians had suffered and died because of this conviction. But just as deeply rooted in the heart of Christianity was the worship of Jesus Christ, not the cult of a deified man (which was common enough in the Roman empire), but the worship of the Son of God who had taken to himself human nature in the Incarnation. These two convictions had to be reconciled.[37]

Conclusion

'What is beyond dispute', writes John P. Meier, 'is that Jesus of Nazareth is one of those perennial question marks in history with which mankind is never quite done. With a ministry of two or three years he attracted and infuriated his contemporaries, mesmerized and alienated the ancient world, unleashed a movement that has done the same ever since, and thus changed the course of history forever.'[38]

I have argued that the much-admired lifestyle of Jesus goes hand in hand with his teaching, and that both are inextricably interwoven with the authoritative claims he makes about his own person and ministry. Indeed, we have seen that the particular combination of lifestyle and claims that is embodied in Jesus marks him out as singularly different from Moses, the Buddha, Muhammad, Confucius or any other historical – or even fictional – character we meet in the world's cultures.

One objection that is often raised is that this is irrelevant, as every religious community claims uniqueness for its 'saviour-figures'. But this, as we have seen, is to sidestep the awkwardness of the *unique nature of the uniqueness* that is claimed by Jesus (or, if one prefers, claimed for Jesus by the early church). There are others who say that to stress the uniqueness of Jesus generates division in societies where there are multiple worldviews. This is perfectly true, but it seems to be based on the assumption that social conflict must be avoided *at all cost*, an assumption that is itself part of a particular worldview that Jesus and his early disciples call into question. To say, as others do, that concepts such as 'resurrection' or 'judgment' are culturally conditioned concepts that can be detached from the Christian message without loss to its 'core experience' is, once again, to assume particular (also culturally con-ditioned) views of culture, religious experience and religious language that the biblical writers challenge. The 'good news' of the death and resurrection of Jesus brings with it an entirely new worldview.

Within this worldview there is mounted a powerful critique of the status quo. The cross reveals the true tragedy of the human condition. For, if the message of the gospel is true, it calls into question the common assumption that it is in the 'religions of the world' that God is known and that it is, therefore, 'religious' people (or, at least, 'civilized' societies) to whom we must turn in our quest for God.

The late Lesslie Newbigin starkly sums up the challenge:

> The same revelation in Jesus Christ, with its burning centre in the agony and death of Calvary, compels me to acknowledge that this world which God made and loves is in a state of alienation, rejection and rebellion against him. Calvary is the central unveiling of the infinite love of God and at the same time the unmasking of the dark horror of sin. Here not the dregs of humanity, not the scoundrels whom all good people condemn, but the revered leaders in church, state, and culture, combine in one murderous intent to destroy the holy one by whose mercy they exist and were created.[39]

The message of the cross is scandalous, for it tells us that it is not the 'good Christian' or the 'sincere Hindu' or the 'devout Muslim' or the 'men and women of good will' who are recipients of the vision of God. Rather, that it is the bad Christian, the bad Hindu, the bad Buddhist – those who know themselves to be moral failures – who may well be closer to the kingdom of God. This can be so simply because salvation is through grace, mediated in the cross of Christ, received in faith. I know of no statement more subversive of the 'world of religions' than Paul's description in Romans 4:5 of the Father of the Lord Jesus Christ as 'him who justifies the ungodly'.

Stephen Neill, a missionary-scholar and an ecumenical statesman of considerable repute, reminds us that 'The historical figure of Jesus of Nazareth is the criterion by which every Christian affirmation has to be judged, and in the light of which it stands or falls'.[40] Jesus calls into question all religious systems, casting the 'shadow of falsehood, or at least of imperfect truth' on them all:

> This Christian claim is naturally offensive ... But we must not suppose that this claim to universal validity is something that can quietly be removed from the Gospel without changing it into something entirely different from what it is. The mission of Jesus was limited to the Jews and did not look immediately beyond them; but his life, his methods and his message do not make sense, unless they are interpreted in the light of his own conviction that he was in fact the final and decisive word of God to men.[41]

Does this mean that disciples of Jesus have nothing to learn from others, or that the story that finds its centre in the cross and resurrection of Jesus cancels all other stories of the divine–human encounter? By no means. It is *this* story that enables us to discern signs of God's new order, inaugurated in Jesus, in all human struggles against fear, greed, violence, sickness, oppression and injustice. It is *this* story, alone among all stories, which gives human beings the firm assurance, rooted in historical event, that their struggles are not ultimately futile. Why? Because death, sin and evil have been overcome. And we have also seen, in the last chapter, that it is *this* story which, more than any other, has historically motivated and guided such struggles in the East as well as in the West. These are themes to which we shall return in later chapters.

Finally, the word of the cross also carries its own revolutionary agenda. The crucifixion can be seen as a point of convergence for two fundamentally opposing visions of what it means to be human. The first is seen in the self-righteous legalism of the Pharisees, the calculating self-preservation and self-seeking of the priestly establishment, the callous pragmatism of their political overlords, and the fickleness of the masses whose lust for revenge has been fuelled by disillusionment. The second is embodied in Jesus himself: a radical surrender to, and dependence on, the One he knew as Father, which issues in the willingness to lay down his life in self-forgetful love for others. Two ways of defining humanness clash: *self-assertion* or *self-giving* – power over others as the highest goal in life, or power to empower others through sacrificial service.

The resurrection of Jesus, then, is the Creator's vindication, within history and in anticipation of the final denouement of all things, of the way of the cross. The resurrection vindicates not only Jesus' unique Sonship, but also the way of self-abandoning love that he embodies.

4
Conversion and cultures

Dealing with diversity

One theme which runs throughout this book takes the form of this question: can we live in a pluralistic environment and continue to make universal truth-claims, while still respecting the diversity of human cultures and religious beliefs?

I suggested in the first chapter that there is a deep ambiguity running through the Islamic response to this question. On the one hand, Muslims hold as a fundamental doctrine the unity of God as Creator and the unity of humankind as the creature and steward (*khalifa*) of God on earth. As long as 'Islam' referred to both a religion and a political community, the universality of its beliefs and calling was never in question. It is only in modern times that a substantial number of Muslims find themselves as minorities in many societies, and Muslim thinkers have only now begun to grapple with the implications of this minority status for their witness (*da'wah*). The treatment of non-Muslim minorities in majority Muslim states, and especially of Muslim converts to other faiths, has often been abysmal, and has invited widespread censure. On the other hand, the way that Islamic states often react to criticism is to deny the validity of universal ethical codes (of human rights, for example) and to urge recognition for Islamic law-codes as a particular instance of cultural respect. This is a form of 'cultural relativism', and it has its sympathizers and defenders among Western writers too.

However, the mystical Sufi tradition in the Islamic world has always been eclectic in its approach to religious experience. It has tended to see in Jesus the embodiment of the Sufi ideals of poverty, ascetic spirituality and sacrificial love. For the Spaniard Ibn 'Arabi, one of the best-known and more pantheistic of medieval Sufis, who died in Damascus in AD 1240, love for God was the essence of all creeds:

> My heart has become capable of every form: it is a
> pasture for gazelles and a convent for Christian monks,
> And a temple for idols, and the pilgrim's Ka'ba,
> and the tables of the Torah and the book of the Qur'an,
> I follow the religion of Love, whichever way his camels take.
> My religion and my faith are the true religion.[1]

In recent years a small band of Muslim writers, usually working in Western universities, has denied that Islam abrogated Christianity and Judaism, and has come to espouse a conciliatory position towards other religious traditions. These writers participate in inter-faith dialogue, and are strongly influenced by the Sufi tradition, or Western advocates of religious pluralism, or both. They all stress the 'inwardness' of faith, distinguish 'faith' from 'belief' and 'doctrine', and welcome the plurality of religions as a phenomenon willed by God.

Hasan Askari, an Indian Shi'ite Muslim who has spent some time at Selly Oak College in Birmingham, England, is a good example. The influences on Askari are Sufism as well as the writings of Wilfred Cantwell Smith and John Hick. What matters for him is the inner spiritual quest of the individual seeker. All claims to finality on the part of any religious tradition must be interpreted 'metaphorically'.[2] The great spiritual teachers – in addition to Muhammad and Jesus, Socrates, the Buddha and Lao-Tse – are compared to different images reflecting a single candle.[3] Muslims need Christians to show them elements which are underemphasized in Islam and Judaism, namely the dimensions of 'the tragic, or suffering, of submission in silence without resistance, of confronting self-righteousness, of upholding the value of humility and poverty, of going inward, of partaking of the burdens, seen and unseen, of the other'.[4]

In the case of Hindu thinkers, I have already pointed out that much of what goes into the melting-pot of 'Hinduism' is of relatively recent origin. The term covers a wide variety of practices and beliefs, many of which seem contradictory to the outside observer. The typical manner of responding to diversity, especially characteristic of the dominant Brahmanical strain of

Hindu practice, is to 'include and hierarchalize' (in Louis Dumont's memorable phrase). I have questioned whether this can properly be called 'tolerance' in the modern sense of the term. To tolerate a belief or practice surely implies that (a) we recognize that belief or practice to be genuinely different from our own, (b) we disagree with the belief (or disapprove of the practice), and (c) we do not coerce or absorb the other into ourselves, but give social and legal space for the other to flourish.

For those outside the Brahmanical tradition in India, Hindu 'hierarchical relativism' is experienced as deeply oppressive, not only in its caste expression, but also in its resistance to criticism. This does not mean, of course, that change is not possible; but, rather, that those who have initiated change have had to step out of Hindu society, and then their difference is later absorbed into what is now redefined as the Hindu mainstream. The Buddha and Buddhist monasticism, Jain vegetarianism and non-violence, local tribal deities and religious myths have all suffered the same absorption. Here it seems that particularity, difference and critique are swallowed up in a suffocating universalism.

The most common way of handling religious pluralism within the Buddhist tradition has been to employ the concept of 'skilful means', central to Mahayana Buddhism as a living religion. The Buddha teaches his message of enlightenment through several vehicles (Sanskrit *yana*) and skilful means (*upaya*) which are fitted to the disposition, temperament, interests and spiritual condition of the listener. It is best illustrated by a story (which, incidentally, has some superficial resemblance to the story of the prodigal son in Luke's Gospel) found in the *Lotus-Sutra*, the most influential of Mahayana texts in East Asia. It is based on the teaching of Nagarjuna and was composed around the second century AD.

The story can be summarized as follows. A young man leaves his father's home and travels abroad for many years. In his absence the father becomes rich and moves to another city where he builds himself a palace. The son falls into poverty and, in the course of his wanderings, turns up in the city where his father lives. The father, who is troubled by the fact that he is ageing and has no heir, recognizes his son who has come to the city as a beggar. But the son does not recognize his father. The latter, realizing that his son is psychologically incapable of grasping the 'absolute truth' that all these riches belong to him, goes about revealing his relationship to him in a roundabout way. He gives him a job as a scavenger near the palace. Gradually he increases his wages, and gives him more responsibility. In this way he builds up the young man's confidence until he can treat him as an adopted son and give him custody of the whole palace. Towards the end of his life the father declares his son to be his true heir before other witnesses. Thus is the 'absolute truth' of the son's relationship revealed.

The *Sutra* itself explains the symbolism. The rich father is the wise Buddha and the son is a typical disciple. The Buddha cannot teach the path to enlightenment directly, so he adopts 'skilful means', depending on the spiritual and psychological disposition of the disciple. The vehicle of Hinayana / Theravada is one such means. It is easy to see how the rigorous meditative practices of Theravada monks, as well as the myriad rituals and folk practices of lay Buddhist communities, can readily be brought into this framework as 'skilful means'. It has also been employed by some modern Japanese Buddhist schools to explain the diversity of religious faiths and to accommodate them without having to grapple with their conflicting truth-claims.

Speaking to a group of Christians in London, the Dalai Lama, the head of Tibetan Buddhism, presented his vision of inter-faith dialogue thus:

> For some people, the Christian traditions, which are based on belief in a Creator, have the most powerful effect on their ethical life and serve to motivate them to act in an ethical and sound way. However, this might not be the case for every person. For others, the Buddhist tradition, which does not emphasize belief in a Creator, may be more effective. In the Buddhist tradition, there is an emphasis on a sense of personal responsibility rather than on a transcendent being.
>
> It is also crucial to recognize that both spiritual traditions share the common goal of producing a human being who is a fully realized, spiritually mature, good, and warm-hearted person. Once we have recognized these two points – commonality of the goal and the clear recognition of the diversity of human dispositions – then I feel there is a very strong foundation for dialogue. It is with these convictions, these two principal premises, that I always enter into dialogue with other traditions.[5]

Christians (and, no doubt, other theists) would want to question both the assumption that belief in a Creator is simply a 'skilful means' to producing 'fully realized' persons, and also whether the two traditions do indeed share a common goal. Within a worldview which sees sentient beings caught up in numerous life-cycles, perhaps it is unreasonable to get too hot and bothered about other people's beliefs and practices. All get the chance to follow the right path to *nirvana* some day. I leave it to the reader to judge whether this form of tolerance truly respects the integrity of the 'other' and is thus morally more attractive than the neo-Vedanta form.

It is not surprising, then, that none of these major faith traditions, despite their universal expression, has seriously engaged with the faiths of others. Early Buddhist scholars, of course, wrote in the context of polemic with Vedic Hindu beliefs and rituals; but, outside of that context, little has been written that demonstrates a familiarity, at once both sympathetic and critical, with the central affirmations of other faiths. I have pointed out the distressing indifference shown by many Muslims to the teaching and lifestyle of Jesus of Nazareth, despite the lofty esteem in which he is held in the Qur'an and Muslim tradition. Most Muslims, like their secular counterparts in Europe or America, would rather read about Jesus as filtered through some dubious medieval or twentieth-century sources than seriously expose themselves to the disturbing issues raised by the early Christian testimony.

If Christian writers have made a far more significant contribution to Islamic, Hindu or Buddhist scholarship than the other way round, it is surely because the impetus to engagement arose out of a universal missionary concern. This is nowadays held as a stigma against those pioneer missionaries, as if the desire to communicate the gospel to people of other faiths tends *inevitably* to nullify the validity of research, to distort the object of study. Missionary scholarship is routinely dismissed as 'orientalist', ever since Edward Said transformed that word into a term of academic abuse. Most contemporary 'Third World' social scientists automatically assume that the missionary enterprise of translation and textual retrieval shared in the exploitative interests of colonialism. But I have quoted Fred Halliday's pertinent criticism of Said in chapter 2 (see p. 64). It is the 'outsider', even the hostile outsider, who is often more accurate in his or her observations and assessments of how things stand than the defensive insider.

Akbar Ahmed, the well-known Muslim social anthropologist, has gently chided his fellow Muslims for jumping too eagerly on the anti-orientalist bandwagon:

> Orientalism itself has become a cliché, and third world literature is now replete with accusations and labels of Orientalism being hurled at critics and at one author by another at the slightest excuse. This has had a stultifying effect on the dispassionate evaluation of scholarship. Thus, for example, in the passion generated by the debate what has been missed out is the great contribution of many Orientalist scholars. The writings of Ibn Khaldun, Ibn Batuta, or the Mughal emperor Babur come to us only through the painstaking scholarship of Orientalists who spent a lifetime deciphering notes in Asian languages and sitting in remote libraries. For them it was a labour of love. To dismiss their

work as simply Orientalism or as an attempt to suppress or subjugate
Muslim peoples denies an important truth.[6]

Were it not for the work of the much-maligned orientalists (whether
secular humanists or evangelical Christians), many of the finest monuments in
the world would have disappeared a long time ago. There are museums across
the Indian subcontinent where priceless artefacts are falling to pieces due to
neglect. Beautiful ancient buildings in Uttar Pradesh, a state ruled by the BJP
since 1991, are in a decrepit state, and museums have no buildings to keep
their treasures. What is the value of history, the visitor is inclined to ask, in a
Hindu consciousness unexposed to European influences? Similarly, in Sri
Lanka, concern for the preservation of priceless Buddhist works of art has
been stimulated, more often than not, by non-Buddhist scholars and Western-
educated élites, rather than by governments or Buddhist monks.

In the nineteenth century, European knowledge of Asian peoples and their
sacred literature was heavily indebted to the Protestant missionary movement.
Most of the early missionaries were not university trained, but their experience
in pioneering situations developed in them scholarly instincts and habits.
Some of them were responsible for developing new disciplines and fields of
study in Western universities, such as linguistics and social anthropology.
From the London Missionary Society alone came four professors in Chinese
for British universities, only one of whom had received a university education
himself.[7]

Some false moves

Any discussion of religious and cultural pluralism among so-called
secularized men and women soon runs into some common misconceptions.

Plausibility and truth

'How can you be right if so many others think differently?'

First, there is the assertion that since we live in a world of diverse and
competing truth-claims we have to give up any notion of ultimate truth where
our own beliefs are concerned. This is sometimes based on a confusion of the
notion of plausibility with that of truth. The plausibility of our beliefs depends
on how much social support they receive. For a believer in, say, a heliocentric
view of the solar system, life in a society consisting of fervent geocentrists
would be almost unbearable. He would be assailed by doubts over his own
position. In moving to a society where the great majority share his beliefs, that

discomfort would be greatly eased. But these feelings of cognitive ease or unease, and the degree of social support that we receive for our beliefs (which are related to those feelings), are not indicators of the truth or falsity of the beliefs in question. All successful scientific theories were born in circumstances of cognitive loneliness, and the same is true of most of the great world faiths. Far from pluralism being a new phenomenon, it is good to be reminded that the Christian movement emerged in a Greco-Roman world as replete with gods, saviour cults and ideologies as our own.

Rationality and truth

'Are you saying that all other religious beliefs are irrational?'

Just as we must not confuse plausibility with truth, so we must not confuse rationality with truth. The rationality of a belief has to do with the way a belief is justified, that is, what reasons can be given in support of it. These reasons often assume the truth of other background beliefs, all of which make up a total worldview. Thus it is rational within a Buddhist or Hindu worldview to believe that a person's present life-situation (e.g. a woman's inability to bear children) has been determined, either in part or wholly, by her actions in a previous life. It was also rational for our forebears to have believed in a geocentric universe when they did not have access to astronomical data and other cosmological theories. (But note that it would not be rational for them to continue to hold them today.) Whether these beliefs are true is another question altogether. So one can accept the rationality of many of the beliefs that we encounter in our pluralist societies, while still denying that most of them are true.

Religious language and truth

'Aren't we all saying the same thing but in different languages?'

Another way of handling divergent truth-claims, equally misconceived though more sophisticated, is so to dilute their content that they cease to make any cognitive assertions. Some modern theologians have become expert at this sort of thing. Religious language, they say, is not to be understood as trying to describe some reality 'out there', let alone explain anything about the world. Rather, it is a special kind of language that expresses our sense of 'absolute dependence' or our commitment to a specific way of life. On this understanding, language about the incarnation of the Word of God in Jesus Christ is as 'mythical' as the *avatars* (theophanies) of Vishnu or the stories of the heavenly Buddhas in Mahayana Buddhism or of the giving of the Qur'an to

Muhammad by the angel Gabriel. Mythical language is not only non-assertive, it is the only way one can express supreme devotion. Conflicts between rival beliefs then disappear, for they would be as illusory as the rivalry between, say, two little girls both of whom proclaim loudly to their friends, 'My daddy is the best daddy in the whole wide world.' We all smile indulgently when we hear such comments, because we take them as 'mythical' pronouncements of loving loyalty, not factual statements about their daddies.

Those theological writers who propose that we should treat conflicting religious truth-claims in the same manner are guilty of a double deceit. First, they do not respect the integrity of the different faith-traditions. In a well-meaning attempt to dissolve conflict, they end up creating a new 'pluralist religion' which looks suspiciously like the lowest common denominator of all other religions. No Christian would accept that the language of incarnation or resurrection is simply expressive of devotion and nothing more, just as no Muslim could accept that no factual assertion is being made when authorship of the Qur'an is ascribed to God. The incarnation is constitutive of Christian faith in a way that the doctrine of *avatara* is not for Hindu faith. Respect for the beliefs of another entails that we take the trouble to explore what those beliefs mean for the believer in the wider context of his or her own life in a believing community, not arbitrarily assigning one's own private meanings to them. Secondly, however, such an approach is not only reductive, it is also simply question-begging. In the case of Christian language about Jesus, for instance, we are still left with the question: what was it about Jesus that made the first Christians call him Lord? The statement 'Jesus is Lord' certainly expresses personal devotion and commitment to a specific way of life; but only because those who sincerely make that statement also believe that Jesus is *in fact* Lord of the world.

Related to this way of dealing with religious pluralism is the notion that all the world religions are simply different, historically conditioned responses to an ultimate divine Reality that is ineffable, beyond linguistic ascription. All we are left with is a number of human languages, each of which is incapable on its own of giving a full account of that reality. Once again, this approach appears at first sight to be a humble way of dealing with diversity, but, on closer inspection, its intellectual arrogance becomes plain. It claims for itself a superior vantage-point from which it can survey the entire world of religious languages and deduce that they are all dealing with the same ultimate reality, and that they are all incomplete and even misguided in places.

It also rules out of court, from the outset, any possibility that the ultimate Reality may be personal – or, to be more precise, a personal God who may seek to make himself known to his creatures. For if we allow for a God who speaks, then the view that all religions are on the same level, as equally flawed human ways of speaking of a transcendent experience, becomes less plausible. So this pluralist scheme is fatally biased against the Semitic traditions and those Indian religious traditions that focus on a personal Deity. It is attractive only to those philosophical idealists who indulge in the arcane vocabulary of 'Absolute Being', 'Transcendent Mystery', 'Ground of Existence', and so on.

The price for resolving conflict between ultimate truth-claims in this way is too costly. It fails to respect true 'otherness'. It savages pluralism in the name of defending it. What is put forward as a humble way of relating to the rich diversity of human religious traditions quickly turns into a reductionist onslaught on the factual affirmations of those traditions, with the Semitic traditions taking the brunt of the assault. What we are left with is a series of Procrustean beds on which a new élite of self-styled 'progressive' theologians dismember the religions of the world.

Historicism and truth

'Since the gospel, like all our beliefs, is conditioned by the historical context, how can it be universally true?'

A form of this argument has been popular since the days of the English Deists in the late seventeenth century and their heirs in the European Enlightenment. These men shared with the ancient religions of the Indian subcontinent a disdain for the epistemic value of historical events. Religious knowledge they took to be timeless and universal. Religious truth must be accessible to all rational human beings through the exercise of their unaided reason or direct personal experience of the divine. History, which is subject to the flux of change and uncertainty, cannot be the source of truths about Deity.

Moreover, the traditional Jewish-Christian notion of divine revelation being mediated through specific events at specific times and places is morally repugnant, because it seems to deny to people at other times and places that direct, immediate access to God which any global religion must entail. All claims to revelation must be subject to the dictates of 'natural religion' which is everywhere the same. History is, at best, a source-book of illustrations of the truths derived from natural religion. Even more repugnant were the notions of human sinfulness and the necessity of divine atonement. For these ran counter to that whole movement in European thought, starting perhaps with Descartes and culminating (paradoxically) in Nietzsche, for human autonomy, self-mastery and self-creation.

It is this intellectual heritage that has come under ruthless scrutiny in recent decades in the debates surrounding what is loosely called 'post-modernism'. The project of modernity is based on a universal vision. History is seen as the unfolding story of a universal immanent process, whether it be the march of reason or of liberty, the self-realization of the Absolute, or whatever. Postmodernism is wary of such universal history, while being on the whole enthusiastic about *histories*. All people possess their own individual and collective histories, and they cannot be ranked on a league table of values, let alone subsumed under one overarching narrative. Postmodernism denies that history is in any sense story-shaped. If the Enlightenment project tried to make universal assertions divorced from historical particularity, the 'post-modern sensibility' rejects the universal in the name of the local, the contingent, the discontinuous. Are we then trapped between a *free-floating universalism*, untethered to particular persons and events, and a *parochial historicism* that cannot make any statements of universal validity and relevance? That seems to be the dilemma of late modern Western academic culture.

The Enlightenment tradition inherited notions of universal justice and equality from Jewish and Christian sources and then used such notions to deride the particular doctrines and practices of those faiths. Is not the claim that Israel was vouchsafed a special disclosure of God's purposes tantamount to contempt for all other nations and cultures? How can the life, death and resurrection of Jesus of Nazareth carry such momentous significance for the life of the whole world as Christians have claimed down the ages? Does this not impugn the goodness of God?

For a relatively recent example of this mentality, consider the following statement by the American theologian John Driver:

> The immoral factor in the 'scandal of particularity' today is its insistence upon a once-and-for-all Christ in a relativistic world … It precludes Christianity's ability to affirm that all people have a right to their place in the sun … If the incarnation of God in finite humanity can occur but once, the religious value of all other human history is nil.[8]

This is, quite frankly, muddle-headed nonsense. Yet it is a commonplace assumption in contemporary society, and, when combined with Western guilt over the colonial and imperialist enterprise, forms a lethal brew that has sapped the vitality of many Christians in the West. For that reason alone it deserves a full refutation. I shall spell out a few arguments here in brief, taking up some of them in greater detail in the next section.

(a) The Christian message is radically historical in its orientation. The doctrine of creation states that we are not timeless, relationless and independent beings, but profoundly contingent and relational creatures. We are rooted in space and time, to bodily, social and cultural existence. The choices we make and the actions we perform shape both our personal future and that of the world we inhabit. Sin and evil too are historical in character, and so it is not surprising that our redemption should pivot on real events in history. And, as we saw in the previous chapter, the manner in which our redemption or salvation is communicated (through a particular people) constitutes the content of that salvation. For part of what it means to be 'saved' is to experience freedom from an illusory 'atomistic' existence and to recover our mutual interdependence in a new human family.

In other words, the universal is always mediated through the particular, in the biblical scheme of things. This resonates with our experience of all artistic, literary and scientific achievement. It simply does not follow, as writers such as Driver seem to assume, that just because all our thoughts, including our thoughts about God, are historically shaped, none of our thoughts can be true for all time and for all peoples. We can read *Hamlet* and recognize that Shakespeare is speaking to a human condition that is shared by people of all ages and cultures, while also freely acknowledging that it could never have been written in the way it was if Shakespeare had been living in 1950, or even in 1750. Similarly, the universal validity of Einstein's theories of Special and General Relativity is unquestioned in scientific circles; and the fact that he was a German Jew, or that his theories could never have emerged at an earlier time in the history of physics, do not impugn that universality.

Universalism and historicism are thus not as polarized as is often assumed. No-one who believes in a doctrine of God as Creator can seriously question the objectivity and universality of truth. No-one who believes that as human creatures we are endowed with dignity and freedom can ever despise the particularity of historical action.

(b) We have seen that the Christian message of God's incarnation in Jesus Christ, as the climax to his dealings with his world, is what ennobles our humanity and enables us to have not merely a 'place in the sun' but a 'home in God'. It is the incarnation, death and resurrection of God in Jesus Christ that enables us to say that human history is finally meaningful, not in the Enlightenment humanist sense that it is a story of continual, linear progress, an ascent from the 'irrational' to the 'rational'; but rather, that in this sorry tale of persistent human arrogance, wretchedness, exploitation and suffering, evil will not have the final word. The triumph of truth, beauty, love and justice is assured.

It is only in the light of this conviction of a once-for-all, public defeat of death and evil that we can affirm the abiding worth of other histories and individual human stories. It is only Christians who can confidently hope that everything that is true, beautiful, just and pleasing to God in every period of human history and in every human culture is not lost for ever, but will be retrieved and restored in the eternal worship of God. The biblical story begins with a picture of a couple in a garden. It ends with that marvellous vision of a city, the New Jerusalem, a place of multicultural cohabitation, where the peoples of the earth will 'bring into it the glory and the honour of the nations' (Rev. 21:22ff.).

(c) We have seen in previous chapters that it was the conviction of the distinctiveness and universality of Jesus Christ that impelled men and women over the centuries to cross geographical and linguistic boundaries, and to offer their lives in the self-giving service of their fellow men and women. It was this conviction that enabled them to recognize the human worth, as well as desperate need, of tribes and cultures long despised by their non-Christian compatriots. It motivated and empowered them to serve the 'dregs' of humanity: the destitute, the disabled and the dispossessed. This is the continuing story of Christian witness and mission in many parts of the world. Far from the doctrine of incarnation breeding any notion of religious or cultural superiority, it humbles human pride.

We have also seen that to identify uncritically the missionary enterprise with European colonialism betrays an ignorance of the historical record. Moreover, in the last chapter, we noted that it betrays a lack of understanding of what the central message of the gospel entails. The belief in the incarnation and atoning death of Jesus can be conveyed only in self-denying love, for that is what the message is all about. That is what the best and most effective missionaries have always grasped.

To say this, of course, is not to deny that the message of the cross has often been linked to domination, avarice and racism. Church history right up to the present day gives ample examples of this ugly and shameful story. But we rightly see these as *betrayals* of the message, rather than as its logical entailment. I would argue that those darkest periods of church history have been the periods when biblical preaching has been at a low ebb and the gospel least understood within the church itself.

(d) The problem of particularity should not be confused with the problem of the ultimate status of those who have not had the opportunity to hear the gospel. The claim that God has revealed his truth in historical events does not entail, at least without further premises, that those who lack this revelation are excluded from the benefits of that revelation. Someone may coherently argue *both* that Jesus' life, death and resurrection are the normative and ultimate revelation of God to humankind *and* that all human beings will eventually come to that knowledge of God in Jesus. Other Christians, more biblically consistent, will reject this form of universalism but still be open to the idea that, even as the Old Testament 'saints' looked forward to God's gracious redemption and trusted in the one in whom that redemption was accomplished – without understanding how that redemption would come about – so there are people who are saved by Christ and serve him without realizing who it is they trust.

It is not my intention here to discuss these issues, but simply to point out that there is no *necessary* connection between the claim that specific historical events uniquely reveal God's saving purpose and the further claim that this is to condemn all who for reasons of history or geography have been denied the chance to respond to that revelation.

(e) The 'once-for-all' character of the incarnation is intrinsic to its meaning. It distinguishes Christian faith from belief in the successive *avatars* of Vishnu or the personification of virtue in the Amitaba Buddha. None of the Indian religions accords any ultimate significance to the human realm. Paradoxically, it is the once-for-all incarnation of Christian belief that guarantees the permanent value and significance of our common humanness. For those who believe in the resurrection of Jesus, humanness is that which is exalted to the right hand of God.

Those theologians who reject the particularity of redemption through the life, death and resurrection of Jesus Christ indulge in a process of theological translation that leaves us with a message that is no longer recognizable as Christian. Thus the 'once-for-allness' of the incarnation is rejected in favour of some presumably more universal account of 'the divine in all human beings' or of 'human transcendence', thereby evoking ancient pagan ideas that the gospel of incarnation once challenged and subverted. As Kierkegaard put it in his scathing criticism of the mighty Hegel: 'That the human race is or should be akin to God is ancient paganism; but that an individual man is God is Christianity.'[9]

These are essentially dishonest ways of universalizing the Christian particulars. They fail to grasp that the universal is already embodied in the particulars of the Christian story. The truth that the early Christians believed had been disclosed in Jesus was *for* the world, because it was *about* the world and its future. This truth revealed both the tragic alienation of the world from its Creator and the glorious hope of its reconciliation and recreation. Thus missionary outreach, both to Jews and to pagans, was not an activity tagged on later to a faith that was basically 'about' something else (e.g. a new metaphysical system); rather, it flowed from the very logic of the death and resurrection of Jesus.

At the end of the nineteenth century, the great German dogmatic theologian Martin Kahler (1835–1912) posed a crucially important question to his academic contemporaries. Surveying the different ways the biblical doctrine of atonement had been interpreted since the days of the so-called European Enlightenment, Kahler asked: 'Has Christ merely provided us with insights concerning an existing state of affairs, or has he *actually brought about a new state of affairs?*'[10] There is all the difference in the world between seeing Christ as, for instance, an 'icon of God's grace' or a 'symbol of humanity's transcendence', and seeing Christ as establishing, through his death on the cross, a fundamentally *new* relationship between God and humanity. It is this latter perspective that entails and compels a universal mission.

Incarnation and translation

The missionary thrust of the early Christians was a force for cultural awakening. Bethlehem, Nazareth and even Jerusalem swiftly receded from view, and the new Christian communities that sprang up, eastwards and westwards, recognized no fixed geographical centre. The church did not make sacred the place of its origins. What is even more remarkable, especially in comparison with the great world religions of Semitic and Asian origin, is that the original language that Jesus used in his preaching was quickly abandoned in favour of country (*koinē*) Greek and 'vulgar' Latin as the uniting media of communication. The entire New Testament was written in a language other than the one in which Jesus preached.

That the eternal counsels of God belonged to the commonplace, everyday speech of ordinary men and women was a view that was, and remains, revolutionary. It resisted the tendency in some parts of the early church to cast the gospel into an élitist gnostic-type discourse. Unlike the widespread 'mystery religions' (and the dominant ethos of traditional Vedic, Tantric and Buddhist religious thought and practice), no attempt was made to develop a professional cultic language or to make a virtue out of élitist secrecy.

This openness of the gospel message, and its endless translatability into languages and cultures outside Palestinian Jewish soil, derive from the heart of its content. For, as Professor Andrew Walls reminds us, the central event on which the Christian movement rests is an astonishing act of divine translation: divinity translated into humanity.[11] Where the great prophetic faiths, Judaism and Islam, tell of a God who speaks to humanity, the Christian faith goes further: the divine speech has *become* a human person. 'The Word became flesh and lived among us' (John 1:14). The statement 'This is what God is like' has been translated into the specific words and actions of an actual human being who spoke a particular language, lived in a particular place at a particular time, and shared a particular ethnic identity. This particular human being now becomes the vehicle of divine meaning.

This fundamental act of divine translation is now re-enacted in countless acts of retranslation into the languages, thought-forms and relational patterns of the world that constitute the history of Christian mission. In fact, Walls points out that translation is an excellent metaphor and working model of Christian mission. We always receive new ideas in terms of the ideas with which we are familiar. In translation, the novel terms of the source language have to be expressed in the vocabulary of the receptor language, whose terms come pre-loaded within an alien context of meanings and connotations. In the process of translation, the receptor language is expanded and put to new uses, with old terms acquiring deeper meanings, some loadings dropping out altogether and some new terms making their way in. There is always the risk of distortion and miscommunication. We can never arrive at a final translation, but keep endlessly revising our translations in the light of changed meanings and expanded repertoires.

We see this translation process beginning within the pages of the New Testament. The first contact that the gospel makes with the Hellenistic-Roman world is through a group of unknown Jewish Christians who made their way to the city of Antioch, the capital of the Roman province of Asia. This was not the result of some grand missionary strategy on the part of the Jerusalem church, but rather the result of persecution. These unnamed refugees, we are told by Luke, began to speak to their Greek pagan neighbours about 'the Lord Jesus' (Acts 11:20). The term is *Kyrios*, not *Christos* or Messiah. In the Septuagint, the Greek translation of the Hebrew Bible, *Kyrios* is the term that is used to translate the Hebrew tetragrammaton 'Yahweh', the personal covenant name of the God of Israel. To the Greeks of Antioch, *Kyrios* would have immediately reminded them of the many cult divinities that were honoured in various parts of the empire: *Kyrios* Serapis, *Kyrios* Osiris, *Kyrios* Isis, and so on. The biblical connotations would have been lost on them. In speaking of Jesus as *Kyrios*, then, these Christian evangelists were taking the risk of presenting Jesus as merely one cultic saviour-figure among legions of others in the pluralist world of the Mediterranean.

The reason this did not happen is undoubtedly that the new converts were brought into a community where the Septuagint was constantly read, and so the biblical associations of *Kyrios* gradually permeated their minds. But as the word of Christ and the word about Christ now had a foothold in Hellenistic culture, it brought about a rich dialogue and confrontation with that culture. It marked a turning-point in Christian history, the beginning of the conversion of the Greek-speaking world. The Greco-Roman world, with its complex array of customs, ideas and belief-systems, was now being subverted from within as its inhabitants found a strange new message being delivered in a language that was recognizably their own. In a conversion process that lasted a few centuries, the gospel addressed the principal concerns, the peculiar anxieties and compulsions, and the shared traditions of the Hellenistic world, turning them all towards the Jewish Christ. And, in so doing, it also raised questions and problems for Christians living in this environment which the Jewish Christians, including the apostles themselves, had never imagined.

Some of these questions surface in the Pauline letters. Indeed, it could be argued that most of Paul's letters are responses to questions arising from this new situation of Gentile (non-Jewish) Christians. In accepting Christ through faith they have been incorporated into the history of Israel without having become Jews. This was an extraordinary situation. To the Jewish mind, it was unthinkable that one could become part of the covenant people of God without the sign of the covenant, circumcision. Moreover, it was unimaginable for obedience to God to lie outside knowledge and submission to the Torah. Paul vigorously combats any attempt on the part of Jewish Christians to impose their cultural patterns on the new Gentile converts. It is here that we see the crucial difference between Christian conversion and proselytism.

In proselytism, as Walls points out, the proselyte simply takes on the ideas and behaviour patterns of the proselytizer. He gives up his old culture for a new culture. Everything is laid down for him, all he has to do is follow precedent. It is essentially a risk-free undertaking. The insecurity that attends leaving his old community is compensated for by his inclusion into a new community. Everybody in that community has only one common identity.

Christian conversion, however, is not the substitution of something new for the old, any more than the incarnation was a substitution of the divine for the human. Nor is it the addition of something new to what was before, any more than the incarnation was the addition of something new to a deficient humanity. In conversion, the word of Christ penetrates the intellect, emotions and attitudes of an individual in such a way that everything that makes him what he is – his past, his network of relationships, his work, his thought-patterns and moral processes – are given a new direction: namely, towards Christ. Conversion is about a radical reorientation, not substitution. It is a risky enterprise, especially in first-generation Christian communities where there is no precedent for what form discipleship to Christ should take in that particular context and culture. Conversion has a beginning, but no end. It's a lifelong process of discovery and transformation.

Evangelism and conversion

Gospel conversion is not limited to individuals. We have seen that the individual is meaningless without a community and a culture. The transformation of the individual carries with it an injection of the word of Christ into that world of shared history and tradition, thought-forms and practices that make up our national identities.

> The commanding heights of a nation's life have to be opened to the influence of Christ; for Christ has redeemed human life in its entirety. Conversion to Christ does not isolate the convert from his or her own community; it begins the conversion of that community. Conversion to Christ does not produce a bland universal citizenship: it produces distinctive discipleships, as diverse and variegated as human life itself.[12]

Perhaps another way we can distinguish authentic evangelism from religious proselytism is that the evangelist is also transformed in the process of conversion. Within the pages of the New Testament the best-known example of this is provided by Peter's encounter with the Roman centurion Cornelius (Acts 10:1 – 11:18). Here we are introduced to a stupendous sight, unimaginable in the ancient world, of a Jewish peasant under the same roof as a Roman military officer. What has brought about this astonishing new phenomenon is a set of events that we could call a 'double conversion'. Cornelius, upright and God-fearing though he was, still needed to hear the message of the gospel from the lips of Peter (not even from those of an angel!) in order that he might receive the forgiveness of sin and the gift of the Holy Spirit. Peter, witnessing the same Holy Spirit at work in a Gentile's life, comes to a recognition of his own cultural prejudice under the deepening impact of the gospel on his thinking. Cornelius has come to a saving knowledge of Christ. Peter has come to a deeper discipleship, a more profound conversion of his cultural and religious heritage towards Christ.

Another way of understanding the dynamic of Christian conversion is in terms of the creative tension between what Walls has called the 'indigenizing principle' and the 'pilgrim principle' in church history. Both these principles derive equally from the gospel. The indigenizing principle witnesses to the truth that God accepts sinners like us as we are, on the basis of Christ's atoning death and resurrection alone. He does not wait for us to correct our ideas or tidy up our behaviour before he welcomes us into his family as adopted sons and daughters. But to accept us 'as we are' implies that he accepts us in our group relations, for (as we have seen) we are not isolated, individual monads, but constituted as human selves by our relationships and our past. So God, in justifying us, accepts us with all our historical and cultural conditioning, and the prejudices, predispositions, suspicions and anxieties that mark our belonging to a particular group and not to another. Christ, so to speak, immerses himself in all that we bring to him in our initial conversion; and 'indigenizes' our discipleship, calling us to live as Christians and as members of our own societies.

There is, however, another side to the gospel. Not only does God in Christ take people as they are, but he takes them in order to make them what they ought to be. So, along with the indigenizing principle, the Christian also inherits a pilgrim principle which 'whispers to him that he has no abiding city and warns him that to be faithful to Christ will put him out of step with his society, for that society never existed, in East or West, ancient time or modern, which could absorb the word of Christ painlessly into its system. Jesus within Jewish culture, Paul within Hellenistic culture, take it for granted that there will be rubs and frictions – not from the adoption of a new culture, but from the transformation of the mind towards that of Christ.'[13]

The indigenizing principle associates Christians with the particulars of their culture and group, testifying to the sanctifying power of Christ within their old relationships. The pilgrim principle, on the other hand, associates Christians with the wider family of faith, bringing them into a new set of relationships with people with whom they would have never associated before and with whom their natural groups have little kinship. The pilgrim principle testifies to the universal scope of the gospel. All those in whom Christ dwells through faith, all who have been accepted by God in Christ, are now family members. The Christian thus has a double nationality: his own former loyalty to biological family, tribe, clan or nation is retained, but is now set within a wider and more demanding loyalty to the global family of Christ.

This new adopted family stretches back in time as well as outward in space. It spans generations as well as cultures and nations. It reaches back to Abraham and to the faithful since Abraham, so that every new convert now finds his or her history drawn into the history of Israel in the Hebrew Bible and that of the people of God of the New Testament age (Rom. 4:11–12; Heb. 11:39–40). What this means is that, for me as an Asian Christian, Augustine and Irenaeus, Teresa of Avila and Mary Slessor, Calvin and Bonhoeffer all become my ancestors, part of my personal family tree. And, for Western Christians, their family tree now includes John of Damascus, Panditha Ramabai, Sadhu Sundar Singh, Kagawa and a host of outstanding Asian Christian men and women. I often wonder what a revolution this simple gospel concept would cause in Western theological education if grasped and applied in the curriculum!

The West African scholar Lamin Sanneh has rebutted the popular charge that Christian mission in Africa and Asia has always led to the destruction of other cultures in the form of Western cultural hegemony. Sanneh points out that the major plank in Protestant mission strategy was always Bible translation. This often involved writing down a vernacular for the very first time, and the creation of grammars and local literatures. Translation of the Bible into over two thousand languages has been the chief instrument of indigenous cultural renewal in many parts of the world. By believing that the vernacular was adequate for participation in the Christian movement, the more serious-minded missionaries and translators have preserved a great variety of languages and cultures from extinction, and lifted obscure tribes and ethnic groups into the stream of universal history. Sanneh writes:

> In many significant cases, these languages received their first breath of life from Christian interest. This is true whether we are speaking of Calvin and the birth of modern French, Luther and German, Tyndale and English, Robert de Nobili or William Carey and the Indian vernaculars, Miles Brunson and Assamese, Johannes Christaller and Akan in Ghana, Moffatt and Sichuana in Botswana, Ajayi Crowther and Yorruba in Nigeria, and Krapf and Swahili in East Africa, to take a random list from many examples … vernacular translation excites vernacular self-confidence, which in turn foments the national sentiment.[14]

Sanneh observes that the Christian view that all cultures may serve God's purpose 'stripped culture of idolatrous liability, emancipating it with the force of translation and usage'.[15] This had momentous social, cultural and political consequences. It is perhaps another of the many ironies of church history that such indigenous renewal should have turned into anti-missionary stridency and later into nationalism.

We may contrast this attitude to culture with that of Hinduism or Islam. To the Hindu and Muslim alike, sacred texts are untranslatable. Sanskrit and Arabic are the divine tongues, and the culture of origin becomes the universal paradigm. Until quite late into the twentieth century, many caste Hindus believed that in venturing beyond India one became ritually contaminated. Since Sanskrit is the language of the gods, it is also that of their human representatives, the Brahmans. It is the language of civilization, and indeed the word *sanskriti* means exactly that. Only men from the 'twice-born' castes can listen to the Vedas chanted in Sanskrit. The Brahmanization of Indian society went hand in hand with the suppression of vernacular tongues in favour of Sanskrit. Indeed, the term 'Sanskritization' has come to be used to describe that process whereby local beliefs and practices have come to be gradually absorbed into the Brahmanical power-structure. We have seen how it was under the influence of Christian missions that vernacular languages and literatures blossomed in India.

While Islam has practised social tolerance, Sanneh points out that the missionary success of Islam is in effect the universalization of Arabic as the language of faith. The Qur'an is fixed in Arabic, kept in heaven for ever. Every Muslim must step into Arabic on entering the mosque to perform his rites, a daily passage that for many reaches its climax in the annual *hajj*, the pilgrimage to Mecca. When one considers that three out of every four Muslims in the world are non-Arabs, it is clear that this implies a downgrading of their mother tongues in the fundamental acts of piety and devotion. Cultural pluralism is regarded, at best, irrelevant or, at worst, a hindrance to faith.

Both the indigenizing and pilgrim principles spring from the gospel, and they need to be held together in creative balance. To emphasize the first at the expense of the latter is to transform Christian faith into 'civil religion' – where the faith is so much at home in the native society that it is used to lubricate the social, political and economic mechanisms that perpetuate injustice or apathy towards other peoples. This is always a temptation in societies where Christians are a numerical majority. The danger of emphasizing the second principle at the expense of the first is to project a universal verbal orthodoxy and to impose it on others, without recognizing that this orthodoxy is shaped by the terms of one's own culture and context. This tendency is seen, paradoxically, both in European theological liberalism, prominent worldwide in the middle years of the twentieth century, and also in some 'fundamentalist' forms of evangelicalism.

What is it, then, that gives coherence to the rich pluralism that the gospel engenders around the world? Or, to use an example that Walls himself uses, what is identifiably 'Christian' about a Jewish Christian assembly in Jerusalem in AD 37, a gathering of Greek- and Latin-speaking bishops in Nicea in AD 325, a group of wild Celtic monks beside the Irish sea in the seventh century, a meeting in the London of the 1840s of enthusiastic Victorian gentlemen, or a congregation of white-robed Nigerian men and women chanting in the streets of Lagos about the power of the Spirit – apart from the fact that all these diverse groups form historical links in the progressive diffusion of the gospel?

The coherence of global Christianity (and here I follow Walls, while slightly altering his way of putting it) lies, principally, in two things.

First, all these groups are conscious that they stand in continuity with ancient Israel, and use both the Scriptures of Israel and the New Testament (except, of course, in the case of the first Jewish Christians) as their normative and regulative guide. This is all the more remarkable, given that most of them have never met or seen a Jew in their entire life! 'It gives them a point of reference outside themselves and their own society.'[16]

Secondly, they all give to Jesus of Nazareth an ultimate significance, and worship him as they do the God of Israel. This is the real test of historic Christian authenticity. Christians explore the conceptual repertoire of their various cultures in order to express the significance of Jesus in the highest ontological categories; and if that repertoire is inadequate, they expand it. 'Every culture has its ultimates, and Christ is the ultimate in everyone's vocabulary.'[17]

Conclusion

Following Andrew Walls's fruitful metaphor, we have looked at the divine act of incarnation in terms of 'translation', and its implication for all peoples and all cultures. The act of translation is prefigured in many acts of divine 'accommodation' in the Hebrew Bible. Students of the Pentateuch know that the patriarchs, including Abraham, worshipped El, the high god of Mesopotamia. It is from El (usually with other epithets, such as El-Shaddai) that they received promises and commands directly, without the intervention of prophets; and they responded to El by building altars and offering sacrifices, as well as in obedience and trust. The writer of Genesis is careful to retain the name El in the dialogue sections of the book, especially where God is the speaker. But in the narrative sections, Yahweh is the name that is used. From the later faith-perspective of Israel, it was Yahweh who had addressed the patriarchs as El and entered into relationship with them (cf. Exod. 6:3).

Now we cannot conclude from this observation that the Bible endorses the validity of the worship of El and his pantheon, let alone the ugly mythology that went with it. The text does not assert that all who worshipped El were thereby brought into a personal relationship with the living and true God; nor does it say anything about the sincerity or otherwise of Abraham's worship. God's speaking to Abraham and calling him into personal relationship is an act of grace, a divine initiative. God accommodates his self-disclosure to fit the religious framework of the patriarchs, including the religious rituals, customs and divine titles of their culture. This is in preparation for an experience of his liberating acts, a deeper and fuller revelation of his character and purposes, one that will in the course of time take them beyond their ancestral religious framework and shatter its central assumptions. Once they have walked with Yahweh in the wilderness, there is no going back (cf. Josh. 24:14–15).[18]

This is very instructive, and of contemporary relevance. It enables us to affirm that the pre-incarnate Son / Word of God has been addressing men and women of cultures and histories other than in Israel, and working with them under forms and names that Christians may find strange and even repellent (cf. John 1:1–3, 9; Heb. 1:1). That, surely, is the self-humbling accommodation of God to a 'fallen' human world. (After all, what can be more repellent than a cross?) This fact, however, far from obviating the need to proclaim the gospel of Christ to all cultures, actually *compels* it. For if it is Christ who has been speaking to human beings in their sin, it is in order to lead them out of what Paul calls (when addressing the learned citizens of Athens) 'the times of human ignorance' (Acts 17:30) that they may understand and experience the freedom that he wrought for them through the cross. The church is the bearer of the good news of freedom, and the Holy Spirit enables the church to discern those 'pointers' to Christ in every human situation, so that the word of Christ may be articulated powerfully and relevantly in every age.

Writing during the dark night of Nazi ascendancy in Germany, Dietrich Bonhoeffer pungently proclaimed that the primary purpose of the gospel was 'not the forming of a world by means of plans and programmes', but, rather, forming a people 'with the one form which has overcome the world, the form of Jesus Christ'.[19] Formation was not a matter of applying Christian values and teaching to the world, and least of all was Christ a 'principle' in accordance with which the world must be shaped. Christian ethics was not an abstract system but, on the contrary, the living process of 'being drawn into the form of Jesus Christ ... as *conformation* with the unique form of him who was made man, was crucified, and rose again'.[20]

For Bonhoeffer, the point of departure for Christian witness in the world is Christian ethics, and the point of departure for ethics is 'the body of Christ, the form of Christ in the form of the Church, and the formation of the Church in conformity with the form of Christ'.[21] The church bears the form which is in truth the proper form of all humanity. 'The Church is the man in Christ, incarnate, sentenced and awakened to new life. In the first instance, therefore, she has essentially nothing whatever to do with the so-called religious functions of man, but with the whole man in his existence in the world and all its implications. What matters in the Church is not religion but the form of Christ, and its taking form amidst a band of men.'[22] Thus, 'It is not Christian men who shape the world with their ideas, but it is Christ who shapes men in conformity with himself.'[23]

5

Secularisms and civility

Modern Western culture, the dominant global culture of our time, is, we are often told, a 'secularized' culture. The term 'secularization' was first used in Europe as a term to describe the legal procedures whereby ecclesiastically owned property was transferred to 'worldly' ownership or use. It has gradually evolved into a description of a process whereby 'religious' beliefs cease to be widely accepted and 'religious institutions' cease to have social, economic or political influence. This process is assumed to be irreversible. It has also been held to be a necessary accompaniment of modernity. Modern institutions displace traditional beliefs and engender a secular (Western) sensibility. The more secular a society, the more irreligious it is.

The evidence, however, does not square with this belief. We have seen how false it is in the case of non-Western societies which have modernized rapidly in recent years. And no-one walking into a bookshop in any Western city or university town can fail to see shelves groaning under the weight of books and magazines on everything from astral channelling to ufology and Zen meditation. Just where 'secularism' seems to be most deeply entrenched, literary critics, physicists and philosophers have started talking again about 'transcendence', 'Spirit' and 'negative theology'. There are over 16,000 new religious movements in Britain, though they represent a relatively small percentage of the population. The extensive European Values Study of 1996 showed that 68% of the population called themselves Christian (but since only three-quarters of these believed in the resurrection, it is doubtful what the rest meant by the term!), and only 4.4% claimed to be committed atheists.[1]

In America, the most secularized of all Western states, religious belief has strengthened down the years. Only 17% of adult Americans belonged to a church when the country broke away from Britain. That rose to 37% by the 1860–65 Civil War, to 50% in the first decade of the twentieth century, and to nearly 70% in the 1990s. Among people born between 1945 and 1954 regular church attendance rose from 33% in 1975 to 41% in 1991.[2] As for the content of religious belief, Robert Wuthnow, a well-known writer on the American religious scene, observes that 'The religion practiced by an increasing number of Americans may be entirely of their own manufacture – a kind of eclectic synthesis of Christianity, popular psychology, *Readers' Digest* folklore and personal superstitions, all wrapped in the anecdotes of the individual's biography.'[3]

Inventing 'religion'

Nicholas Lash of Cambridge University has pointed out that every definition of the 'secular' carries with it 'concomitant *re*definitions of "religion"'.[4] Those who write so glibly about secular society assume that the concept of 'religion' refers today to the same objects as before the process of secularization got under way; namely, to the 'metaphysical', the 'mystical', or the 'supernatural'. But not so. Lash reminds us that words such as 'mysticism' and 'supernatural' were used for the first time as substantive nouns only in seventeenth-century England and France. Prior to that period, 'supernatural', for example, was used either adverbially or adjectivally to refer to an object (or a person) that is enabled to behave in a manner beyond its (or his or her) natural state. So, if you saw a chimpanzee which composed sonnets, that chimp was empowered with a supernatural gifting, and was performing supernaturally. Similarly, normally self-centred human beings are enabled by divine grace towards supernatural works of generosity, sacrifice and kindness.

On this understanding, it is only God to whom the term 'supernatural' could *never* be applied. For who or what can elevate the nature of divinity? For God to show kindness and to act truthfully is precisely *not* to act 'supernaturally'.

> In the seventeenth century, for the first time, 'supernatural', the substantive, began to connote a realm of being, a territory of existence, 'outside' the world we know. With 'nature' now deemed single, homogeneous and self-contained, we labelled 'supernatural' that 'other' world inhabited (some said) by ghosts and poltergeists, by demons,

angels, and suchlike extraterrestrials – and by God ... By the end of the seventeenth century, 'believing in God', which, for Augustine and Aquinas, had been a matter of setting as our heart's desire the holy mystery disclosed in Christ towards whose blinding presence we walk in company on pilgrimage, had become a matter of supposing that there is, outside the world we know, a large and powerful entity called 'God'.[5]

'Religion', too, is hardly a biblical word. For the biblical writers, all that men and women do, in every sphere of life, whether it be dubbed 'religious' or 'secular', is expressive of their response to their Creator, who is the Source, the Judge and the Goal of all existence. Conversion, as we have seen, is the re-orientation to God in Christ of all that has claimed for itself an illusory autonomy and so lost its proper direction. Similarly, neither the Indian languages nor the Chinese have a term corresponding to the modern Western concept of 'religion'.

In the medieval period of European history, the term 'religion' is used very infrequently. As an adjective, 'religious' identifies those who belong to a monastic order, as distinguished from lay Christians, or 'secular' clergy. Wilfred Cantwell Smith has reminded us that, during this period, often described by non-Christian writers as the 'most religious' period of Christian history, no-one 'ever thought to write a book specifically on "religion"'.[6] In fact he suggests that the rise of the concept 'religion' is in some ways linked to a decline in the practice of religion itself.[7] Thomas Aquinas devotes only one question of his massive *Summa Theologiae* to *religio*. This names a virtue which directs a person to God. Religion refers specifically to the liturgical practices of the church. According to Aquinas, 'The word religion is usually used to signify the activity by which man gives the proper reverence to God through actions which specifically pertain to divine worship, such as sacrifice, oblations, and the like.' As a virtue, *religio* is a habit, and virtuous persons are embedded in communal disciplines of body and soul that give their lives direction towards the good.

Thus the rise of the modern concept of religion is associated with the decline of the church as the particular locus of the communal practice of *religio*, and the rise of the modern state. *Religio* turns from being a virtue into a system of propositions to which individuals choose to give assent. This process leads in the eighteenth century to the 'genus and species' approach to handling religious diversity: there is one essential, universal religion which is accessible to all rational human beings, and the multiplicity of creeds and sects are culturally distorted branches of that one religion.

In the modern liberal state, there arose a strict division between the 'secular' and 'religious' realms, whose boundaries blended neatly with that between the 'public' and the 'private'. Now what is significant is not so much the privatization of religion, but the denial that religion is to be associated with truth. Religious beliefs and practices are to be treated as we do art and music, that is as expressions of the Beautiful. Occasionally they may be regarded as contributing to the Good, especially where they inculcate the moral sensibility required to foster respect for law and order and raise support for the nation-building projects of the state. Yet they can never be regarded as speaking matters of Truth in the public square. The public square is ruled by the rationality of science – cool, neutral and universal.

We have seen that this was the view of the world's progress that shaped some of the framers of the post-Independence Indian Constitution, most notably Nehru and others who had had a liberal humanist education. In an influential essay written before the rise to power of the Hindu nationalists, T. N. Madan, an eminent Indian social scientist, trenchantly argued that this notion of secularism has been a failure in India. For Professor Madan, secularism as an ideology emerged from the 'dialectic of modern science and Protestantism' in Europe. He observes: 'Models of modernization ... prescribe the transfer of secularism to non-Western societies without regard for the character of their religious traditions or for the gifts that these might have to offer.'[8] Madan believes that 'secularism in South Asia as a generally shared credo of life is *impossible*, as a basis for state action *impracticable*, and as a blueprint for the foreseeable future *impotent*.'[9]

It is impossible as a credo of life because the great majority of the people of South Asia understand themselves to be followers of some religious faith. 'Secularism is the dream of a minority which wants to shape the majority in its own image, which wants to impose its will upon history but lacks the power to do so under a democratically organized policy.'[10] Madan claims that the privatization of religion is an option only for Protestant Christians. He characterizes all of South Asia's major religions as being both 'totalizing' and 'hierarchical'. By 'totalizing' he means that they claim 'all of a follower's life, so that religion is constitutive of society'. They are hierarchical in the sense that the sacred or moral domain encompasses the secular or temporal power. The indices of this are the valuation of the world renouncer *(bhikku)* as superior to the world conqueror *(chakkavarti)* in Buddhism; the holy book *(Granth Sahab)* being placed at a higher level than the sacred sword in every Sikh *gurudwara*; and, in Hinduism, *dharma* being valued as superior to and encompassing *artha* (the pursuit of political and economic ends).

For Madan, secularism is impracticable because the stance of religious neutrality is 'difficult to maintain since religious minorities do not share the majority's view of what this entails for the state'. And it is impotent as a blueprint for the future because 'by its very nature it is incapable of countering religious fundamentalisms and fanaticism'. More fundamentally, a secularism that is unable to empathize with the religious faiths of the people only provokes reaction. 'In truth it is the marginalization of religious faith, which is what secularization is, that permits the perversion of religion.'[11]

Madan ends his essay on a poignant note by confessing his inability to offer any political alternatives to secularism. He cites Ashis Nandy's own perplexity in the face of the rising tide of Hindu nationalism: 'There is now a peculiar double-bind in Indian politics: the ills of religion have found political expression but the strengths of it have not been available for checking corruption and violence in public life.'[12]

It is indeed ironic that Madan should speak disparagingly of Protestant Christianity as representing the privatization of religion when, as we have seen in chapter 2, both modern Indian society and the Hindu reform movements owe a deep debt to Protestant missions. But we have also seen that this is a blind spot widespread among Indian intellectuals of both secularist and Hindu persuasions. Madan's misunderstanding of Protestant Christianity is also shared by most Muslim writers and several non-Christian social scientists in the West. However, the godly magistrate who would administer the laws of God was as much a sixteenth-century Reformation ideal as it was in the medieval age. Indeed, most of the Reformers took over, almost unchanged, the medieval conception of the religious state. Luther's 'two-kingdom' ethic, while separating the realms of temporal, 'worldly' society (Latin *saeculum*) and the church as the body of Christ, nevertheless affirmed the Christian's responsibility towards both and God's sovereignty over both.

The more radical Reformers and the later English Puritans insisted on a strict institutional separation of church and state, but that separation was not intended to mean that Christian faith was no longer to be applied to the life of society. The institutional separation of powers must be maintained precisely in order that the church may not be corrupted and distracted from its vocation by the exercise of coercive power, and so that the state may be held accountable to divine judgment and prevented from encroachment upon other social institutions.

For the first few centuries, Christians in the West were an oppressed and politically powerless minority. Christians in Asia, beginning with the first-century Syrians and Persians right through to the vast majority today, continue in that position. Many of the pioneers in the development of ideas of civil liberty and human rights in Britain and America were Christian dissidents who themselves had experienced persecution at the hands of an 'establishment religion'. As the Frenchman Alexis de Tocqueville found out to his great surprise on his visit to the United States in 1836, it was a people animated by a robust Christian faith that had made possible both the separation of church and state and a religious orientation to the social order. Thus the church possesses a unique perspective on the totalitarian tendencies of the state, more so perhaps than do the majority of Hindus, Muslims and Buddhists. To fail to listen to this history would be foolish, if not arrogant.

In the interests of clarity, perhaps we need to distinguish the different senses in which 'secularism' makes its claims in the modern world. There is the secularism which Madan rightly calls an 'ideology', which actively seeks to promote as a social good the 'secularization' of life, and is defined as 'The process whereby religious institutions become less powerful in a society and religious beliefs less easily accepted'.[13] This is a secularism that, until relatively recently, has been identified as inseparable from the project of modernity and the triumph of scientific rationality.

There is also a secularism which, while not being hostile to religious truth-claims and often welcoming of religious cultures, nevertheless promotes a practical, rather than theoretical, atheism. Belief in God, at the end of the day, is irrelevant to the daily affairs of the *polis*. In areas of economics, science, politics, business, law and suchlike, 'God' and other so-called 'traditional religious beliefs' are redundant, whether as explanations, as guides or as sources of empowerment. Such secularists may well be nominal adherents of traditional faiths, and may be seen in a church building on a Sunday or in a mosque on a Friday. The committed Christian or Muslim, of course, would doubt whether such a person has any inkling of what belief in 'God' means.

Although conceptually distinct, both these versions of secular sensibility are, for practical purposes, identical. They dominate the discourse of modern Western academia and that of non-Western intellectuals who have had their professional training in the West. It is often what prompts a critical response on the part of more thoughtful Christians, Muslims, Buddhists, Hindus and others, who rightly suspect that what is often put forward as a 'reasonable', 'scientific' or 'neutral' stance on public issues is ideologically loaded. It is itself a particular worldview, shaped by a context-specific tradition of discourse (namely, that of the seventeenth- and eighteenth-century *salons* of Western Europe) which has become globally hegemonic.

However, there is another use of 'secularism' which need not carry such hegemonic associations. This is a strictly political use of the term, and refers to the attempt on the part of the state to deal impartially with all religious communities that constitute the *polis*. This is an issue that is particularly important in pluralist societies such as in South Asia, and has generated much discussion since the mid-twentieth century. Perhaps we should call this 'constitutional secularism', and distinguish it from the social or cultural secularism described above, though these terms are, admittedly, ill-defined.

In America, debates about secularism revolve around moral issues such as abortion, or more narrowly Christian concerns such as the place of prayer and biblical instruction in state-funded schools, or the provision of state support for private denominational colleges. Such debates centre on the interpretation of the 'establishment of religion' clause in the United States Constitution, which declares that government shall neither prescribe nor proscribe religion.

Discussions about secularism in the Indian context are coloured by the bloody experience of Partition and the post-Partition riots that have left their scars on Indian society. The challenge to forge one united nation out of a diversity of religious traditions, cultures and regional languages brought the question of secularism to the fore, as did the concern of Nehru and others that the Hindu majority should respect the sensibilities of the large Muslim minority left in the country after Partition. In the 1950 Constitution, the Constituent Assembly implied, but did not actually inscribe, that India should be a secular state. The word 'secular' was, however, consciously inserted into the preamble of the Constitution in 1976.

There were, however, many ambiguities in the Constitution, and inconsistencies in its implementation; and the failure of the Indian governments of the 1950s and 1960s to deal with such ambiguities and inconsistencies contributed to what many have called the 'crisis of secularism' in India today. Nehru and other Congress liberals probably avoided an 'establishment' clause similar to that in the US Constitution because they saw the role of the state as the primary engine of social progress. The state had therefore to legislate against the Hindu caste system and other 'non-egalitarian' practices such as denial of temple-entry to *Dalits* or the early marriage of female children. At the same time, the Congress-dominated Parliament was hesitant to antagonize the Muslim population by ruling against 'undemocratic' or 'non-egalitarian' practices on their part. We have seen how this incongruity, which erupted in the celebrated Shah Bano case of 1985, gave ammunition to the militant Hindu voices in Indian society.

The Shah Bano case raised an important issue for India and all other polities made up of plural cultural communities of long standing. Is it necessary to have a uniform civil code that applies to all citizens of the country, or should the customary 'personal laws' of different communities be permitted to flourish? And, if different systems of personal laws are recognized as legitimate, how do we deal with the case when they conflict with provisions that are regarded as fundamental rights applicable to all citizens? For example, the fundamental rights recognized in the Indian Constitution, and to which all laws must be subject, include equal protection of the law for all citizens and non-discrimination of persons on the basis of race, caste, sex, religious affiliation, place of birth, etc.

Unlike the US Constitution, Article 30 of the Indian Constitution gives educational institutions run by religious groups the right to receive grants from the state. This raises unresolved questions about the status of India's secularism. Does this, for instance, signify mandatory state subsidies for all religious institutions? Does that therefore discriminate unfairly against bodies that do not claim any religious affiliation? Also, how does that relate to another Article (Art. 25) which, while recognizing religious freedom, subjects it not only to fundamental rights but also to the state's authority to regulate or restrict any financial, political or secular activity associated with religious practice? Is financial help from the state a way of controlling religious instruction? And, even more fundamentally, how can we realistically separate financial or political and other so-called 'secular' aspects from the so-called 'religious' aspects of any movement that seeks to propagate its faith and make its contribution to national life?

These are issues to which we shall return shortly. It has often been taken for granted, both by much mainstream Western political writing over the last two hundred years and by many among the first generation of post-colonial leaders in the Third World, that constitutional secularism is inseparable from social and cultural secularism – indeed, that the former both requires and promotes the latter. This is why the modern liberal state has received a severe battering since the mid-1970s by a wide and unrelated assortment of critics around the world – 'communitarians', 'public theologians' and 'civic republicans' in America, and movements of 'religious nationalism' elsewhere.

Secularist myths

We have seen that the spread of modernization, far from encouraging religious scepticism, has spawned new religious movements and revitalized many old ones. But the more dangerous myths that need to be exposed have to do with the self-images of the modern secular nation-state. Three such myths have received considerable attention in recent political and theological thought. They overlap and intertwine with each other, but I shall attempt to separate them out for the sake of clarity in exposition.

The myth of the benign peacemaker

This is the legitimizing narrative of modern liberalism, and could also be called its 'myth of origins'. Religious faiths are inevitably confrontational and prone to violent conflict, we are told, and the only way we can ensure a peaceful social order is to keep them out of the public square. Entry to the latter requires acceptance of the modern secularized state as peacemaker, that which takes up and reconciles the conflicts and contradictions in society. The so-called 'Wars of Religion' of sixteenth- and seventeenth-century Europe, following in the wake of the Protestant Reformation, are usually evoked as the founding moment of the modern secular state. Jeffrey Stout, for example, repeats the familiar litany: 'Liberal principles were the right ones to adopt when competing religious beliefs and divergent conceptions of the good embroiled Europe in the religious wars ... Our early modern ancestors were right to secularize public discourse in the interest of minimizing the ill effects of religious disagreement.'[14]

This is a gross and dangerous over-simplification of history, similar to the way Samuel Huntington's account of timeless civilizational conflicts serves to hide from view the underlying realities of the power struggle in the global theatre which began to develop in the late twentieth century. The so-called 'Wars of Religion', as William Cavanaugh has pointed out, 'were not the events which necessitated the birth of the modern State; they were in fact themselves *the birthpangs of the State*. These wars were not simply a matter of conflict between "Protestantism" and "Catholicism", but were fought largely for the aggrandizement of the emerging State over the decaying remnants of the medieval ecclesiastical order.'[15]

This argument goes much deeper than merely questioning the sincerity of the religious convictions of the warring factions.

> What is at issue behind these wars is the creation of 'religion' as a set of beliefs which is defined as personal conviction and which can exist separately from one's loyalty to the State. The creation of religion, and thus the privatization of the Church, is correlative to the rise of the State. It is important therefore to see that the principal promoters of the wars in France and Germany were in fact not pastors and peasants, but kings and nobles with a stake in the outcome of the movement toward the centralized, hegemonic state.[16]

While it is beyond my competence, as well as beyond the scope of this chapter, to chronicle the story of the European 'Wars of Religion', it may be useful to summarize a few of the examples that Cavanaugh himself gives to illustrate his argument.

(a) The Catholic princes of Germany, the Catholic Habsburgs of Spain and the Catholic Valois of France had all extracted concessions from the Pope well before the Reformation was under way, and these considerably increased their control over the church within their realms. Charles V, Holy Roman Emperor, attacked Rome, not any Protestant city, in 1527. When he eventually turned his attention to the Protestants in 1547, igniting the first major War of Religion, his assault on the Lutheran states was an attempt to consolidate Imperial authority rather than an expression of doctrinal zealotry. When in 1552–53 the Lutheran princes (aided by the French Catholic King Henry II) defeated the Imperial forces, the German Catholic princes refused to intervene.

(b) The rise of a centralized bureaucratic state in France preceded the French civil wars in the second half of the sixteenth century, and was based on the fifteenth-century assertion of civil dominance over the church in France. The Queen Mother, Catherine de Medici, who unleashed the notorious massacre of Huguenots (Calvinists) on St Bartholomew's day was not a religious zealot but a disciple of Machiavellian statecraft, anxious to forestall the Huguenot nobility's increasing influence and consequent challenge to the absolutization of royal power. After 1576, when Catholic and Huguenot nobles together rose up in rebellion against King Henry III, it was impossible to distinguish Catholic from Protestant in the French civil wars. At issue in these wars was not simply Catholic versus Calvinist, transubstantiation versus spiritual presence. It was about royal pretensions to absolute power.

(c) Likewise, in the Thirty Years War (1618–48), the cruellest of the so-called 'Wars of Religion', ecclesiastical loyalties were not easy to sort out. The war was prompted by Emperor Ferdinand II's ambition to consolidate his patchwork empire into a modern state, ruled by one sovereign, uncontested authority. France's interest lay in keeping Ferdinand's Habsburg empire fragmented, and France's interest superseded that of the French church. The last thirteen years of the war – the bloodiest – were essentially a struggle between the Habsburgs and the Bourbons, the two great Catholic dynasties of Europe.

Cavanaugh does not argue that no Christian ever butchered another over zealously held beliefs. What he does show is how the dominance of the state over the church in the sixteenth and seventeenth centuries allowed temporal rulers to direct doctrinal conflicts to secular ends. 'The new State required unchallenged authority within its borders, and so the domestication of the Church. Church leaders became acolytes of the State as the religion of the State replaced that of the Church, or more accurately, the very concept of religion as separable from the Church was invented.'[17]

Anthony Giddens, in his monumental study on the modern nation-state, has shown how the scope of modern warfare has been greatly enlarged by the rise of the modern nation-state.[18] The territories of medieval rulers were often porous and ill-defined, and residents of a territory might owe varying allegiances to several different nobles, and only nominal allegiance to a distant king. The emergence of the nation-state saw territorial frontiers now transformed into borders, lines demarcating an exclusive domain of centralized, sovereign power. The state now claimed a monopoly on the legitimate means of violence. Ultimate loyalty was transferred to the sovereign state. Politics in the nation-state system had become a matter of protecting, consolidating and enlarging borders, all of which necessitated the eventual creation of large standing armies.

Far from ending violent strife, the modern nation-state and its ideology of secular nationalism has been the biggest single cause of warfare over the past two hundred years. By claiming the ultimate loyalty of its citizens, the essentially religious character of the modern state is revealed. The state now becomes the sole sanction for violence. Martyrdom is redefined as laying down one's life for one's nation. Blasphemy, the worst sin in a religous milieu, has been transformed into treason. The nation-state offers protection from violence, both internal and external, in exchange for the willingness to kill other human beings on its behalf. Usually the threats from which the state offers protection are the results of its own activities. It demands access to our bodies, and our money to fuel its war-making machinery.

Both religious and secular nationalisms provide an overarching moral framework, locating the individual in a larger collectivity. For secular nationalism, emotional identification with the geographical area of one's birth and the people of that locality is not only natural but is assumed to be a universal moral good. This affective dimension to nationalism is nurtured by religious myths and rituals. For example, mythic stories of the nation's past glories and historical exemplars of true patriotism; the composition of a national anthem as the collective hymn to the nation; the hoisting of a national flag and the collective chanting of the national anthem at all civic occasions. Despite all the contemporary mantra of globalization among liberal economists, the great bulk of the wealth created by transnational corporations remains within their originating nation-states; and the directors who reap the huge profits of a corporation's transnational operations all carry the same passports.[19]

In the twentieth century, Lenin, Mao Zedong and Ataturk were notorious for the savage ruthlessness with which they transformed ancient, religious societies into modern, secular nation-states. While not as brutal as Lenin and Mao, Ataturk's strong-arm methods were not practised in response to internal religious conflicts. He sought to modernize institutions that were no longer able to compete with the economic and political power of the West and of Russia. For Ataturk, modernization meant Westernization. He abolished the caliphate in 1923, and followed it up by romanizing the Turkish script and banning traditional Turkish dress. A radically secularized state could be maintained only at the expense of democracy by excluding the convictions and habits of the people from everything defined as 'public'. He decreed, and by military power imposed, a naked public square. What is ironic is to find Western liberal states supporting the secularist fanaticism of a state in which democratic opinion has been sidelined, while vociferously denouncing religious fanaticism elsewhere.

The cruelties perpetrated by religious conflicts in Western history pale into relative insignificance when compared with the global suffering unleashed by liberal Western nation-states in the twentieth-century alone. Just one example will suffice. Recently declassified official documents from the period of the Vietnam War reveal the full extent of American terrorism in southeast Asia. The US invaded a neutral country, Cambodia, in 1970, and in one six-month period in 1973 American B-52 bombers dropped more bombs on that country than were rained on Japan during the whole of the Second World War. Between 1969 and 1973 US bombers killed an estimated 750,000 Cambodian peasants in an attempt to destroy North Vietnamese supply lines, many of which did not exist. It was these atrocities that paved the way for the rise of Pol Pot and the Khmer Rouge, a small band of extreme nationalists with Maoist pretensions. What the Americans began in Cambodia, the Khmer Rouge completed. For most of the 1980s the US was secretly funding Pol Pot forces in exile in Thailand. Neither any Western government nor any liberal academic philosopher has so far called for the US leadership at the time to be brought before a war-crimes tribunal and charged with crimes against humanity.[20]

The myth of the empty shrine

The term was coined by the contemporary American writer Michael Novak, but the concept goes back to early political liberalism. In a truly pluralistic society, there can be no one public purpose, no overarching structure of significance applicable to all. We have a multiplicity of ends and meanings, plural conceptions of what constitutes human flourishing. The secular, liberal state enables all such narratives to prosper, while remaining attached to none.

Novak writes that 'At the spiritual core' of such a society:

> ... there is an empty shrine. That shrine is left empty in the knowledge that no one word, image, or symbol is worthy of what all seek there. Its emptiness, therefore, represents the transcendence which is approached by free consciences from a virtually infinite number of directions ... Believer and unbeliever, selfless and selfish, frightened and bold, naive and jaded, all participate in an order whose *centre* is not socially imposed.[21]

Is this contradicted by the widespread use of 'God' on US dollar bills and in American political rhetoric? In Novak's vision, 'In God we trust' is a statement whose meaning is left to each individual to define. 'God' has no content, it is a cypher pointing to an unnameable transcendence. Such transcendence inspires faith in progress and continual reform. It invites 'more' of whatever an individual sets his or her heart on, provided that such an individual recognizes that such desires may not be fulfilled within the present limits of what Novak calls 'worldly power'.

> Is not God at the centre? For those who so experience reality, yes. For atheists, no. Official religious expressions ... have a pluralistic content. No institution, group, or person in the United States is entitled to define for others the content signified by words like 'God', the 'Almighty' and 'Creator'. These words are like pointers, which each person must define for himself ... Such symbols are not quite blank; one may not fill them in with any content at all. They point beyond worldly power. Doing so, they guard the human openness to transcendence.[22]

The 'empty shrine' of pluralism is simply a restatement of eighteenth-century 'natural religion' with its aversion to particular convictions, to specific narratives of human hope. For Novak, what lies between the 'now' of struggle and the 'beyond' of unspecifiable transcendence is the 'wasteland of democratic capitalism'. This is 'like a field of battle, on which individuals wander alone, in some confusion, amid many casualties. Nonetheless like the dark night of the soul in the inner journey of the mystics this desert has an indispensable purpose ... It is swept clean out of reverence for the transcendent.'[23]

Note the way that specific religious terminology and imagery enters through the back door. The shrine, after all, is not empty. It only *looks* empty because, in the process of 'secularization', the traditional 'religious' stories that people told each other have now been lumped together in the margins. But the way Novak tells it, 'democratic capitalism', like 'secularization', enacts a tale, performs a master narrative. It functions as a traditional religious mythology, an explanation of *why the world is as it is*. In the new mythology, the public world is made up not of sinful human agents, but of impersonal, rational forces which we try to understand and control. In the outworking of these forces, some end up as winners and others as losers. That's simply how the world is. There is no point in assigning blame to anyone. If the poor are poor, that's how the 'system' functions. It is all very rational and orderly. Let us not upset it with utopian dreams, whether of 'the kingdom of God', or of 'socialism'. This, then, is the modern Western equivalent of ancient Eastern doctrines of *karma*. Or, to change the metaphor, the losers on the margins of society are the sacrificial victims we offer to the new gods who have taken over the public shrine.

It is dangerous for Christians to fall for the 'empty shrine' myth. The temples of modern secular society are not primarily to be found on the peripheries, among the new religious movements. Secular narratives mask the essentially religious character of the foundational beliefs and public practices of modern institutions. Banks, stock exchanges, and corporation boardrooms are hallowed ground on which ardent acolytes perform their daily liturgies in honour of the god of 'market forces'. Government bureaucracies, the military, and secondary schools are sacred establishments devoted to nurturing the pure worship of the 'nation-state'. Rituals of obeisance are enacted daily on our TV screens in the cults of hedonism and consumerism. The billion-dollar cosmetics, fashion and entertainment industries combine to lure the young to prostrate themselves at the feet of the latest icons of beauty and 'style'.

Deep in every human heart lies a propensity for worship. And if men and women do not worship their Creator, they end up worshipping the creature, in the form of an idea, an artefact, an institution, a feeling, or an individual. Just as nature abhors a vacuum, social shrines do not remain empty for long. The displacement of the biblical God from the realm of truth 'merely unleashes the horsemen of the Apocalypse, leaves our propensity for idolatry unchecked and unconstrained, with devastating consequences'.[24]

Those who insist that the public square be untouched by any particular moral or spiritual vision are those who have themselves seized the commanding heights of the square and will not tolerate anything that stands in the way of their political domination. The pluralism of goods that liberal, secular societies protect exists only at the private level. In the public square, the liberal state defends and imposes a particular set of goods (for instance, a free-market economy, unlimited technological progress, national sovereignty), on behalf of which wars are fought with other states.

Communitarian critics of liberalism have pointed out that the liberal state promotes a particular understanding of individual autonomy which presupposes a particular (and impoverished) theory of human nature, which, far from commanding universal assent, is itself one tradition among other rival traditions in Western history. Civic republicans have pointed to the absurdity of supposing that the good life is a private affair, while the business of enabling the good life is the stuff of politics. To divorce ethics from politics in this way is to destroy the latter. There can be no 'private virtues' or a conception of the good life which is mine alone. To exercise virtue, to realize my capacities and powers as a self-determining being, involves my participation with others in the *polis*.

Similarly, socialist critics point to the one-sidedness of the liberal vision of the good. Thus Terry Eagleton, Professor of English at Oxford University, notes:

> What is wrong with the disinterestedness of the liberal state is not that it speciously masks some interest, but that it quite explicitly enshrines one: the all-important interest of individual choice. It is not flawed because it has a notion of the good which it furtively conceals, but because it has a drastically one-sided idea of the good to which other goods are unduly subordinated.[25]

This is to charge with incoherence the liberal concept of the state. Following Charles Taylor, Eagleton argues that to assign a right implies that the 'capacity protected by that right should be positively nurtured'. It would be 'odd to single out some need or capacity in this way and then be blithely indifferent as to whether it flourished or not. But this in turn implies fostering, through our political participation, the kind of social order which would allow this to happen, which might then be taken as challenging the liberal assumption of the primacy of political rights.'[26]

The myth of Archimedean autonomy

Archimedes was the ancient Greek experimenter who is famous for discovering the principle of buoyancy while climbing into his bath-tub one day. He is also known for his discovery of the principle of the lever, and boasted that he could move the universe itself if given a long stick and a place completely outside the universe.

The idea of a 'place completely outside the universe' seems to haunt some versions of secular liberalism. The quest is for a set of political beliefs that are sufficiently abstract and universal to be able to stand alone, free of any embedding in a particular social narrative. It is commonly asserted that democracy, human rights, and individual human freedom and equality qualify in this respect and must, therefore, command universal assent.

However, anyone familiar with the history of European and American thought knows that this is false. The doctrine of 'human rights' emerges from a particular theological narrative, rooted in the biblical notion of humanity made in the image of God and further developed by Aquinas and Puritan writers. As the Polish philosopher Leszek Kolakowski observes:

> There is no substantial difference between proclaiming 'the right to life' and stating that natural law forbids killing. Much as the concept may have been elaborated in the philosophy of the Enlightenment in its conflict with Christianity, the notion of the immutable rights of individuals goes back to the Christian belief in the autonomous status and irreplaceable value of the human personality.[27]

Similarly, Michael Perry, an American law professor, has recently argued that the idea of human rights is 'ineliminably religious – that there is, finally, no intelligible secular version of the idea of human rights, that the conviction that human beings are sacred is inescapably religious'.[28] He points out, however, that this is not to deny that many who do take human rights very seriously are agnostics and atheists where religious convictions are concerned. But it does raise serious doubts whether a vision of human rights can be both argued for coherently and sustained effectively in societies which lack an appropriate religious understanding of the human person. In this regard Perry quotes Jeffrie Murphy who, while insisting that he finds it 'very difficult – perhaps impossible – to embrace religious convictions', none the less claims that 'the liberal theory of rights requires a doctrine of human dignity, preciousness and sacredness that cannot be utterly detached from a belief in God or at least from a world view that would be properly called religious in some metaphysically profound sense'. Murphy continues: 'The idea that fundamental moral values may require [religious] convictions is not one to be welcomed with joy [by non-religious enthusiasts of the liberal theory of rights]. This idea generates tensions and appears to force choices that some of us would prefer not to make. *But it might be true for all that.*'[29]

A historical digression may serve to underline the value of these observations. Alexis de Tocqueville was a young French aristocrat who was sent by his government in 1831 to investigate the working of prisons in

America. Tocqueville wrote his report on the prison system, but his imagination was seized by the grander subject of how democracy in America worked. He was impressed by the stability of democracy in America compared to its precariousness in France. So he travelled extensively across the continent over a seventh-month period, making copious notes and interviewing scores of people. The burning question that guided his research was: why had the French Revolution led to the Terror and the rise of Napoleon, while the American Revolution had led peacefully to constitutional democracy? Out of his study emerged a political masterpiece, *Democracy in America*.

Tocqueville perceived that democracy, revolution and republicanism in America could not be understood simply as secular movements. It was not democracy that paved the way for the freedom of worship, but freedom of worship that made democracy possible. 'Religion in America takes no direct part in the government of society, but it must be regarded as the first of their political institutions.'[30] The love of liberty, and a general social and economic equality, had been nurtured in the small townships and congregations of New England ever since the first Puritan settlements there in the early sixteenth century. Then, when the War of Independence broke out, 'the doctrine of the sovereignty of the people came out of the townships and took possession of the state'.[31] Tocqueville also wrote: 'Liberty regards religion as its companion in all its battles and its triumphs, as the cradle of its infancy and the divine source of its claims. It considers religion as the safeguard of morality, and morality as the best security of law and the surest pledge of the duration of freedom.'[32]

Tocqueville realized that the citizens of the United States (whom he refers to as the 'Anglo-American people'), though divided among twenty-four sovereignties, were far less diverse in outlook than their contemporaries in Europe who may live under one sovereign and a single legislative code. For him the *customs* of a nation were more important than geographical situation, or even a body of protective law, in nurturing and sustaining a love for freedom. He uses the word 'customs' to refer not merely to the collective manners of a people, but 'to the various notions and opinions current among men and to the mass of those ideas which constitute their character of mind. I comprise under this term, therefore, the whole moral and intellectual condition of the people.'[33]

I am convinced that the most advantageous situation and the best possible laws cannot maintain a constitution in spite of the customs of a country while the latter may turn to some advantage the most unfavourable position and the worst laws. The importance of custom is a common truth to which study and experience necessarily direct our attention ... So seriously do I insist upon this head that, if I hitherto failed in making the reader feel the important influence of the practical experience, the habits, the opinions, in short, of the customs of the Americans upon the maintenance of their institutions, I have failed in the principal object of my work.[34]

Tocqueville also warned that, where material inequalities widened, liberty would be jeopardized. The rise of a 'mercantile aristocracy' and the decline of a religious sensibility would alike spell the erosion of popular sovereignty: 'Habits are formed in the heart of a free country which may someday prove fatal to its liberties.'[35]

Thus, the moral cohesion of a political community cannot rest on the force of law alone, and the health of any community will finally depend on the moral character of its individual citizens. Democracy does not arise in a vacuum. It requires disciplined citizens if it is to thrive; citizens nurtured in a culture that prizes not only the love of freedom but voluntary self-restraint. Contemporary studies by the sociologist Robert Bellah and his associates seem to indicate that where people are too preoccupied with the cult of self-gratification and private consumption, not only do the bonds of citizenship decay but so does commitment to any social project.[36]

In his biography of the famous economist John Maynard Keynes, Lord Skidelsky notes that Keynes was acutely aware of how much the economy depended on the moral capital that religious beliefs conferred. He quotes him as saying, 'I begin to see that our generation ... owed a great deal to our fathers' religion. And the young ... who are brought up without it will never get much out of life. They're trivial: like dogs in their lusts. We had the best of both worlds. We destroyed Christianity and yet had its benefits.'[37]

Civility and the common good

If, then, there is no Archimedean vantage-point from which an independent secularist ethic can be formulated, and if the aim of a public square from which all particular religious confessions have been excluded is not only ill-conceived but unlikely to make headway in much of the non-Western world (while being subject to growing criticism even in the West), what alternatives do we have for the peaceful coexistence of people of different faiths or ultimate commitments?

The original basis of the American separation seems to have been to keep the federal government from intervening in those states of the Union which had established churches. The goal of political secularism would then be a state which dealt even-handedly with the different religious confessions, to prevent a state which backed one confession rather than another, but not to make religious commitments irrelevant to public life and policy. This aim was subsequently transformed into a situation where the strict exclusion of religion from public affairs became binding on all levels of government. We have seen how the Indian Constitution aims at a secularism that is not hostile to religious claims, but seeks to accommodate them within a framework of mutual respect.

One strategy in this process is to look for common beliefs among the different religious confessions that make up a society. The aim would be to abstract from the various doctrinal and ethical commitments of religious traditions a common foundation that could provide a set of rules for peaceful coexistence. This could take the form of a 'natural law' ethic, as in European tradition from Aquinas onwards, which, while arising from a Christian worldview, none the less could be defended without referring to specific Christian doctrines. Similarly, in an Indian context, it is often stated that a common belief in Infinite Spirit or Supreme Being undergirds individual and social life. This looks suspiciously like the 'empty shrine' dedicated to an unknown – and unnameable – God. It is hard to see how such a nameless deity can provide ethical grounds for life together.

More importantly, this approach flounders as the plurality of ultimate commitments in a society enlarges. For instance, as long as all people in India profess a vague kind of theism, a formulation such as the above may be acceptable as a common ground. But there are many atheists and Theravada Buddhists in India who also need to be made to feel that this is a society to which they belong, and that what they have to contribute is as valued as that of any professing theist. Otherwise, the common ground is going to be perceived as yet another party position by those groups who do not share the common ground.

The litmus test, I suggest, is the actual treatment of minorities in any society. Here I see no alternative to a secular constitution, perhaps one on the model of the Indian one, but without its ambiguities and inconsistencies. The reason for my position is simply that democratic legitimacy requires it. Not that democracy is a sacred cow, but we have not arrived at a better alternative; and any political progress in the foreseeable future will take the form not of throwing out democracy altogether but of making it more true to itself and applicable on a wider scale.

At the heart of democracy is the notion that people must in some sense have a say in the decisions that affect their lives. If any segment of the population feels that its needs and aspirations are not getting an adequate hearing in the public square, and that it is the victim of systematic neglect or discrimination, then the legitimacy of that government is put in question. The only options open to such a group are total physical separation from the nation-state, if that is geographically and economically viable, or to press for a political constitution and legislation that publicly recognize their plight. Of course, constitutions and legislation do not, in themselves, bring about an end to oppression and discrimination, but often they are necessary, albeit not sufficient, conditions for social justice.

Many 'religious nationalists' argue that secular governments are undemocratic in that they do not recognize the demands of the religious majority. This has been a constant theme in the propaganda of the Muslim Brotherhood in Egypt, or of the VHP/BJP in India, or of Sinhala Buddhist organizations in Sri Lanka. But this is a naïve understanding of democracy, which opens the way for the tyranny of the majority. Given the history of many of these movements in recent times, minority groups belonging to other persuasions are rightly suspicious.

Is it not possible – and here I can only be tentative and cautious, for far better minds than mine have grappled with these vexed issues – to envisage a *plurality of secularisms* emerging around the world, each specific to its historical, cultural and political context? What this would involve is not a 'top-down' secularism imposed on society by a Western-educated élite, but a more 'grass-roots' secularism that emerges through negotiation, dialogue and compromise among all the communities that comprise a given polity.

What could emerge from such an enterprise could be a context-specific charter of rights and duties, designed to protect the integrity and freedoms of human persons. Christians in such a dialogue would want to safeguard such things as the right to life, which would include protection for the unborn and the disabled, protection from arbitrary arrest and punishment, and a commitment to satisfying the basic needs of all citizens; also freedom of conscience, association and conversion; and an independent judiciary.

There is nothing in this list of Christian concerns that cannot be accepted by many adherents of the major world faiths. We have seen that the major faiths are not static, monolithic entities, but are dynamic and complex wholes which often include many different traditions and schools of thought within their ambit. The 'right to life', for example, would be defended from within a Buddhist tradition in terms of the doctrine of *ahimsa* or non-violence towards all sentient beings; and in Christian tradition in terms of the image of God that all human beings embody.

The Christian strategy in this dialogue would be to appeal to reasons *internal* to the faith traditions of other communities, and not only explicitly Christian arguments, to press for legislation and public policy that Christians believe would enhance human flourishing. Would it not be possible, say, for Christians to encourage Islamists to see that traditional interpretations of *shar'ia* are not as consistent with Qur'anic teaching as they are assumed to be? Or to help Buddhists in Sri Lanka to see that any religion that requires state patronage for its survival loses its moral authority and becomes vulnerable to corruption?

What about 'hate-speech', intended to incite hatred towards persons of a particular social, religious or cultural background? In societies with a history of such violent conflict, legal prohibitions against such speech may be agreed upon by all traditions as being in the interests of social harmony. For Western liberals to complain that this is intolerance is itself an act of cultural intolerance. Tolerance can never be an end in itself, but must be a means to approximating the good society. Political freedom is not just the absence of limitations; it is freedom to do the good. The fact that coercion may be necessary for such work does not deny the basis of democratic polity. Even the most liberal of societies has to draw limits. There are some things that we simply do not tolerate: racism, slavery, rape, paedophilia, etc. We even have libel laws to prevent character assassination.

For Christians, politics can never be simply a matter of balancing individual or group interests. We are not individuals who come to the social order to get what we can from it, but rather, to be fully individuals, we must be socially constituted. The common good is not simply the sum of individual or group interests, but it is genuinely a good that is common. It cannot be abstractly determined, however, but needs to be worked out through public debate and negotiation within the contingencies of each society's historical circumstances. There is an inescapable 'contextual' dimension to any genuine understanding of the common good.

In such a scenario, the state would refuse to identify itself with any particular religious identity, and not permit any religious group to manipulate the state apparatus for its own chauvinistic ends. But, unlike in most Western secular democracies, the state would also actively encourage public dialogue and debate among the various faith-traditions, and also seek their views on matters of state policy. If open intellectual persuasion is not fostered as a positive virtue in society, then coercion and manipulation result.

This may sound an idealistic situation. I am, of course, aware that profound obstacles stand in its path. One of the problems we have seen from the Indian situation is the tendency for the secular state to listen (and pander) to the more strident voices in a given religious or ethnic community. Thus, in the

Shah Bano case, for example, the protests of many Muslim women were ignored in favour of the more militant mullahs. The state would have to pay close attention to the multiple voices within even the most seemingly unified communities if it is to carry legitimacy.

I am also aware that neither a political ethic nor any charter of rights is self-interpreting. The same schedule of rights may be understood somewhat differently when read from within different background beliefs. In a strongly diversified society, with a wide range of worldviews and ultimate commitments, the most we can hope to share may be the same principles of social harmony but without the underlying reasons or background justifications.

This suggestion is very similar to John Rawls's celebrated notion of an 'overlapping consensus',[38] but it does not require that we accept Rawls's concept of justice as fairness, or his theory of how we get there. The basic idea behind an 'overlapping consensus' is that people can come to agree on a set of working principles (a 'thin' consensus) while they may disagree profoundly on the reasons for doing so (or, to use Rawls's language, they have different 'comprehensive theories of the good'). People can 'sign up' to the consensus, so to speak, from differing starting-points. Rawls believes not only that a limited consensus of this sort is possible in a pluralist society, but also that it leads to a more stable social unity than would be obtained on the basis of traditional liberal scepticism, indifference, or a prudent *modus vivendi*.

Thus, in a democratic and pluralist society, social convergence is sought around a set of politico-ethical guides for action in the public square. But, unlike the post-Enlightenment myth of a universally acceptable foundation which lies over and above the particular religious narratives of society, it is openly acknowledged that no such common foundation exists. Nor can it be expected without the danger of tending towards tyranny.

Separating the ethic from its embedding in a particular view of the good is, no doubt, problematic, as many critics of Rawls have pointed out, but I think that this provides a model that is worth exploring in different contexts around the world. Instead of focusing on the abstraction of 'thin' universals and neglecting the 'thick' particularities as irrelevant to public life (as Rawls himself tends to do, despite occasional disclaimers), I would stress that public civility is cultivated by fostering genuine debate over the truth-values of particular conceptions of human ends. Moreover, as I have indicated, the 'overlapping consensus' need not be limited to procedures for conflict management, but can also enshrine beliefs about a (context-specific) common good. The important thing, however, is that it must emerge out of actual dialogue and debate, not abstract theorizing.

Conclusion

To summarize, the secularization of modern society has spawned new constructions of 'religion', not only at the margins but at the very centre of social and political life. The alleged neutrality of the 'secular state' raises the question: neutral with regard to what? A state that is 'neutral' with regard to traditional religious loyalties may be ruthlessly active in promoting its own version of religion. Christians rooted in the gospel's narrative of human idolatry are summoned by that same gospel to unmask the religious character of the new 'secular' identities and binding practices of the nation-state, whether liberal or autocratic. At the same time the gospel enables us to promote a mode of political secularism that insists that a people's religious, ethnic or any other affiliation is a matter of indifference where their legal and political rights are concerned.

'Citizenship' is the primary political identity of the modern world. It runs counter to the Christian's primary identity, which is citizenship in another kingdom, one that transcends the divisions of ethnicity and of nation-states. Thus Christians always stand in a position of critical tension vis-à-vis their political identities. They seek to be responsible servants of their *polis*, refusing to claim special privileges for the church or 'rights' that are not truly universal. However, that responsibility is discharged within a wider vision of a new, global humanity. To surrender the social and political dimension of the gospel is to transform the church from being the body of Christ, the sign, pledge and agent of his kingdom, into simply another voluntary association of like-minded individuals. This may be the way the state sees the church, but it can never be the way Christians see it.

This is why, from its beginnings in Roman Asia, the Christian movement has been viewed with suspicion and concern by political authorities. The ideologues of the nation-state at the beginning of the modern period in Europe were equally concerned to trim the sails of Christian globalism. For Thomas Hobbes (1588–1679), it was crucial for the sovereignty of the commonwealth to deny the universal nature of the church and make each member of the church depend, not on fellow members, but directly on the sovereign. The Scriptures were reinterpreted by the sovereign to make resistance to the state impossible, for the church was now reinterpreted as the *civil state*. Christian faith was a matter of pure interiority, shorn of any transnational visions and goals.[39] John Locke (1632–1704), while admirably arguing against the state's coercion of the religious conscience, grounded his argument in the solitary nature of religious judgment: 'All the life and power of true religion consist in the inward and full persuasion of the mind.'[40] This emphasis led him to deny explicitly the social nature of the church, which is now redefined as a free association of like-minded individuals.[41]

The disciplines of the modern state seek to create disciples of the nation-state. The disciplines of the church – the practices of prayer and corporate worship, of Bible reading and mutual caring, of evangelical proclamation and costly solidarity with the outsider and the oppressed – seek to form disciples of Jesus Christ. This disciple-community cuts across the lines which demarcate the public from private, one nation-state from another. It thus makes possible a different political practice, one that rejects the nationalist politics of sacrifice and victimization and espouses a politics of global responsibility.

For Christians in America and Britain, say, to identify publicly with the plight of their brethren among the Kurds and Iraqis, and to take up their cause against the foreign policies of their governments, would be to make visible the body of Christ in the world. Similarly, to speak on behalf of the 40,000 children in the world who die every day from malnutrition or easily preventable diseases – and to do so with the same fervour that they do over abortion in the West – would be to expose the pitiful contributions of the US and Britain towards organizations such as the World Health Organization and the United Nations Children's Fund. When Christians in India and Pakistan challenge the jingoistic militarism of their respective nation-states, or when Christians in Europe confront the hypocrisy of 'foreign aid' to Third World nations and choose to live in a way that exposes the dependence of the rich in the West on the suffering of the poor elsewhere, they likewise practise a different discipleship, contrary to that which their nations encourage. They show themselves to be freed from the captivity of other gods.

Moreover, Christian global praxis, emerging out of the church as a truly multicultural and missionary community, lies at the leading edge of the world's future. We live in a world where the lives of most people are shaped increasingly by choices and decisions enacted elsewhere, in another part of the world. This makes much of the discussion of democracy and secularism in political circles hopelessly outdated. These discussions seem to move in a world devoid of nuclear missiles, of acid rain or tropical deforestation, of transnational corporations or financial deregulation. Whether such challenges can be tackled merely by an expanded notion of 'human rights' and the organizing of more interregional and international conferences is highly dubious. Self-regarding interest, in whatever guise it appears (and even the language of rights descends to self-interest when the theological roots of that language are forgotten), is an inadequate basis for moral action.

For Nicholas Lash, the gospel can be summed up in the simple statement 'We have been made capable of friendship' – with God and with one another.

To say this, seriously, against our actual background of brutality and devastation, of ancient and deep-rooted group and individual egotism, of terror, isolation and exhausted disbelief, is to say something either very foolish or, if sensible, then very dark and strange indeed. And yet, I have been taught by that particular people which identifies me more deeply than does my British nationality – namely, by Catholic Christianity – that I must learn to place my fundamental loyalty with no people, no possibility of friendship, more restricted than the human race.[42]

Epilogue

The Christian encounter with other faiths, 'religious' or 'secular', brings both enrichment and conflict. We have seen that to be a Christian is to indwell a particular story, embedded in historical event and borne by a global community, whose distinctiveness is disclosed in engagement with rival stories. The Christian needs the 'other' in order to learn that story rightly. Evangelism, whenever authentic, is discovery as well as witness. But conflict and suffering have always accompanied faithful gospel witness, not least because the gospel message relativizes all human authority-claims (whether of Brahmans or parliaments), and conversion to Christ leads to new social and political alignments. Persecution of Christians is more commonplace today than it has ever been since the first few centuries of the Christian era.

The Christian movement was born into a world every bit as pluralistic in ideology and behaviour as our own. Yet there is one major difference that Christians today face, a challenge that to some appears so overwhelming that it has led to a colossal loss of nerve where the proclamation of the gospel is concerned. First-century Christians were newcomers in the Greco-Roman and Persian worlds, with no history or land of their own, the objects of curiosity and puzzlement. Christians today are, in many countries, identified with a history which, at several points, has served to obscure the gospel from the gaze of the non-Christian: a history that includes bloody crusades and inquisitions, social intolerance and intellectual bigotry, the selective use of biblical texts to justify slavery, sexism, colonial expansionism and a host of other evils. Much

167

ink has been spilled, ever since the heyday of the so-called European Enlightenment, in exposing the betrayals of the gospel by the church. In self-righteous indignation, the thinkers of the Enlightenment and the founders of the modern nation-state relegated Christianity to a position of social marginality, a domesticated 'religion' incapable of mounting a challenge to the new ideology of self-salvation and the cult of 'autonomous man'. Hindu, Buddhist and Muslim thinkers, many of them emerging only relatively recently from a world of Western colonialism, have seized upon the anti-Christian polemic of some Western writers in order to make their own faiths attractive to (post)modern men and women.

That Christians, as a community of forgiven sinners, should not be ashamed to confess their sins and those of their forebears before their non-Christian neighbours, is, surely, an expectation that the gospel demands. To identify the truth of the gospel with the moral superiority of Christians would be to turn the gospel on its head. For it is with a flawed and faithless people that the Christ has stooped to pitch his tent and link his name. Any sharing of the gospel within a pluralist world, after two millennia of 'Christianity', has to begin with the humble acknowledgment of betrayals of the gospel by the church itself. These betrayals have to be identified concretely, not covered over in generalizations, and they will vary from one cultural context to another. We have given several examples of contemporary betrayals in earlier chapters.

We have also seen that there is another story about Christian mission that needs to be told. Perhaps the greatest betrayal of the gospel by the Western church would be the forgetting of that story in an over-reaction of post-colonial guilt. Positive aspects of that story have been brought to light at various points in this book, and a few examples here by way of recollection would suffice: the contribution of Persian Christians to the birth of Islamic as well as European civilization; the renewal of indigenous cultures all over the world by the courageous act of Bible translation; the defence of native peoples against colonial exploiters by Christian missionaries; the emancipation of women, slaves and children by Christians in every continent; the pioneering of modern health-care systems and the impact on social reform by Christians in many non-Christian societies, far out of proportion to their numerical size; the study and dissemination of the religious texts of non-Christian peoples by Christian missionary-scholars; and, perhaps more than anything else, the selfless devotion of men and women, often to the point of martyrdom or serious debilitation through illness, to people of another faith and culture. This is a unique story that needs to be recounted with humility and courage in a world that is losing touch with history.

We have also observed some of the ironies in this story of the gospel's trajectory among the nations. The resurgence of religious faiths in the Indian subcontinent owes much to the example and impact of Christian missions as well as to the social critiques of secular humanism. The resurgence is as much innovation as it is recovery. Much of what is invoked by religious nationalists as 'ancient tradition' is, on closer inspection, seen to be of fairly recent origin. Hindu (and Buddhist) nationalists often repeat stereotypes of their 'indigenous religions' culled from early orientalist scholarship in India. 'Hinduism' and 'Buddhism', as practised in India and Sri Lanka respectively, also cannot be understood apart from their links with Christian movements, foreign and native, since the early nineteenth century. The myth of self-enclosed civilizations, like myths of racial purity and 'pure indigeneity', needs to be laid to rest once and for all.

On a more global scale, postmodernist critiques of the Enlightenment project have served to expose the unconscious dependence of many anti-Christian thinkers on assumptions and values that make sense only within a Christian worldview. Those radical writers who take their cue from Nietzsche have simply drawn out the implications of his vision of a world that no longer has an integrating centre: if God is dead, then morality is dead, and man is dead. All attempts to smuggle in 'transcendence', to shore up a joyless, valueless world, end in personal despair and social nightmares.

Writing in the midst of one such nightmare, Dietrich Bonhoeffer reminded his fellow Christians

> It is not Christ who must justify himself before the world by the acknowledgement of the values of justice, truth and freedom, but it is these values which have come to need justification, and their justification can only be Jesus Christ. It is not that a 'Christian culture' must make the name of Jesus Christ acceptable to the world, but the crucified Christ has become the refuge and the justification, the protection and the claim for the higher values and their defenders that have fallen victim to suffering. It is with the Christ who is persecuted and who suffers in his Church that justice, truth, humanity and freedom now seek refuge; it is with the Christ who found no shelter in the world, the Christ who was cast out from the world, the Christ of the crib and the cross, under whose protection they now seek sanctuary, and who thereby for the first time displays the full extent of his power.[1]

In 1948, the famous French writer Albert Camus was invited to address the Dominican Monastery at Latour-Maubourg on the theme 'What do unbelievers expect of Christians?' Camus surprised his audience by saying that what the world today needed was for Christians to remain Christians. He shared how during the 'frightful years' of oppression and war, he and others like him had waited for 'a great voice to speak up in Rome'. 'I, an unbeliever? Precisely. For I knew that the spirit would be lost if it did not utter a cry of condemnation when faced with force.'[2] Camus continued:

> It has been explained to me since that the condemnation was indeed voiced. But that it was in the style of the encyclicals, which is not at all clear. The condemnation was voiced and it was not understood! ... What the world expects of Christians is that Christians should speak out, loud and clear, and that they should voice their condemnation in such a way that never a doubt, never the slightest doubt, could rise in the heart of the simplest man. That they should get away from abstraction and confront the blood-stained face history has taken on today. The grouping we need is a grouping of men resolved to speak out clearly and to pay up personally ... Perhaps we cannot prevent this world from being a world in which children are tortured. But we can reduce the number of tortured children. And if you don't help us, who else in the world can help us do this?[3]

Courageous words, challenging to pietists and communitarians as much as to theologians. No doubt the Roman Catholic Church has been far more bold in condemning social evils since the Second World War than Protestant churches worldwide. Camus's exhortation has proved salutary, but the church does not take its agenda from him. Camus spoke out of a culture that still retained memories of the Hebrew-Christian story: the intrinsic value of a child's life; the 'blood-stained face' of history was a moral aberration, a clue that something was radically out of joint, not the outworking of biological or logical necessity. Whether such a repugnance towards evil can be vigorously sustained in the hedonist, ethically relativist cultures of the late modern world remains to be seen. So, while being open to the challenge of men and women like Camus who remain outside the Christian community, we also need to ask them: what is the story of the world that makes sense of your moral outrage? Can we divorce values from facts – or public condemnation from the public telling of the gospel story within which that condemnation finds its force?

Christians who are rightly sensitive to the complicity of the church in legitimizing the status quo have often tended to adopt the same selective hermeneutic to legitimize every protest against the status quo. But both are betrayals of the gospel. They obscure the unique perspectives that the gospel brings to bear on the human predicament. We repent of sinful complicity so that we may engage with integrity in the joyful privilege of sharing the Good News of Jesus Christ as Lord to all peoples. Unless the quest for justice among the nations is guided by passion for the glory of God, and is rooted in what God has done for the world in Jesus Christ, it quickly becomes another form of domination. God's gracious, reconciling love in Jesus Christ towards us human beings is the ground and pattern for our response to injustice and conflict. This takes the righting of historic wrongs seriously, but the ultimate aim is the transformation of sinful men and women through their reconciliation to one another and to their Creator.

Thus Christian witness cannot stop with the public condemnation of evil, whether alone or in collaboration with sensitive others outside the church. Christian witness is a never-ending interplay of repentance and remembrance, condemnation and celebration, proclamation and practice. Word and deed are held together, above all, in the formation of a multicultural community of men and women that is growing into the likeness of the True Human. The world does not set the agenda for the church (*pace* some ecumenical theologies), nor does the church set the agenda for the world. Rather, the church, as the body of the risen Christ, *is* the agenda for the world. It is the eschatological community, modelling a different understanding of humanness, embodying both the indictment of the world and its eternal hope. It is here that the redemption of our humanity is taking place. The church influences the world most when it seeks to be truly *church*, and not a political or evangelistic organization. If we want to discern God's purposes for the nations, it is not at the 'blood-stained face of history' that we look, but at a blood-stained cross. The latter reveals a God whose will is nothing less than the formation of Christ in us: the healing of a fractured humanity and the glorification of a spoiled creation. Compared to this, every other vision of the world appears bleak, narrow, escapist or simply sick.

When Graham Staines, an Australian missionary working among lepers and tribal peoples in Orissa, India, was brutally murdered, along with his two young sons, by a Hindu mob on 22 January 1999, many in that country and abroad were rightly outraged. His grieving widow told a newspaper reporter, 'I am deeply upset. But I am not angry. For Jesus has taught us how to love our enemies.' Here the path of evangelical mission is displayed. To suffer joyfully for the gospel, and to forgive and serve those who inflict that suffering, is to be taught by Christ to walk the way of the cross. It is only such a church, radical in its obedience, that makes known the beauty, truth and power of the Christian message to the world.

Bibliography

The following books and articles are those either quoted from, or referred to, in the text. This selection is not intended to be a comprehensive list.

A. Ahmed, *Postmodernism and Islam: Predicament and Promise* (London and New York: Routledge, 1992).

A. Ahmed and H. Donnan, 'Islam in the Age of Postmodernity', in A. Ahmed and H. Donnan (eds.), *Islam, Globalization and Postmodernity* (London and New York: Routledge, 1994).

A. Amaladass SJ (ed.), *Christian Contribution to Indian Philosophy* (Madras: CLS, 1995).

J. N. D. Anderson, *Law Reform in the Muslim World* (London: Athlone Press, 1976).

—— *Islam in the Modern World: A Christian Perspective* (Leicester: Apollos, 1990).

W. Anderson and S. Damle, *The Brotherhood in Saffron* (Boulder, CO: Westview Press, 1987).

A. A. An-Na'im, *Towards an Islamic Reformation: Civil Liberties, Human Rights and International Law* (Syracuse: Syracuse University Press, 1990).

H. Askari, 'Within and Beyond the Diversity of Religious Experience', in J. Hick and H. Askari (eds.), *The Experience of Religious Diversity* (London: Gower, 1985).

M. 'Ata ur-Rahim, *Jesus, a Prophet of Islam* (London, 1979).

P. Bannerman, *Islam in Perspective: A Guide to Islamic Society, Politics and Law* (London: Routledge, 1988).

J. Barr, '"Abba" isn't "Daddy"', *Journal of Theological Studies* 39 (1988).

A. L. Basham, 'Introduction', in B. L. Smith (ed.), *Essays on Gupta Culture* (New Delhi: Motilal Banarsidass, 1983).

T. Basu, P. Datta, S. Sarkar, T. Sarkar and S. Sen, *Khaki Shorts and Saffron Flags* (Delhi: Orient Longman, 1993).

R. J. Bauckham, 'The Sonship of the Historical Jesus in Christology', *Scottish Journal of Theology* 31 (1978).

R. Bellah et al., *Habits of the Heart: Individualism and Commitment in American Life* (Berkeley, CA: University of California Press, 1985).

N. Bhattacharya, 'Myth, History and the Politics of Ramjanmabhumi', in Gopal (ed.), *Anatomy of a Confrontation*.

A. Bishara, 'Islam and Politics in the Middle East', in Hippler and Lueg (eds.), *The Next Threat: Western Perceptions of Islam*.

D. Bonhoeffer, *Ethics* (1949; ET London: SCM, 1955; New York: Simon & Schuster, Touchstone ed., 1995).

R. A. Burridge, *What are the Gospels? A Comparison with Greco-Roman Biography* (Cambridge: Cambridge University Press, 1992).

A. Camus, *Resistance, Rebellion, and Death*, trans. J. O'Brien (1960; New York: Random House, Vintage International ed. 1995).

W. T. Cavanaugh, ' "A Fire Strong Enough to Consume the House": The Wars of Religion and the Rise of the State', *Modern Theology* 11.4 (1995).

B. Chandra, *Communalism in Modern India* (Delhi: Vikas Publishing House, 1984).

B. Chandra, M. Mukherjee, A. Mukherjee, K. N. Panikkar and S. Mahajan, *India's Struggle for Independence 1857–1947* (Delhi: Penguin, 1989).

C. Chapman, *Cross and Crescent: Responding to the Challenge of Islam* (Leicester: Inter-Varsity Press, 1996).

N. Chaudhuri, *Hinduism* (London: Chatto & Windus, 1979).

K. Cragg, *The Call of the Minaret* (1956; London: Collins, 1986).

The Dalai Lama, *The Good Heart* (Boston, MA: Wisdom Publications, 1996).

J. T. K. Daniel and R. E. Hedlund (eds.), *Carey's Obligation and India's Renaissance* (Serampore: Serampore College Press, 1993).

R. H. Davies, 'The Iconography of Rama's Chariot', in Ludden (ed.), *Making India Hindu*.

C. Dexter, *Service of All the Dead* (London: Pan, 1980).

L. Dumont, 'World Renunciation in Indian Religions', *Contributions to Indian Sociology* 4 (1960).

—— *Homo Hierarchicus: The Caste System and its Implications* (Chicago and

London: University of Chicago Press, complete revised Eng. ed. 1980).

T. Eagleton, *The Illusions of Postmodernism* (Oxford: Blackwell, 1996).

J. L. Esposito, *The Islamic Threat: Myth or Reality?* (New York: Oxford University Press, 1992; 2nd ed. 1995).

C. B. Firth, *An Introduction to Indian Church History* (Madras: CLS, 1961; rev. ed. 1976).

G. Flood, *An Introduction to Hinduism* (Cambridge: Cambridge University Press, 1996).

R. T. France, *Jesus and the Old Testament* (London: Tyndale, 1971).

A. Giddens, *The Nation-State and Violence*, vol. 2 of *A Contemporary Critique of Historical Materialism* (Berkeley and Los Angeles: University of California Press, 1985).

R. F. Gombrich, 'Introduction: The Buddhist Way', in *The World of Buddhism: Buddhist Monks and Nuns in Society and Culture*, eds. H. Bechert and R. Gombrich (London: Thames & Hudson, 1984).

—— *Theravada Buddhism: A Social History from Ancient Benares to Modern Colombo* (London: Routledge & Kegan Paul, 1988).

S. Gopal (ed.), *Anatomy of a Confrontation* (Delhi: Penguin, 1991).

F. Halliday, *Islam and the Myth of Confrontation: Religion and Politics in the Middle East* (London and New York: Tauris, 1995).

R. P. C. Hanson, 'The Achievement of Orthodoxy in the Fourth Century AD', in R. Williams (ed.), *The Making of Orthodoxy* (Cambridge: Cambridge University Press, 1989).

M. Hasan, *Nationalism and Communal Politics in India, 1885–1930* (Delhi: Manohar, 1991).

—— (ed.), *India's Partition: Process, Strategy and Mobilization* (Delhi: Oxford University Press, 1993).

J. Hippler and A. Lueg (eds.), *The Next Threat: Western Perceptions of Islam* (London: Pluto Press, 1995).

P. Hirst and G. Thompson, *Globalization in Question: The International Economy and the Possibilities of Governance* (Cambridge: Polity Press, 1996).

T. Hobbes, *Leviathan* (1651; New York: Collier Books, 1962).

C. R. A. Hoole, *Modern Sannyasins: Protestant Missionary Contributions to Ceylon Tamil Culture* (Berne: Peter Lang, 1995).

S. P. Huntington, *The Clash of Civilizations and the Remaking of World Order* (New York: Simon & Schuster, 1996).

A. Inder Singh, *The Origins of the Partition of India, 1936–1947* (Delhi: Oxford University Press, 1987).

M. Juergensmeyer, *Religious Nationalism Confronts the Secular State* (University of California Press, 1993; Delhi: Oxford University Press, 1996).

B. Jupp, 'The Persistence of Faiths', *Demos* 11 (1997).

N. Keddie, 'Iranian Revolutions in Comparative Perspective', in A. Hourani, P. Khoury and M. Wilson (eds.), *The Modern Middle-East: A Reader* (London and New York: Tauris, 1993).

S. Kierkegaard, *Training in Christianity*, trans. W. Lowrie (Princeton, NJ: Princeton University Press, 1941).

S. Khilnani, *The Idea of India* (London: Hamish Hamilton, 1997).

S. Kim, *The Son of Man as the Son of God*, WUNT 30 (Tübingen: J. C. B. Mohr [Paul Siebeck], 1983).

P. Knitter, *No Other Name? A Critical Survey of Christian Attitudes Toward the World Religions* (London: SCM, 1985).

L. Kolakowski, *Modernity on Endless Trial* (Chicago: University of Chicago Press, 1990).

W. Lane, *The Gospel of Mark* (London: Marshall, Morgan & Scott, 1974).

N. Lash, *The Beginning and the End of 'Religion'* (Cambridge: Cambridge University Press, 1996).

J. Locke, *Two Treatises of Government* with a *Letter on Toleration*, ed. J. W. Gough (1690, 1689: Oxford: Blackwell, 1956).

D. Ludden (ed.), *Making India Hindu: Religion, Community and the Politics of Democracy in India* (Delhi: Oxford University Press, 1996).

A. Lueg, 'The Perception of Islam in Western Debate', in Hippler and Lueg (eds.), *The Next Threat.*

A. McGrath, *The Making of Modern German Christology, 1750–1990* (Leicester: Apollos, 2nd ed. 1994).

T. N. Madan, 'Secularism in Its Place', *Journal of Asian Studies* 46.4 (1987).

I. H. Marshall, *The Gospel of Luke: A Commentary on the Greek Text* (Grand Rapids: Eerdmans, 1978).

D. Martin, *A General Theory of Secularization* (Oxford: Blackwell, 1978).

A. Mayer, *Islam and Human Rights: Tradition and Politics* (Boulder, CO: Westview Press; London: Pinter Publishers, 1991).

J. P. Meier, *The Mission of Christ and His Church: Studies in Christology and Ecclesiology* (Wilmington, DE: Michael Glazier, 1990).

K. Murad, *Da'wah Among Non-Muslims in the West: Some Conceptual and Methodological Aspects* (Leicester: Islamic Foundation, 1986).

A. Nandy, *Intimate Enemy: Loss and Recovery of Self under Colonialism* (Delhi: Oxford University Press, 1983).

A. Nandy, S. Trivedy, S. Mayaram and A. Yagnik, *Creating a Nationality: The Ramjanmabhoomi Movement and Fear of the Self* (Delhi: Oxford University Press, 1997).

M. Nazir-Ali, *Islam: A Christian Perspective* (Exeter: Paternoster, 1983).

S. Neill, *Christian Faith and Other Faiths* (Oxford: Oxford University Press, 1970).

L. Newbigin, *The Gospel in a Pluralist Society* (London: SPCK; Grand Rapids: Eerdmans, 1989).

R. A. Nicholson, *The Mystics of Islam* (1914; London: Routledge & Kegan Paul, 1963).

M. Novak, *The Spirit of Democratic Capitalism* (New York: Simon & Schuster, 1982; London: IEA Welfare and Health Unit, 1991).

W. D. O'Flaherty, 'The Image of the Heretic in the Gupta Puranas', in B. L. Smith (ed.), *Essays on Gupta Culture* (New Delhi: Motilal Banarsidass, 1983).

G. Pandey, *The Construction of Communalism in Colonial North India* (Delhi: Oxford University Press, 1990).

K. N. Panikkar, 'A Historical Overview', in Gopal (ed.), *Anatomy of a Confrontation*.

M. J. Perry, *The Idea of Human Rights: Four Inquiries* (Oxford and New York: Oxford University Press, 1998).

J. Pilger, 'Pol Pot: The Monster We Created', *The Guardian Weekly*, 26 April 1998.

W. R. Pinch, 'Soldier Monks and Militant Sadhus', in Ludden (ed.), *Making India Hindu*.

S. Radhakrishnan, *The Hindu View of Life* (London and New York: Macmillan, 1969).

R. Ramanathapillai, *Sacred Symbols and the Adoption of Violence in Tamil Politics in Sri Lanka* (unpublished MA thesis, McMaster University, Canada, 1991).

A. Rambachan, 'Keynote Address, Hindu–Christian Consultation, Varanasi, India, October 23–27, 1997', *Current Dialogue* 31 (1998).

J. Rawls, *Political Liberalism* (New York: Columbia University Press, 1993).

The Runnymede Trust, *Islamophobia: A Challenge For Us All* (London: Runnymede Trust, 1997).

E. W. Said, *Orientalism* (1978; London: Penguin, 1995).

L. Sanneh, 'Pluralism and Christian Commitment', *Theology Today* 45 (April 1988).

V. D. Savarkar, *Hindutva: Who is a Hindu?* (1923; New Delhi: Bhatiya Sahitiya Sadan, 6th ed. 1989).

A. Siddiqi, *Christian–Muslim Dialogue in the Twentieth Century* (London: Macmillan Press and New York: St Martin's Press, 1997).

W. C. Smith, *The Meaning and End of Religion* (1962; Minneapolis: Fortress Press, 1991).

J. Stout, *The Flight from Authority: Religion, Morality, and the Quest for*

Autonomy (Notre Dame, IN: University of Notre Dame Press, 1981).

R. Thapar, *Ancient Indian Social History: Some Interpretations* (Delhi: Orient Longman, 1979).

—— 'A Historical Perspective on the Story of Rama', in Gopal (ed.) *Anatomy of a Confrontation.*

R. Thapar, H. Mukhia and B. Chandra, *Communalism and the Writing of Indian History* (Delhi: Peoples Publishing House, 2nd ed. 1977).

M. M. Thomas, 'The Christian Contribution to an Indian Philosophy of Being and Becoming Human', in Amaladass SJ (ed.), *Christian Contribution to Indian Philosophy.*

S. P. Tillman, *The United States in the Middle East: Interests and Obstacles* (Indiana: Indiana University Press, 1982).

A. de Tocqueville, *Democracy in America* (1841; abridged, with introduction, by P. Renshaw; Ware: Wordworth ed. 1998).

P. van der Veer, *Gods on Earth: The Management of Religious Experience and Identity in a North Indian Pilgrimage Centre* (Delhi: Oxford University Press, 1989).

—— 'Hindu Nationalism and the Discourse of Modernity: The Vishva Hindu Parishad', in M. Marty and S. Appleby (eds.), *Accounting for Fundamentalisms* (Chicago: University of Chicago Press, 1991).

—— *Religious Nationalism: Hindus and Muslims in India* (Berkeley and Los Angeles: University of California Press, 1994).

—— 'Writing Violence', in Ludden (ed.), *Making India Hindu.*

J. Verkuyl, *Contemporary Missiology, An Introduction* (Grand Rapids: Eerdmans, 1978).

G. Vermes, *Jesus the Jew* (London: Collins, 1973).

Swami Vivekananda, *The Complete Works of Swami Vivekananda* (Calcutta: Advaita Ashrama, 1964–71).

A. F. Walls, *The Missionary Movement in Christian History: Studies in the Trans-mission of Faith* (Maryknoll, NY: Orbis; Edinburgh: T. & T. Clark, 1996).

W. M. Watt, *Islamic Philosophy and Theology* (Edinburgh: University of Edinburgh Press, 1962; 2nd ed. 1985).

B. Witherington III, *The Christology of Jesus* (Philadelphia: Fortress, 1990).

—— *Jesus the Sage: The Pilgrimage of Wisdom* (Minneapolis: Fortress, 1994).

—— *The Third Quest: The Search for the Jew from Nazareth* (Downers Grove, IL: InterVarsity Press; Carlisle: Paternoster, 1995).

C. J. H.Wright, *Living as the People of God: The Relevance of Old Testament Ethics* (Leicester: Inter-Varsity Press, 1983).

—— 'The Christian and Other Religions: The Biblical Evidence', *Themelios* 9.2 (January 1984).

N. T. Wright, *The New Testament and the People of God* (London: SPCK, 1992).

R. Wuthnow, *The Struggle for America's Soul* (Grand Rapids: Eerdmans, 1989).

B. Ye'or, *The Decline of Eastern Christianity Under Islam: From Jihad to Dhimmitude* (Eng. trans. M. Kochan and D. Littman (London: Associated University Presses, 1996).

R. Young, 'Ripple or Wave? Protestant Missions and the "Protestantization" of Religion in Nineteenth-Century Sri Lanka', unpublished paper delivered in Colombo, Sri Lanka, 8 February 1992.

Y. Zaki, 'The Politics of Islamophobia', *Q-News*, 1–20 November 1997.

K. Zebiri, *Muslims and Christians Face to Face* (Oxford: Oneworld, 1997).

Notes

1. Islam and new religious wars?

1. Samuel P. Huntington, *The Clash of Civilizations and the Remaking of World Order* (New York: Simon & Schuster, 1996).
2. Ibid., p. 21.
3. Ibid., p. 28.
4. Ibid., p. 43.
5. Ibid., p. 125.
6. Ibid., p. 183.
7. Ibid., p. 321.
8. For a selection of such reports, see *The Economist*, 1 August 1992, pp. 34–35.
9. Quoted in M. Juergensmeyer, *Religious Nationalism Confronts the Secular State* (Berkeley, CA: University of California Press, 1993; Delhi: Oxford University Press, 1996), p. 155.
10. Huntington, *Clash of Civilizations*, p. 217.
11. Azmy Bishara, 'Islam and Politics in the Middle East', in J. Hippler and A. Lueg (eds.), *The Next Threat: Western Perceptions of Islam* (London: Pluto Press, 1995), pp. 109–110.
12. Fred Halliday, *Islam and the Myth of Confrontation: Religion and Politics in the Middle East* (London and New York: Tauris, 1995), p. 6.
13. Ibid., p. 111.
14. John L. Esposito, *The Islamic Threat: Myth or Reality?* (New York: Oxford University Press, 1992; 2nd ed. 1995), pp. 193–194.
15. Halliday, *Islam and the Myth*, pp. 119–120.
16. Ibid., p. 126.
17. Ibid., pp. 125–126.

18. The first four 'rightly-guided caliphs' were Abu Bakr (AD 632–634), 'Umar (634–644), Uthman (644–656) and 'Ali (656–661). There were numerous Kharijite uprisings in the reign of 'Ali as well as during the following Umayyad period.
19. Ibn Rushd's influence on European thought far outweighed his influence on the Islamic world. For a brief but useful survey of medieval Islamic thought, see W. Montgomery Watt, *Islamic Philosophy and Theology* (Edinburgh: University of Edinburgh Press, 1962; 2nd ed. 1985).
20. Bat Ye'or, *The Decline of Eastern Christianity Under Islam: From Jihad to Dhimmitude*, Eng. trans. Miriam Kochan and David Littman (London: Associated University Presses, 1996), p. 217.
21. Ibid., pp. 231–232.
22. Ibid., p. 233.
23. Ibid., p. 265.
24. Edward W. Said, *Orientalism* (1978; London: Penguin, 1995), pp. 43–44.
25. Quoted in Andrea Lueg, 'The Perception of Islam in Western Debate', in Hippler and Lueg (eds.), *The Next Threat*, p. 9.
26. Bishara, 'Islam and Politics', in Hippler and Lueg (eds.), *The Next Threat*, p. 92.
27. See Nikki Keddie, 'Iranian Revolutions in Comparative Perspective', in A. Hourani, P. Khoury and M. Wilson (eds.), *The Modern Middle-East: A Reader* (London and New York: Tauris, 1993).
28. Halliday, *Islam and the Myth*, p. 116.
29. Ibid., p. 114.
30. Bishara, 'Islam and Politics', p. 93.
31. These schools are the Hanafi, Hanbali, Maliki and Shafi'I. The classic works on Islamic law are those by Noel J. Coulson, *A History of Islamic Law* (Edinburgh: Edinburgh University Press, 1964) and Joseph Schacht, *An Introduction to Islamic Law* (Oxford: Clarendon Press, 1964).
32. Norman Anderson, *Law Reform in the Muslim World* (London: Athlone Press, 1976), p. 10. Anderson also notes that the *shari'a* was 'originally fashioned out of the raw material of local customary law and administrative practice, systematized and islamicized by the work of early scholar-jurists. Yet the fact remains that no place whatever is expressly given, in the traditional doctrine, to customary law as such' (ibid.).
33. Michael Nazir-Ali, *Islam: A Christian Perspective* (Exeter: Paternoster, 1983), p. 52.
34. Ibid., p. 53 (italics as in text).
35. Norman Anderson, *Islam in the Modern World: A Christian Perspective* (Leicester: Apollos, 1990), p. 114.
36. Bishara, 'Islam and Politics', p. 88.
37. Quoted in ibid., p. 85.
38. A Muslim scholar who seriously attempts to develop a methodology that arrives at international human-rights norms from Islamic values and principles is Professor Abdullahi Ahmed An-Na'im of Syracuse University, formerly of Khartoum University Law School. See his *Towards an Islamic Reformation: Civil Liberties, Human Rights and International Law* (Syracuse: Syracuse University Press, 1990).
39. Ann Mayer, *Islam and Human Rights: Tradition and Politics* (Boulder, CO: Westview Press; London: Pinter Publishers, 1991), pp. 53–54.
40. Colin Chapman, *Cross and Crescent: Responding to the Challenge of Islam* (Leicester: Inter-Varsity Press, 1996), p. 270.
41. Ibid., pp. 277–278.
42. See Ye'or, *Decline of Eastern Christianity*, ch. 6.

43. Mayer, *Islam and Human Rights*, pp. 144–145.
44. See Taha's *The Second Message of Islam*, trans. by Abdullahi An-Na'im (Syracuse: Syracuse University Press, 1987).
45. Mayer, *Islam and Human Rights*, pp. 186–187.
46. Both quotations in Chapman, *Cross and Crescent*, p. 270.
47. The full quotation is as follows: 'Islamophobia is as old as Islam; it began with Quraish. Its intensity varies according to time and place, but hatred of Islam and Muslims is *endemic* in the European psyche – *endemic* if at times it becomes epidemic. We are living through such an epidemic now' (Dr Yaqub Zaki, 'The Politics of Islamophobia', *Q-News*, 1–20 November 1997 [emphasis mine]).
48. A. Ahmed, *Postmodernism and Islam: Predicament and Promise* (London and New York: Routledge, 1992), p. 247 (emphasis mine). Immediately preceding this comment, we read: '[Western women] are now the open target of men's wildest fantasies and most violent plans. In these they are to be sadistically raped, strangled, chopped up, and – especially in recent years – eaten in little bits and pieces. They face the serial killer as much as the sexual pervert. The stifling horror of boredom in the home may well appear attractive in comparison.'
49. *Islamophobia: A Challenge For Us All* (London: Runnymede Trust, 1997).
50. Earlier in his book, Ahmed gives some positive descriptions of the West (cf. pp. 98–100) and also explicitly distances himself from 'occidentalist' writers (p.243). However, let the reader judge, both from note 48 above and from passages like the one below, whether Ahmed has freed himself completely from occidentalism / westophobia: 'The problem with this civilization is the hole where the heart should be, the vacuum inside; there is no moral philosophy or set of principles that drives it. What gives it its dynamic energy is individualism, the desire to dominate, the sheer drive to acquire material items, to hoard. Every technological development must be gathered into your home; it is the obsession to out-buy, out-eat and out-sex the Joneses next door' (p.109).
51. Kate Zebiri, *Muslims and Christians Face to Face* (Oxford: Oneworld, 1997), p. 173.
52. Ibid., p. 174.
53. Ibid., p. 89.
54. *The Economist*, 9 March 1996, p. 27. Mahathir is also, apparently, an 'orientalist' and 'biological determinist' in the way he speaks of his own people. *The Economist* of 8 July 1995 reports: 'In 1970, Dr Mahathir published a book, "The Malay Dilemma", which said, in effect, that, because of heredity and environment, Malays were lazy. The book was banned in Malaysia until Dr Mahathir became prime minister fourteen years ago [1981]. In his 1995 edition, it retains that deadly sentence, "Deep under, the inherent traits and characteristics acquired over the centuries persist" ' (p. 27).
55. Huntington, *Clash of Civilizations*, p. 29.
56. R. Bellah et al., *Habits of the Heart: Individualism and Commitment in American Life* (Berkeley, CA: University of California Press, 1985).
57. Cited in S. P. Tillman, *The United States in the Middle East: Interests and Obstacles* (Indiana: Indiana University Press, 1982), p. 46.
58. Cited in ibid., pp. 45–46.
59. Esposito, *Islamic Threat*, p. 190.
60. Ibid., p. xv.
61. Lueg, 'The Perception of Islam', in Hippler and Lueg (eds.), *The Next Threat*, p. 7.
62. Patrick Bannerman, *Islam in Perspective: A Guide to Islamic Society, Politics and Law* (London: Routledge, 1988), p. 219, cited in Esposito, *Islamic Threat*, p. 191.
63. Khurram Murad, *Da'wah Among Non-Muslims in the West: Some Conceptual and*

Methodological Aspects (Leicester: Islamic Foundation, 1986), p. 18.

64. The only manuscript of the so-called *Gospel of Barnabas* that we have is in Italian, previously in the Papal Library and now in the National Library in Vienna. It was translated into English by Canon and Mrs Ragg and published by the Clarendon Press in 1907. Montague James in *The Apocryphal New Testament*, published in 1924, regards the existence of a 'Gospel under the name of Barnabas' to be 'most doubtful ... the extant book under that name (ed. Ragg, 1907) is in Italian, a forgery of the late fifteenth or sixteenth [century], by a renegade from Christianity to Islam'. For a survey of the history of the claims regarding this document, see Norman Anderson, 'The So-called "Gospel of Barnabas"', Appendix to *Islam in the Modern World*.

65. Muhammad 'Ata ur-Rahim, *Jesus, a Prophet of Islam* (London: MWH Publishers, 1979), p. 39.

66. 'Jesus answered: "I am indeed sent to the house of Israel as a prophet of salvation; but after me shall come the Messiah sent of God for all the world, for whom God hath made the world"' (*Gospel of Barnabas*, ch. 82).

67. One example from a relatively irenical Muslim writer will suffice: 'The [East India] company, which not only supplied arms and textiles, but also carried missionaries, gradually shifted from commerce and curiosity to conversion of the local people, and this eventually paved the way, arguably, for the colonization of India' (Ataullah Siddiqi, *Christian–Muslim Dialogue in the Twentieth Century* [London: Macmillan; New York: St Martin's Press, 1997], p. 53).

68. Kenneth Cragg, *The Call of the Minaret* (1956; London: Collins, 1986), pp. 219–220.

2. Hinduism and the search for identity

1. Jawaharlal Nehru, *Construction of the New Capital at Chandigarh: Project Report* (no date), quoted in Sunil Khilnani, *The Idea of India* (London: Hamish Hamilton, 1997), p. 131.

2. Khilnani, ibid., p. 132.

3. Ibid., p. 133.

4. Ibid., p. 135.

5. V. D. Savarkar, *Hindutva: Who is a Hindu?* (1923; New Delhi: Bhatiya Sahitiya Sadan, 6th ed. 1989).

6. M. S. Golwalkar, *We or Our Nationhood Defined* (Nagpur: 1947 ed., pp. 55–56), quoted in Bipan Chandra et al., *India's Struggle for Independence 1857–1947* (Delhi: Penguin, 1989), p. 437.

7. See Tapan Basu, Pradip Datta, Sumit Sarkar, Tanika Sarkar and Sambuddha Sen, *Khaki Shorts and Saffron Flags* (Delhi: Orient Longman, 1993); Walter Anderson and S. Damle, *The Brotherhood in Saffron* (Boulder, CO: Westview Press, 1987).

8. See Ashis Nandy, Shikha Trivedy, Shail Mayaram and Achyut Yagnik, *Creating a Nationality: The Ramjanmabhoomi Movement and Fear of the Self* (Delhi: Oxford University Press, 1997), pp. 86–95.

9. Quotations from issues of the weekly paper of the RSS, *The Organizer*, cited in Neeladri Bhattacharya, 'Myth, History and the Politics of Ramjanmabhumi', in Sarvepalli Gopal (ed.), *Anatomy of a Confrontation* (India: Penguin, 1991).

10. Bhattacharya, ibid., pp. 125–126.

11. Richard H. Davies, 'The Iconography of Rama's Chariot', in David Ludden (ed.), *Making India Hindu: Religion, Community and the Politics of Democracy in India* (Delhi: Oxford University Press, 1996), p. 35.

12. Peter van der Veer, 'Hindu Nationalism and the Discourse of Modernity: The Vishva Hindu Parishad', in Martin Marty and Scott Appleby (eds.) *Accounting for Fundamentalisms* (Chicago: University of Chicago Press, 1991), p. 666.

13. Thus Golwalkar: 'Alien traits found today in the life of Muslims and Christians of Bharat may be traced to history. Both these sects were imported into Bharat by foreign rulers, and thrived under their patronage, as their instruments. These foreign rulers did not nationally establish the superiority of their faith before propagating it. Instead, they used terror to alienate our nationals from our ancient traditions, and used the converts to prop up their rule. A large number of people embraced these faiths out of fear or greed, and simultaneously they adopted foreign ways of life too. These faiths, therefore, symbolize our slavery' (*Shri Guruji, the Man and His Mission*, Delhi: B. N. Bhargava, pp. 67–68).

14. Romila Thapar, 'A Historical Perspective on the Story of Rama', in Gopal (ed.), *Anatomy*, p. 159.

15. See, e.g., the studies by Bipan Chandra, *Communalism in Modern India* (Delhi: Vikas Publishing House, 1984); Romila Thapar, Harbans Mukhia and Bipan Chandra, *Communalism and the Writing of Indian History* (Delhi: Peoples Publishing House, 2nd ed. 1977); Mushirul Hasan, *Nationalism and Communal Politics in India, 1885–1930* (Delhi: Manohar, 1991); Gyanendra Pandey, *The Construction of Communalism in Colonial North India* (Delhi: Oxford University Press, 1990). For a healthy corrective to some of these readings, which place exclusive blame on the colonial state for constructions of Indian communalism, see Peter van der Veer, *Religious Nationalism: Hindus and Muslims in India* (Berkeley and Los Angeles: University of California Press, 1994).

16. *Newsweek*, 22 December 1992, p. 46; *The Washington Post*, 29 January 1993, p. A20.

17. *The Independent*, 1 June 1998, p. 15 (emphasis in text).

18. On a first reading this section (pp. 58–63) can be left out. It is an expansion of the argument of the previous section, and fills out some of the historical background to the present conflicts in Indian society.

19. K. N. Panikkar, 'A Historical Overview', in Gopal, *Anatomy of a Confrontation*, ch. 2; Peter van der Veer, *Gods on Earth: The Management of Religious Experience and Identity in a North Indian Pilgrimage Centre* (Delhi: Oxford University Press, 1989).

20. Less than twenty-five years after Partition, East Pakistan ceded from West Pakistan as Bengali Muslims felt they had little in common with the Punjabi élite that they believed controlled the Pakistani state. This led to a bloody war and the creation of the state of Bangladesh. Similar ethnic conflicts between Muslims have continued to destabilize Pakistani politics and society.

21. Mushirul Hasan (ed.), *India's Partition: Process, Strategy and Mobilization* (Delhi: Oxford University Press, 1993), p. 5.

22. See van der Veer, *Religious Nationalism*, pp. 86–94.

23. The scholarly literature on the subject of India's nationalist movement and the events leading up to Partition is enormous. In my discussion I have drawn mostly on the following works: the essays in Hasan (ed.), *India's Partition*; Anita Inder Singh, *The Origins of the Partition of India, 1936–1947* (Delhi: Oxford University Press, 1987); and Chandra et al., *India's Struggle*.

24. Inder Singh, *The Origins*, p. 245.

25. Hasan, 'Introduction', in Hasan (ed.), *India's Partition*, p. 41.

26. Lord Wavell to Sir A. Chow, *Transfer of Power*, vol. 8, Document 414, 7 October 1946, cited by Gopal, 'Introduction', in *Anatomy of a Confrontation*, p. 13.

27. Nandy et al., *Creating a Nationality*, p. viii.

28. Ibid., p. ix.
29. A. Nandy, *Intimate Enemy: Loss and Recovery of Self under Colonialism* (Delhi: Oxford University Press, 1983), p. ix.
30. P. van der Veer, 'Writing Violence', in Ludden (ed.), *Making India Hindu*, p. 257.
31. Ibid., p. 258.
32. Fred Halliday, *Islam and the Myth of Confrontation: Religion and Politics in the Middle East* (London: Tauris, 1996), pp. 213–214.
33. Gavin Flood, *An Introduction to Hinduism* (Cambridge: Cambridge University Press, 1996), p. 53.
34. Ibid., p. 12.
35. Ibid.
36. Ibid., p. 59.
37. *Rg Veda* 10.90.11–12.
38. Louis Dumont, *Homo Hierarchicus: The Caste System and its Implications* (Chicago and London: University of Chicago Press, complete revised Eng. ed., 1980), p. 259.
39. Flood, *An Introduction to Hinduism*, p.59.
40. Charles R. A. Hoole, *Modern Sannyasins: Protestant Missionary Contributions to Ceylon Tamil Culture* (Berne: Peter Lang, 1995), p. 39.
41. See A. L. Basham, 'Introduction', in B. L. Smith (ed.), *Essays on Gupta Culture* (New Delhi: Motilal Banarsidass, 1983), p. 7.
42. See Wendy Doniger O'Flaherty, 'The Image of the Heretic in the Gupta Puranas', in Smith (ed.), ibid., pp. 107–127.
43. Ibid., p. 108.
44. Ibid., pp. 120–121.
45. Ibid., p. 116.
46. William R. Pinch, 'Soldier Monks and Militant Sadhus', in Ludden (ed.), *Making India Hindu*, p. 153.
47. Ibid., p. 156.
48. Ibid., p. 145.
49. Van der Veer, 'Writing Violence', in Ludden, *Making India Hindu*, p. 260.
50. Rajmohan Ramanathapillai, *Sacred Symbols and the Adoption of Violence in Tamil Politics in Sri Lanka* (unpublished MA thesis, McMaster University, Canada, 1991).
51. Ibid., p. 134. A similar case could be made for the Sinhalese south of Sri Lanka, where the legendary Pali Chronicles, the *Dipavamsa* and the *Mahavamsa*, have assumed a canonical status among the island's Buddhists. They depict the triumphs in battle of Buddhist kings over Hindu invaders.
52. *The Complete Works of Swami Vivekananda* 1 (Calcutta: Advaita Ashrama, 1964–71), p. 18.
53. Gopal, *Anatomy of a Confrontation*, p. 14.
54. Sarvepalli Radhakrishnan, *The Hindu View of Life* (London and New York: Macmillan, 1969), pp. 42–43.
55. Ibid., p. 24.
56. *Current Dialogue* 29 (Geneva: World Council of Churches, January 1996), p. 18.
57. A. Rambachan, 'Keynote Address, Hindu–Christian Consultation, Varanasi, India, October 23–27, 1997', in *Current Dialogue* 31 (Geneva: World Council of Churches, 1998), p. 34.
58. Louis Dumont, 'World Renunciation in Indian Religions', *Contributions to Indian Sociology* 4 (1960), p. 47.
59. Romila Thapar, *Ancient Indian Social History: Some Interpretations* (Delhi: Orient Longman, 1979), pp. 63–105.

60. Dumont, 'World Renunciation in Indian Religions', p. 47. I am indebted to Charles Hoole for introducing me to Dumont's work and its application to Christian mission in India.
61. Thapar, *Ancient Indian Social History*, p. 75.
62. See the essays in the bicentennial volume *Carey's Obligation and India's Renaissance*, eds. J. T. K. Daniel and R. E. Hedlund (Serampore: Serampore College Press, 1993). For the impact of Protestant missions on the revival of Tamil culture in Northern Sri Lanka, see Hoole, *Modern Sannyasins*, chs. 13 and 14.
63. R. Young, 'Ripple or Wave? Protestant Missions and the "Protestantization" of Religion in Nineteenth-Century Sri Lanka' (unpublished paper delivered in Colombo, Sri Lanka, 8 February 1992).
64. C. B. Firth, *An Introduction to Indian Church History* (Madras: CLS, 1961; rev. ed. 1976), p. 208.
65. The examples below are taken from Young, 'Ripple or Wave?'
66. Quoted in 'Modern-Day Martyrs', *Time*, 11 May 1998, p. 15.
67. Khilnani, *The Idea of India*, pp. 8–9.
68. Ibid., p. 190.
69. From Flood, *An Introduction to Hinduism*, p. 267.
70. Van der Veer, *Religious Nationalism*, p. 136.
71. Ibid., p. 137.
72. Khilnani, *The Idea of India*, p. 9.
73. Ibid., p. 41.
74. M. M. Thomas, 'The Christian Contribution to an Indian Philosophy of Being and Becoming Human', in A. Amaladass SJ (ed.), *Christian Contribution to Indian Philosophy* (Madras: CLS, 1995), pp. 217–218.

3. The Jesus enigma

1. Colin Dexter, *Service of All the Dead* (London: Pan, 1980), p. 250.
2. E.g. Tacitus, *Annals* 15.44.3.
3. Justin, *First Apology* 13.4.
4. For an incisive critique of the methodology of the Jesus Seminar, see Ben Witherington III, *The Third Quest: The Search for the Jew from Nazareth* (Downers Grove, IL: InterVarsity Press; Carlisle: Paternoster, 1995), ch. 2. The whole book is an excellent survey of various images of Jesus in recent Western scholarship.
5. Richard A. Burridge, *What are the Gospels? A Comparison with Greco-Roman Biography* (Cambridge: Cambridge University Press, 1992), p. 143.
6. Ibid., p. 258.
7. See, e.g., Eccles. 12:9–12; Sirach 33:18; 39:1–3; 51:23–26.
8. Josephus, *Antiquities* 18.63.
9. B. Witherington III, *Jesus the Sage: The Pilgrimage of Wisdom* (Minneapolis: Fortress Press, 1994), p. 177.
10. Ibid., p. 178 (emphasis in text).
11. Ibid., p. 386.
12. The answer given to Moses when he asks to know the 'name' of the God who was sending him to Pharaoh (Exod. 3:14) is variously translated 'I am who I am' or 'I shall be what I shall be' or even 'I shall be what I am'. Perhaps the best way to understand this is that God declares that he will be known personally only through his future actions. Israel will come to know the personal 'name' of God (which sums up his

eternal character) through his redemptive actions in history.

13. For Yahweh's sovereign activity in the histories of other nations, see also Exod. 9:13–16; Is. 10:5–19; Jer. 27:5–7; Amos 9:7; Is. 44:28 – 45:13. It is interesting to note, too, that Israel's destruction of the Canaanites and occupation of the land was held back by Yahweh for four hundred years until the wickedness of the Canaanites had 'reached its full measure' (Gen. 15:16).

14. E.g. Deut. 10:14ff.; Lev. 19:1–2; Lev. 25. For the radical distinctiveness of Israel's social system (rooted in her theological distinctiveness) compared with both the Canaanite system she displaced and other ancient West Asian cultures, see the classic study by N. K. Gottwald, *The Tribes of Yahweh: A Sociology of the Religion of Liberated Israel, 1250–1050 BCE* (London: SCM, 1980), and the (more readable) works by the British Old Testament scholar C. J. H.Wright, e.g. *Living as the People of God: The Relevance of Old Testament Ethics* (Leicester: Inter-Varsity Press, 1983).

15. J. Verkuyl, *Contemporary Missiology, An Introduction* (Grand Rapids: Eerdmans, 1978), p. 95.

16. C. J. H. Wright, 'The Christian and Other Religions: The Biblical Evidence', *Themelios* 9.2 (1984), p. 7.

17. Judas Maccabeus, the eldest of five sons of a village elder, Mattathias. Judas led a popular revolt (166–142 BC) that overthrew the hellenizing Seleucid Syrian rulers. This inaugurated a period of substantial political independence for Judah. In 140 BC, Maccabean rule was further consolidated when Simon acquired the function of high priest, thereby founding the Hasmonean dynasty (after Hashmon, an ancestor of the Maccabees), which lasted until Roman conquest in 63 BC.

18. Cf. *Antiquities* 18.60–62; *Jewish War* 2.175–177.

19. G. Vermes, *Jesus the Jew* (London: Collins, 1973), p. 224.

20. R. F. Gombrich, *Theravada Buddhism: A Social History from Ancient Benares to Modern Colombo* (London: Routledge & Kegan Paul, 1988), p. 205.

21. N. Chaudhuri, *Hinduism* (London: Chatto & Windus, 1979), p. 315.

22. Ibid., p. 325.

23. The link between the appointing of the twelve and the twelve tribes of Israel is indicated by Matt. 19:28; Luke 22:30.

24. By forgiving sins in his own name (that is, as the Son of Man), Jesus implicitly claims a divine prerogative and thus provokes the theologians of his day; see S. Kim, *The Son of Man as the Son of God*, WUNT 30 (Tübingen: J. C. B. Mohr [Paul Siebeck], 1983); I. H. Marshall, *The Gospel of Luke: A Commentary on the Greek Text* (Grand Rapids: Eerdmans, 1978), p. 213.

25. Many commentators draw attention to the contrast with Jewish and pagan charismatic exorcists. For instance, William Lane, *The Gospel of Mark* (London: Marshall, Morgan & Scott, 1974), pp. 74–75: 'In contrast to contemporary exorcists, who identified themselves by name or by relationship to some deity or power, who pronounced some spell or performed some magical action, Jesus utters only a few direct words, through which his absolute authority over the demonic power that held the man captive was demonstrated.'

26. For a summary of the monotheism of Second Temple Judaism, see N. T. Wright, *The New Testament and the People of God* (London: SPCK, 1992), pp. 248–259.

27. The Aramaic word *Abba* that Jesus used was preserved in the early church and used by Christians (Rom. 8:15; Gal. 4:6). The most exhaustive study of the word and the authenticity of the sayings in which it occurs remains that of Joachim Jeremias, *Abba* (Göttingen: Vandenhoeck & Ruprecht, 1966) and *The Prayers of Jesus* (ET, London: SCM, 1967), pp. 11–65. The significance Jeremias attaches to the word *Abba* has been

challenged by James Barr, '"Abba" isn't "Daddy"', *Journal of Theological Studies* 39 (1988), pp. 28–47. Although Barr is correct to question the use of the term as a child's word for 'Daddy', this does not affect the fundamental point that for a Jew to speak of God as his Father was rare in Palestinian Judaism, and to use it in the exclusive way Jesus did was unique.

28. For the Semitic character of this saying, see Jeremias, *Abba*, pp. 47–51. A defence of its authenticity is found in B. Witherington III, *The Christology of Jesus* (Philadelphia: Fortress, 1990), pp. 221–228. See also R. J. Bauckham, 'The Sonship of the Historical Jesus in Christology', *Scottish Journal of Theology* 31 (1978), pp. 245–260.
29. The theme of Sonship is especially prominent in the fourth gospel (John), though by no means absent in the synoptics.
30. Cf. R. T. France, *Jesus and the Old Testament* (London: Tyndale, 1971), pp. 125–132, 148–150.
31. Witherington, *Jesus the Sage*, pp. 147–208.
32. For the authenticity of this saying and its basis in Is. 52:13 – 53:12, see, e.g., France, *Jesus and the Old Testament*, pp. 116–121.
33. For the idea of redemptive covenant blood, see especially Exod. 24:8 and Zech. 9:11. It is interesting that the latter appears immediately after the prophecy of the humble king riding into Zion on a donkey. Note also how the fourth Servant Song of Isaiah (52:13 – 53:12), with its theme of substitutionary atonement, follows on the heels of 52:7 which announces Yahweh's return to Zion and the inauguration of his universal reign. For the understanding, in some circles, of the second-century BC Maccabean martyrdoms as atoning sacrifices for the sins of the nation (under the influence, no doubt, of Is. 53 and Gen. 22), see 4 Macc. 6:29; 17:21ff. (cf. 2 Macc. 6 – 7).
34. R. F. Gombrich, 'Introduction: The Buddhist Way', in *The World of Buddhism: Buddhist Monks and Nuns in Society and Culture*, eds. Heinz Bechert and Richard Gombrich (London: Thames and Hudson, 1984), p. 13. In a famous simile, the Buddha compared his doctrine to a raft (*Majjhima Nikaya* 1, 134–135). Just as one uses a raft to cross a river, but only a fool would then carry the raft on the further shore, so the Buddha's teaching was intended to help men across the ocean of *samsara*; once they were across, they could go their way without depending on his words.
35. 2 Macc. 7:9, 14, 21–29. See also 12:43–45; 14:45ff.
36. See N. T. Wright, *The New Testament and the People of God*, pp. 320–334.
37. R. P. C. Hanson, 'The Achievement of Orthodoxy in the Fourth Century AD', in R. Williams (ed.), *The Making of Orthodoxy* (Cambridge: Cambridge University Press, 1989), p. 149.
38. J. P. Meier, *The Mission of Christ and His Church: Studies in Christology and Ecclesiology* (Wilmington, DE: Michael Glazier, 1990), p. 31.
39. Lesslie Newbigin, *The Gospel in a Pluralist Society* (London: SPCK; Grand Rapids: Eerdmans, 1989), p. 175.
40. S. Neill, *Christian Faith and Other Faiths* (Oxford: Oxford University Press, 1970), p. 9.
41. Ibid., p. 16.

4. Conversion and cultures

1. From R. A. Nicholson, *The Mystics of Islam* (1914; London: Routledge & Kegan Paul, 1963), p. 105. Nicholson calls Ibn al-'Arabi 'the greatest theosophist the Arabs have produced' (p. 102).
2. H. Askari, 'Within and Beyond the Diversity of Religious Experience', in J. Hick and H.

Askari (eds.) *The Experience of Religious Diversity* (London: Gower, 1985), pp. 208–209.
3. Ibid., p. 210.
4. Ibid., pp. 205–206. An excellent summary and critique of such writers is found in K. Zebiri, *Muslims and Christians Face to Face* (Oxford: Oneworld, 1997), ch. 4.
5. The Dalai Lama, *The Good Heart* (Boston, MA: Wisdom Publications, 1996), p. 80.
6. Akbar Ahmed and Hastings Donnan, 'Islam in the Age of Postmodernity', in Akbar Ahmed and Hastings Donnan, *Islam, Globalization and Postmodernity* (London and New York: Routledge, 1994), p. 5.
7. Andrew Walls, 'The Nineteenth-Century Missionary as Scholar', in *The Missionary Movement in Christian History: Studies in the Transmission of Faith* (Maryknoll, NY: Orbis; Edinburgh: T. & T. Clark, 1996).
8. J. Driver, *Christ in a Changing World: Toward an Ethical Christology*, quoted in P. Knitter, *No Other Name? A Critical Survey of Christian Attitudes Toward the World Religions* (London: SCM, 1985), p. 165.
9. S. Kierkegaard, *Training in Christianity*, trans. W. Lowrie (Princeton, NJ: Princeton University Press, 1941), p. 64.
10. M. Kahler, *Doctrine of Reconciliation* (1898), cited in A. McGrath, *The Making of Modern German Christology, 1750–1990* (Leicester: Apollos, 2nd ed. 1994), p. 136 (my emphasis).
11. Walls, *The Missionary Movement*, ch. 3.
12. Ibid., p. 51.
13. Ibid., p. 8.
14. L. Sanneh, 'Pluralism and Christian Commitment', *Theology Today* 45 (April 1988), pp. 21–33.
15. Ibid., p. 27.
16. Walls, *The Missionary Movement*, p. 23.
17. Ibid., p. 24.
18. Cf. C. J. H. Wright, 'The Christian and Other Religions: The Biblical Evidence', *Themelios* 9.2 (January 1984). Joshua challenges the people to get rid of all other gods and serve Yahweh alone in accordance with the covenant. Wright notes that among 'other gods' Joshua cites 'the gods your forefathers worshipped beyond the River'. The inference here is that however God may have initially accommodated his relationship with the patriarchs to their previous worship and concepts of deity ... now that their descendants have an unambiguous knowledge of Yahweh in the light of the exodus, Sinai and the conquest, such concepts are inadequate and indeed incompatible with covenant loyalty' (p. 7).
19. D. Bonhoeffer, *Ethics* (1949; ET London: SCM, 1955; New York: Simon & Schuster, Touchstone ed. 1995), p. 81.
20. Ibid., pp. 81–82 (emphasis in text).
21. Ibid., p. 85.
22. Ibid.
23. Ibid., p. 82.

5. Secularisms and civility

1. B. Jupp, 'The Persistence of Faiths', *Demos* 11 (1997), p. 3.
2. Cf. 'The Counter-Attack of God', *The Economist*, 8 July 1995, pp. 19–21.
3. R. Wuthnow, *The Struggle for America's Soul* (Grand Rapids: Eerdmans, 1989), pp. 116–117.

4. N. Lash, *The Beginning and the End of 'Religion'* (Cambridge: Cambridge University Press, 1996), p. 188.
5. Ibid., pp. 168, 169.
6. Wilfred Cantwell Smith, *The Meaning and End of Religion* (1962; Minneapolis: Fortress Press, 1991), p. 32.
7. Cantwell Smith observes that when Calvin's *Institutio Christiana Religio* was first translated into English, '*Christiana religio* was rendered not as "the Christian religion", an as yet unfamiliar concept … but "Christian religion", which is very different … The matters set forth in Calvin's *magnum opus* – a pattern of doctrines, Church practices, interpretations of Scripture and of the Lord's Supper, etc – are not themselves *religio*. They are, rather, things that he hoped would institute or induce in people or guide them to or instruct them in a personal, dynamic, and worshipful "recognition" of God to which he gave that name (*Christiana religio*). A century later men were calling by this name not that personal vision but the matters such as he set forth to lead to it: the system of beliefs and practices, considered as a system, irrespective of whether or not they elicited in the human heart a genuine fear of and love for God. The difference is momentous' (ibid., pp. 37, 39).
8. T. N. Madan, 'Secularism in Its Place', *Journal of Asian Studies* 46.4 (1987), p. 754. The article has been reproduced in many collections, e.g. T. N. Madan (ed.), *Religion in India* (India: Oxford University Press, 1991), pp. 394–409.
9. Ibid., p. 748 (my emphasis).
10. Ibid.
11. Ibid., p. 749.
12. Ibid., p. 757.
13. D. Martin, *A General Theory of Secularization* (Oxford: Blackwell, 1978), p. 12.
14. J. Stout, *The Flight from Authority: Religion, Morality, and the Quest for Autonomy* (Notre Dame, IN: University of Notre Dame Press, 1981), p. 241, quoted in William T. Cavanaugh, ' "A Fire Strong Enough to Consume the House": The Wars of Religion and the Rise of the State', *Modern Theology* 11.4 (1995).
15. Cavanaugh, ibid., p. 398 (my emphasis).
16. Ibid., p. 403.
17. Ibid., p. 408.
18. A. Giddens, *The Nation-State and Violence*, vol. 2 of *A Contemporary Critique of Historical Materialism* (Berkeley and Los Angeles: University of California Press, 1985).
19. Cf. P. Hirst and G. Thompson, *Globalization in Question: The International Economy and the Possibilities of Governance* (Cambridge: Polity Press, 1996), pp. 95–98, 117.
20. Source of this information is John Pilger, 'Pol Pot: The Monster We Created', *The Guardian Weekly*, 26 April 1998.
21. M. Novak, *The Spirit of Democratic Capitalism* (New York: Simon & Schuster, 1982; London: IEA Welfare and Health Unit, 1991), p. 53.
22. Ibid., p. 54.
23. Ibid., pp. 54–55.
24. Lash, *The Beginning and End of 'Religion'*, p. 110.
25. T. Eagleton, *The Illusions of Postmodernism* (Oxford: Blackwell, 1996), p. 80.
26. Ibid.
27. Leszek Kolakowski, *Modernity on Endless Trial* (Chicago: University of Chicago Press, 1990), p. 214, quoted in Michael J. Perry, *The Idea of Human Rights: Four Inquiries* (Oxford and New York: Oxford University Press, 1998), p. 3.
28. Perry, ibid., p. 35.
29. Jeffrie Murphy, 'Afterword: Constitutionalism, Moral Skepticism, and Religious

Belief', in Alan S. Rosenbaum (ed.), *Constitutionalism: The Philosophical Dimension* (1988), p. 248, quoted (and emphasis added) in Perry, ibid., p. 41.

30. Alexis de Tocqueville, *Democracy in America* (1841), abridged, with introduction, by Patrick Renshaw (Ware: Wordworth ed. 1998), p. 120.
31. Ibid., p. 31.
32. Ibid., p. 21.
33. Ibid., p. 117.
34. Ibid., p. 127.
35. Ibid., p. 103.
36. Robert Bellah et al., *Habits of the Heart: Individualism and Commitment in American Life* (Berkeley, CA: University of California Press, 1985).
37. Cited by Bob Tyrell, 'Belief in Business', *Demos* 11 (1997), p. 10.
38. John Rawls, *Political Liberalism* (New York: Columbia University Press, 1993), pp. 133–172.
39. Thomas Hobbes, *Leviathan* (New York: Collier Books, 1962), chs. 42 and 29.
40. John Locke, *Two Treatises of Government* with a *Letter on Toleration*, ed. J. W. Gough (Oxford: Blackwell, 1956), p. 143.
41. Ibid., p. 131.
42. Lash, *The Beginning and End of 'Religion'*, p. 214.

Epilogue

1. D. Bonhoeffer, *Ethics* (1949; ET London: SCM, 1955; New York: Simon & Schuster, Touchstone ed., 1995), p. 61.
2. A. Camus, *Resistance, Rebellion, and Death*, trans. Justin O'Brien (1960; New York: Random House, Vintage International ed. 1995), p. 71.
3. Ibid., pp. 71, 73.